Biblical Faith and Other Religions

Biblical Faith and Other Religions

An Evangelical Assessment

DAVID W. BAKER
General Editor

Biblical Faith and Other Religions: An Evangelical Assessment

© 2004 by David W. Baker

Published by Kregel Publications, a division of Kregel, Inc., P.O. Box 2607, Grand Rapids, MI 49501.

Cover design: John M. Lucas

Library of Congress Cataloging-in-Publication Data
Biblical faith and other religions: an evangelical assessment / by David W. Baker.
　　p.　cm.
Includes bibliographical references and index.
　　1. Christianity and other religions.　I. Baker, David W. (David Weston).
BR127.B52　2004
261.2—dc22　　　　　　　　　　　　　　　　　　2004019251

ISBN 0-8254-2026-1

Printed in the United States of America

04　05　06　07　08 / 5　4　3　2　1

Contents

Contributors 7

Preface 9

Introduction 11
    David M. Howard Jr.

Abbreviations 17

1. Religious Pluralism and the Question of Truth 21
    Harold A. Netland

2. Other Religions in Old Testament Theology 43
    Daniel I. Block

3. Other Religions in New Testament Theology 79
    Gregory K. Beale

4. God So Loved the World: Theological Reflections on
   Religious Plurality in the History of Christianity 106
    Richard J. Plantinga

5. Biblical Faith and Traditional Folk Religion 138
    Tite Tiénou

6. Biblical Faith and Islam 148
   J. Dudley Woodberry

   Scripture Index 163
   Subject Index 167

Contributors

David W. Baker, Ph.D., University of London
Professor of Old Testament and Semitic Languages
Ashland Theological Seminary, Ashland, Ohio

Gregory K. Beale, Ph.D., Cambridge University
Kenneth T. Wessner Chair of Biblical Studies and Professor of New Testament
Wheaton College Graduate School, Wheaton, Illinois

Daniel I. Block, D.Phil., University of Liverpool
John R. Stampey Professor of Old Testament Interpretation
The Southern Baptist Theological Seminary, Louisville, Kentucky

David M. Howard Jr., Ph.D., The University of Michigan
Professor of Old Testament
Bethel Theological Seminary, St. Paul, Minnesota

Harold A. Netland, Ph.D., Claremont Graduate School
Naomi A. Fausch Chair of Missions and Associate Professor of Philosophy of
    Religion and Mission
Trinity Evangelical Divinity School, Deerfield, Illinois

Richard J. Plantinga, Ph.D., McMaster University
Professor of Religion
Calvin College, Grand Rapids, Michigan

Tite Tiénou, Ph.D., Fuller Theological Seminary
Senior Vice President of Education, Academic Dean, and Professor of Theology
of Mission
Trinity Evangelical Divinity School, Deerfield, Illinois

J. Dudley Woodberry, Ph.D., Harvard University
Professor of Islamic Studies and Dean Emeritus of the School of World Mission
Fuller Theological Seminary, Pasadena, California

Preface

SINCE THE BIRTH OF CHRISTIANITY, our mandate has been to look to Jerusalem, Judea, and Samaria, and to the ends of the earth (Acts 1:8). Too often, though, we have tended only to our Jerusalem, abandoning two-thirds of our Lord's commission. In this era of growing communication and personal contact, however, the world has become smaller because our access to it has increased. Greater mobility, too, has transformed what was traditionally considered the mission field into those we now call our neighbors. In dialogue with friends, and even family, what has been religious belief in the third person ("what he/she/they believe") must now be translated into the second person ("what you believe"). An understanding of the relationship between biblical faith and other religions has become, then, more than simply an objective, academic exercise; it has taken on existential importance.

The essays in this volume are the written records of oral presentations. As such, the reader will find documentation at numerous points, but this volume is not meant solely to present finished academic products for the academy. While scholars will indeed find the material of interest, this book is intended for a much wider readership. From these pages, the church at large will attain better understanding of different faith traditions as it engages with them at numerous levels. We trust that the God of peace who raised from the dead our Lord, Jesus Christ, might still show himself as such in this time of conflict, still providing resurrection life for those without peace and hope.

—DAVID W. BAKER

Introduction

DAVID M. HOWARD JR.

AT THE NOVEMBER 1998 Annual Meeting of the Evangelical Theological Society (ETS), held in Orlando, the members of the ETS Executive Committee decided to make the topic for the 2002 Annual Meeting in Toronto "Evangelical Christianity and Other Religions." Their rationale in choosing this was twofold. First, they judged that it was again time to address this subject—the last time it had been considered was in 1989, when the theme was "The Gospel and World Religions." Second, they judged that this topic would follow logically upon the topics of 2000 ("Israel—Past, Present, and Future") and 2001 ("Defining Evangelicalism's Boundaries"), especially at a time when religious pluralism was becoming more and more widespread.

The chosen topic was indeed timely, given that in recent decades Christianity in so much of the West has been in decline, while other religions have been rapidly ascendant. These other religions range from classic "old" religions such as Islam, Buddhism, Hinduism, and Confucianism to "new" religions or sects such as Mormonism, Jehovah's Witnesses, and any number of New Age movements. The Executive Committee envisioned a lively meeting with many papers presented on a broad variety of topics under the umbrella of the conference theme.

No one on the Executive Committee, however, dreamed how much more timely the topic would become after the events of September 11, 2001. Almost instantly, Islam, and the relationship between Islam and Christianity, became topics of discussion in circles where religion had scarcely ever been discussed. In the United States, interfaith services everywhere proclaimed the message that

11

we all worship the same God and that Islam is a religion of peace. Curiosity about the teachings of Islam skyrocketed among the general populace, as it did about the teachings of other world religions. Thus, the Executive Committee's decision to designate "Evangelical Christianity and Other Religions" as the Annual Meeting theme for 2002 proved to be especially appropriate—even, perhaps, providential. And the location in Toronto proved to be a most apt setting as well, given its status as one of the world's most cosmopolitan cities.

At the Annual Meeting, more than sixty-five papers were presented on the main theme, almost twenty percent of the total. Interest in Islam ran the highest, naturally enough, with fourteen papers addressing it directly and many others addressing it indirectly. But the other papers covered a wide range within the main theme, including general papers on relating Christianity to cultures and religions everywhere, and more specific papers on such topics as Rastafarianism, African traditional religion, Brazilian spiritism, Bahaism, and the other major world religions (Buddhism, Hinduism, Confucianism, Taoism, Judaism). Papers were also presented on how the church has related to other religions throughout its history, and even on the interface between Old Testament and New Testament faith and religions of their respective day.

I was privileged to be the ETS program chair for the Annual Meeting in 2002, with responsibility for putting together the slate of plenary speakers who would address the topic of "Evangelical Christianity and Other Religions." An early clarification I sought from members of the Executive Committee was the intent behind the term "Evangelical Christianity." Did they refer to evangelicalism as a relatively recent religious or sociological phenomenon, say, in the past few decades, or in the last century or two? Or did they mean something more general, such as "orthodox Christianity," which would extend much further back? I was assured that the latter was more generally in view, not the former.

In formulating the lineup for the plenary sessions, I was faced with many decisions. One was to ensure inclusion of papers from both Old Testament and New Testament perspectives, as a reminder that the Bible itself provides guidelines for how to relate to other faiths. This is so in part because it was itself written against the backdrop of diverse religious systems. Old Testament writers faced religious challenges from Egypt, Canaan, Assyria, Babylonia, and Persia, at a minimum, while New Testament writers faced vastly different challenges from Greece and Rome.

Given, though, that one plenary session of the Annual Meeting focused on the Old Testament perspective, a designation such as "evangelical (or orthodox) Christianity" for inclusion was a bit of a misnomer. An attempt to more accurately reflect the subject matter herein led to the title chosen for this book: *Biblical Faith and Other Religions*. We evangelicals certainly affirm that our core beliefs arise directly from "biblical faith," and so this broader title captures the intent behind the conference theme. At the same time, it embraces papers dealing with Old and New Testament attitudes toward other religions of the respective biblical periods, as well as later periods.

Another early decision was to include one paper addressing the broad philosophical questions concerning Christianity's relationship to other religions today, including, among other things, the question of truth. Filling in the rest of the topics was then relatively easy—one paper from a church historian, and at least one paper on a major world religion today. In the end, the final topic to be added dealt with folk religious expression today, and it turned out to be a felicitous choice for rounding out the program for this volume.

It was a joy and a delight to put together this program. Because the study of world religions is not my area of professional expertise—which is the Old Testament—I solicited recommendations from a number of trusted colleagues from around the country. I was delighted with the final lineup of contributors, because in each case, the first person I asked accepted the invitation, and in each case we were able to secure one of the world's leading authorities on the topic at hand. And now we are indebted to David W. Baker, editor of the ETS Monograph Series, and to Jim Weaver, director of Academic and Professional Books at Kregel Publications, for making these addresses available to the broader reading public.

The book starts on a philosophical note, with Harold A. Netland addressing the topic of "Religious Pluralism and the Question of Truth." In his essay, Netland builds upon his experience as a missionary—having spent nine years in Japan—and as a scholar interested in questions of religious epistemology and religious pluralism. His books include *Dissonant Voices: Religious Pluralism and the Question of Truth* and *Encountering Religious Pluralism: The Challenge to Christian Faith and Mission,* and a volume he coedited with Edward Rommen, *Christianity and the Religions.*[1] In his essay Netland focuses upon some epistemological challenges to Christian faith that have emerged from our increased awareness of religious diversity in the West. He presents a clear

---

1. Harold A. Netland, *Dissonant Voices: Religious Pluralism and the Question of Truth* (Grand Rapids: Eerdmans, 1991); idem, *Encountering Religious Pluralism: The Challenge to Christian Faith and Mission* (Downers Grove, Ill.: InterVarsity, 2001); and Edward Rommen and Harold A. Netland, eds., *Christianity and the Religions* (Pasadena, Calif.: William Carey Library, 1996).

and cogent case for asserting that rational reflection can sift through competing truth claims and arrive at some measure of truth, arguing that "a strong
case for the truth of Christian theism can be established through the careful
accumulation and analysis of a wide variety of data from various dimensions
of our experience and the world."

Daniel I. Block is eminently qualified to address the topic of "Other Religions in Old Testament Theology." Much of his work has addressed the relationship between biblical and ancient Near Eastern worldviews, beginning with
his D.Phil. dissertation on "The Foundations of National Identity: A Study in
Ancient Northwest Semitic Perceptions," and continuing in major commentaries on *Ezekiel*, NICOT; *Judges*, NAC; and *Deuteronomy*, NIVAC.[2] He addresses
the issue of comparative religious worldviews most directly in his ETS monograph, *The Gods of the Nations: Studies in Ancient Near Eastern National Theology.*[3] In his essay in this volume, Block creatively discusses, first, how Old
Testament faith *parallels* certain pagan religious ideas and practices; second,
how it *appropriates* others, using them in certain ways without giving assent to
their veracity; and third, how it explicitly *repudiates* still others as completely
antithetical to genuine belief.

The New Testament does not address the issues arising from conflicting
truth claims or practices in nearly as self-conscious a way as does the Old
Testament. For one thing, the New Testament is much shorter, and, for another, it is much more limited in its time frame. Nevertheless, significant things
can be said about "Other Religions in New Testament Theology." Gregory K.
Beale brings to his essay an extensive background of study in the book of Revelation, as well as the use of the Old Testament in the New Testament. This
background is most notable in his monumental commentary, *The Book of Revelation*, NIGTC, as well as in such works as *The Use of Daniel in Jewish Apocalyptic Literature and in the Revelation of St. John* and *John's Use of the Old
Testament in Revelation.*[4] In his essay, Beale focuses in depth on two loci in the

---

2. Daniel I. Block, "The Foundations of National Identity: A Study in Ancient Northwest Semitic
   Perceptions" (D.Phil. dissertation, University of Liverpool, 1981); idem, *Ezekiel, Chapters
   1–24*, NICOT (Grand Rapids: Eerdmans, 1997); idem, *Ezekiel, Chapters 25–48*, NICOT
   (Grand Rapids: Eerdmans, 1998); idem, *Judges*, NAC (Nashville: Broadman & Holman,
   1999); and idem, *Deuteronomy*, NIVAC (Grand Rapids: Zondervan, forthcoming).
3. Daniel I. Block, *The Gods of the Nations: Studies in Ancient Near Eastern National Theology*, 2d ed. (Grand Rapids: Baker, 2000).
4. Gregory K. Beale, *The Book of Revelation*, NIGTC (Grand Rapids: Eerdmans, 1998); idem,
   The Use of Daniel in Jewish Apocalyptic Literature and in the Revelation of St. John (Lanham,
   Md.: University Press of America, 1984); and idem, *John's Use of the Old Testament in
   Revelation*, JSNTSup 166 (Sheffield, England: Sheffield Academic Press, 1998).

New Testament: Paul's Areopagus speech in Acts 17, and various passages in Revelation. He makes a major contribution in studying these texts, showing how they not only address conflicts with Greco-Roman religious outlooks, but do so with an eye to specific Old Testament texts as well, demonstrating how the New Testament writers self-consciously used the Old Testament in their cases against the pagan systems.

Richard J. Plantinga is a theologian and the editor of a superb collection of readings on the subject of religious pluralism throughout church history titled *Christianity and Plurality: Classic and Contemporary Readings.*[5] He had the daunting task of surveying the church's attitudes and approaches toward other religions through two millennia. Nevertheless, in his essay "God So Loved the World: Theological Reflections on Religious Plurality in the History of Christianity," he succeeds admirably in highlighting the most important thinkers and Christian responses to religious pluralism across the centuries. In the process, he challenges the standard typology of exclusivism, inclusivism, and pluralism often used in theological scholarship, preferring to qualify a Christian approach to other religions in a more nuanced fashion, such that a Christian theologian should be "a qualified apocalyptic inclusivist, a qualified epistemic inclusivist, a qualified alethetic inclusivist, a soteriological exclusivist, and an empathetic phenomenologist in the study of religion."

Turning to the contemporary scene, Tite Tiénou, in his essay titled "Biblical Faith and Traditional Folk Religion," addresses the issue of folk religions, particularly as they find expression in African religion(s). Born in Mali, Tiénou has lived and taught theology and mission in Burkina Faso and Côte d'Ivoire. Among his writings, two of his books have especially focused on the folk aspect of Christianity and world religions: *The Theological Task of the Church in Africa* and *Understanding Folk Religion: A Christian Response to Popular Beliefs and Practices,* the latter written with Paul G. Hiebert and Daniel R. Shaw.[6] He has also written the articles "African Theology" and "African Traditional Religions" in the *Evangelical Dictionary of World Missions,* edited by A. Scott Moreau.[7] Tiénou argues that, for missiological reasons as well as because folk

---

5. Richard J. Plantinga, ed., *Christianity and Plurality: Classic and Contemporary Readings* (Oxford: Blackwell, 1999).
6. Tite Tiénou, *The Theological Task of the Church in Africa* (Achimota, Ghana, W. Africa: Africa Christian Press, 1990); and Paul G. Hiebert, R. Daniel Shaw, and Tite Tiénou, *Understanding Folk Religion: A Christian Response to Popular Beliefs and Practices* (Grand Rapids: Baker, 1999).
7. Tite Tiénou, "African Theology" and "African Traditional Religions," in *Evangelical Dictionary of World Missions,* ed. A. Scott Moreau (Grand Rapids: Baker, 2000).

religions in various guises have made their way into Western societies, evangelicals should make a better effort to understand folk religious expressions of all types (not just African).

J. Dudley Woodberry brings a lifetime of experience in the Muslim world to his topic, "Biblical Faith and Islam." He spent many years ministering in Pakistan, Afghanistan, and Saudi Arabia, and has consulted on Islam for many missions and government agencies, including the U.S. State Department. His writings include the following edited books: *Muslims and Christians on the Emmaus Road: Crucial Issues in Witness among Muslims; Reaching the Resistant: Barriers and Bridges for Mission*, and *Missiological Education for the Twentieth-first Century: The Book, the Circle, and the Sandals: Essays in Honor of Paul E. Pierson*, coedited with Charles Van Engen and Edgar J. Elliston.[8] In his essay, Woodberry traces nine elements of religious expression found in both Christianity and Islam, indicating the points of contact—which can be starting points in Muslim evangelization—and the points of difference. He does so in creative fashion, weaving a compelling personal tale of his and his wife's presence in Pakistan and Afghanistan on September 11, 2001—and the days thereafter—with a scholarly analysis of the points of contact and difference.

The affirmation of the truth of the Christian message, which is made explicitly in the first essay, is to be found in all of the essays in one form or another. Such is a heartening phenomenon, given that the six original addresses were prepared without reference to the others. Each author comes at the question of how true biblical faith interfaces with other religious systems differently—some emphasizing points of commonality and others points of difference—and each highlights different ways to best engage other religions today. But, in the end, each author believes passionately in the truth of the Christian message and has devoted his life to it. In this we can be encouraged, and we can learn from the instruction of these authors concerning ways of proclaiming and defending that message in a religiously pluralistic world.

---

8. J. Dudley Woodberry, ed., *Muslims and Christians on the Emmaus Road: Crucial Issues in Witness among Muslims* (Monrovia, Calif.: MARC, 1989; Grand Rapids: Baker, 1991); idem, *Reaching the Resistant: Barriers and Bridges for Mission*, Evangelical Missiological Society, no. 6 (Pasadena, Calif.: William Carey Library, 1998); and J. Dudley Woodberry, Charles Van Engen, and Edgar J. Elliston, eds., *Missiological Education for the Twentieth-first Century: The Book, the Circle, and the Sandals: Essays in Honor of Paul E. Pierson*, American Society of Missiology, no. 23 (Maryknoll, N.Y.: Orbis, 1996).

Abbreviations

AB	Anchor Bible
AHw	*Akkadisches Handwörterbuch,* W. von Soden, 3 vols. (Wiesbaden: Harrassowitz, 1965–81)
ANET	*Ancient Near Eastern Texts Relating to the Old Testament,* ed. J. B. Pritchard, 3d ed. with supplement (Princeton, N.J.: Princeton University Press, 1969)
ASMS	American Society of Missiology Series
AT	*Annales theologici*
BAR	*Biblical Archaeology Review*
BDB	*The New Brown, Driver, Briggs Hebrew and English Lexicon of the Old Testament* (Oxford: Oxford University Press, 1907)
BHS	*Biblia Hebraica Stuttgartensia,* ed. K. Elliger and W. Rudolph (Stuttgart: Deutsche Bibelgesellschaft, 1983)
BR	*Biblical Research*
BZAW	Beilhefte zur Zeitschrift für die alttestamanetliche Wissenschaft
CAT	Commentaire de l'Ancien Testament
CBOT	Coniectanea Biblica: Old Testament Series
CBQ	*Catholic Biblical Quarterly*
CIS	*Corpus inscriptionum semiticarum*
DDD	*Dictionary of Deities and Demons in the Bible,* ed. K. van der Toorn, B. Becking, and P. W. van der Horst (Leiden: Brill, 1995)
DNWSI	*Dictionary of North-West Semitic Inscriptions,* J. Hoftijzer and K. Jongeling, 2 vols. (Leiden: Brill, 1995)
EMS	Evangelical Missiological Society

EncJud	*Encyclopedia Judaica*, 16 vols. (Jerusalem: Encyclopedia Judaica; New York: Macmillan, 1972)
ETS	Evangelical Theological Society
EvQ	*Evangelical Quarterly*
HALOT	*The Hebrew and Aramaic Lexicon of the Old Testament*, L. Koehler, W. Baumgartner, and J. J. Stamm, trans. and ed. under the supervision of M. E. J. Richardson (Leiden: Brill, 1994–99)
HSM	Harvard Semitic Monographs
HSS	Harvard Semitic Studies
ICC	International Critical Commentary
IVPNTC	InterVarsity Press New Testament Commentary
JSNTSup	Journal for the Study of the New Testament: Supplement Series
JSOTSup	Journal for the Study of the Old Testament: Supplement Series
JTS	*Journal of Theological Studies*
KAI	*Kanaanäische und aramäische Inschriften*, H. Donner and W. Röllig, 2d ed. (Wiesbaden: Harrassowitz, 1966–69)
NAC	New American Commentary
NCBC	New Century Bible Commentary
NIBC	New International Biblical Commentary
NICNT	New International Commentary on the New Testament
NICOT	New International Commentary on the Old Testament
NIDOTTE	*New International Dictionary of Old Testament Theology and Exegesis*, ed. W. G. VanGemeren, 5 vols. (Grand Rapids: Zondervan, 1997)
NIGTC	New International Greek Testament Commentary
NIVAC	New International Version Application Commentary
NovT	*Novum Testamentum*
NovTSup	Novum Testamentum Supplements
NSBT	New Studies in Biblical Theology
NTS	*New Testament Studies*
OTL	Old Testament Library
SBB	Stuttgarter biblische Beiträge
SBL	Society of Biblical Literature
SBLWAW	Society of Biblical Literature Writings from the Ancient World
TDOT	*Theological Dictionary of the Old Testament*, ed. G. J. Botterweck and H. Ringgren, trans. J. T. Willis, G. W. Bromiley, and D. E. Green, 8 vols. (Grand Rapids: Eerdmans, 1974–)
THAT	*Theologisches Handwörterbach zum Alten Testament*, ed. E. Jenni,

	with assistance from C. Westermann, 2 vols. (München: Chr. Kaiser Verlag; Zurich: Theologischer Verlag, 1971–76)
TLOT	*Theological Lexicon of the Old Testament*, ed. E. Jenni, with assistance from C. Westermann, trans. M. E. Biddle, 3 vols. (Peabody, Mass.: Hendrickson, 1997)
UBL	Ugaritisch-biblische Literatur
UT	*Ugaritic Textbook*, C. H. Gordon, Analecta Orientalia 38 (Rome: Pontifical Biblical Institute, 1965)
VT	*Vetus Testamentum*
VTSup	Vetus Testamentum Supplements
WBC	Word Biblical Commentary
WUNT	Wissenschaftliche Untersuchungen zum Neuen Testament
ZNW	*Zeitschrift für die neutestamentliche Wissenschaft und die Kunde der älteren Kirche*
ZTK	*Zeitschrift für Theologie und Kirche*

1

Religious Pluralism and the Question of Truth

HAROLD A. NETLAND

IN CONSIDERING THE SUBJECT OF the Christian faith and other religions, it is help-ful to begin with a basic question: Why should someone be a Christian? Pre-sumably, one should be so because the central claims of the Christian faith about God, Jesus Christ, humankind, sin, and salvation are true. I accept this, and certainly this conviction has been at the heart of orthodox Christianity throughout the centuries. But most people in the world today do not accept the truth of those claims. Most embrace religious or nonreligious worldviews that are very different from that of the Christian faith.[1]

The Christian faith has always faced intellectual and cultural challenges that call into question the truth of the gospel. During the nineteenth and twentieth centuries, Christians in the West thought of these challenges largely in terms of religious agnosticism or atheism. But at the beginning of the twenty-first century the cultural and intellectual landscape is rapidly changing. The

---

1. Reliable statistics on such matters are notoriously difficult to come by, but David Barrett's analysis provides a helpful comparison. According to Barrett, in 2002 worldwide there were 2 billion Christians of all kinds, 1.2 billion Muslims, 836 million Hindus, 367 mil-lion Buddhists, 24 million Sikhs, 14 million Jews, and 780 million "nonreligious." See David Barrett, "Annual Statistical Table on Global Mission: 2002," *International Bulletin of Missionary Research* 26, no. 1 (January 2002): 23. For an insightful analysis of global Christianity today, see Philip Jenkins, *The Next Christendom: The Coming of Global Chris-tianity* (New York: Oxford University Press, 2002).

challenges from secularism and philosophical naturalism remain formidable, to be sure, and they continue to require careful responses from reflective Christians. In addition, though, complex and troubling questions are being prompted by a general increased awareness of religious diversity and the accompanying ideology of religious pluralism.

The late Bishop Lesslie Newbigin raised the question, "Can the West be converted?"[2] What would be entailed, he asked, in a genuine missionary encounter with pagan Western culture? Among the issues with which Newbigin was concerned was the drift toward religious pluralism. Thus, a responsible missiological engagement with the West must certainly include proper understanding of, and response to, the values and assumptions of what has come to be called religious pluralism. In doing so, multiple issues are involved, which are becoming increasingly complex in our rapidly changing societies. But in an incisive observation, sociologist Peter Berger takes us to the heart of the challenge from pluralism: "We do have a problem of belief, and it not only raises the question of why we should believe in God but why we should believe in *this* God. There are others, after all, and today they are made available in an unprecedented way through the religious supermarket of modern pluralism."[3]

Why should one today be a Christian rather than a Muslim or Buddhist or atheist? With this question we confront the problem of competing claims to religious authority and truth. As a Christian I believe that God has revealed himself definitively in the Incarnation and the written Scriptures, and thus I am not only entitled but obligated to reject anything that is incompatible with Scripture. Moreover, as a Christian I should assess alternative worldviews on the basis of principles and criteria internal to the Christian faith.

But the issue at hand operates from a logically more basic level: In a world of competing claims to religious authority, on what epistemological basis should one accept the Christian claims rather than other alternatives as true? We must not forget that each of the major religions claims to be true and each has its own distinctive authority structure. The Christian appeals to the Bible as the supreme authority; the Muslim rejects the Bible in favor of the Qur'an; the Zen Buddhist claims to have direct access to ultimate reality through the expe-

---

2. Lesslie Newbigin, "Can the West Be Converted?" *International Bulletin of Missionary Research* 11, no. 2 (1987): 27; idem, "The Cultural Captivity of Western Christianity as a Challenge to a Missionary Church," in *A Word in Season: Perspectives on Christian World Mission* (Grand Rapids: Eerdmans, 1994), 66.
3. Peter Berger, *A Far Glory: The Quest for Faith in an Age of Credulity* (New York: Free Press, 1992), 146–47.

rience of enlightenment or *satori;* the Advaita Vedantin Hindu appeals to the authority of the Upanishads and the experience of *samadhi;* and so on. Merely appealing to divine authority in and of itself settles nothing. Which "authority" is, in fact, ultimately authoritative? The question cannot be dismissed as just another academic quibble, for it is increasingly pressed today by ordinary people trying to make sense of the cacophony of religious voices, each claiming distinctive religious authority.

This essay thus focuses upon some epistemological challenges to the Christian faith that are prompted by the West's growing awareness of religious diversity. While the issues considered pertain primarily to philosophy of religion, those issues have significant implications as well for apologetics, evangelism, and theology. First, then, this essay notes some significant changes within recent religious epistemology, after which it will be argued that, while these changes have been effective in some ways in responding to the classical critiques of atheism, they are not so helpful in dealing with the issues raised by religious pluralism. This essay then concludes by suggesting in very broad terms a way forward.

But first some clarification of terminology. The term *religious pluralism* has two distinct meanings. First, it can be used descriptively to refer to the empirical fact of religious diversity. Globalization and the massive demographic changes of the twentieth century have greatly deepened Western awareness of religious others. The demographic changes in the United States have been so great that Diana Eck of Harvard calls the United States the world's most religiously diverse nation. "Nowhere, even in today's world of mass migrations, is the sheer range of religious faith as wide as it is in the United States."[4] Religious alternatives that were unavailable even fifty years ago are now available to many, and even those who choose to become or remain Christian do so with the conscious awareness of other options. Moreover, all indications suggest that such diversity is likely to increase, not diminish, in the coming decades.

---

4. Diana Eck, *A New Religious America: How a "Christian Country" Has Become the World's Most Religiously Diverse Nation* (New York: HarperCollins, 2001), 5. Eck's claim about the extent of religious diversity in the United States has been vigorously contested by Jenkins, *The Next Christendom*, 10–45; and idem, "Here for Good: Religion and the New Immigrants," *Books and Culture*, May–June 2002, 12–13. Jenkins points out that Eck minimizes the still dominant Christian presence in the United States, and the significant numbers of immigrants to the United States who are themselves Christian, but Eck is surely correct in her main thesis that a remarkably broad range of religious traditions is becoming part of the American social and religious landscape. Whether this qualifies the United States for the title "the world's most religiously diverse nation" is a moot point.

The second meaning of religious pluralism goes beyond mere description of diversity and embraces a particular view, a normative judgment, about the relation among the different religions. Pluralism in this sense maintains that the major religions are all to be accepted as more or less equally legitimate ways in which culturally and historically conditioned humankind responds to the one divine reality. This essay uses the term *religious pluralism* to refer to this normative view about religions.

Religious pluralism in this latter sense is an increasingly attractive perspective in Europe and North America. It finds sophisticated expression in the academic world, but popular culture as well is shaped by what we might call the "pluralistic ethos." By this is meant a set of assumptions and values that celebrate religious diversity as something good, and is deeply suspicious of attempts to privilege any one tradition or perspective as normative for all people. While skeptical about claims that any particular religion is exclusively true, religious pluralism is open to the multiplicity of ways of accessing the divine. At its heart is the conviction that sincere and morally respectable people simply *cannot* be mistaken about basic religious beliefs, especially when such beliefs and practices seem to have beneficial effects for the participants.

No one has done more to champion the cause of religious pluralism in the academic world than the philosopher and theologian, John Hick.[5] Hick began his academic career in the 1950s as an able defender of Christian orthodoxy, but by the late 1970s he had abandoned orthodoxy for a thoroughgoing religious pluralism. Three claims are at the center of his model of religious pluralism: (1) there is a religious ultimate reality—the Real—to which the major religions are all legitimate responses; (2) the various religions are historically and culturally conditioned interpretations of this divine reality; (3) soteriological or moral transformation is occurring roughly to the same extent across the major religions.

The religions are thus to be regarded as culturally and historically conditioned human responses to "an ultimate ineffable Reality that is the source and ground of everything, and which is such that in so far as the religious

---

5. Hick's writings on religious pluralism are voluminous. Among the more significant are John Hick, *God Has Many Names* (Philadelphia: Westminster, 1980); idem, *An Interpretation of Religion: Human Responses to the Transcendent* (New Haven, Conn.: Yale University Press, 1989); idem, *The Metaphor of God Incarnate: Christology in a Pluralistic Age* (Louisville: Westminster John Knox, 1993); idem, *A Christian Theology of Religions: The Rainbow of Faiths* (Louisville: Westminster John Knox, 1995); and idem, *Dialogues in the Philosophy of Religion* (New York: Palgrave, 2001). For an overview of the development of Hick's thought, see Harold Netland, *Encountering Religious Pluralism: The Challenge to Christian Faith and Mission* (Downers Grove, Ill.: InterVarsity, 2001), chap. 5.

traditions are in soteriological alignment with it, they are contexts of salvation/liberation. These traditions involve different human conceptions of the Real, with correspondingly different forms of experience of the Real, and correspondingly different forms of life in response to the Real."[6]

According to Hick's model, then, no single religion is uniquely true or definitive, and all religions are roughly equally legitimate and effective. Why then, should one be a Christian rather than, say, a Buddhist? Hick, in effect, dismisses the question, for with pluralism there is no need to make the choice. Or if one does choose Christianity over Buddhism, one does so not because Christianity is distinctively true or rationally preferable to Buddhism; the decision simply reflects personal preferences based upon other contingent factors. Hick has thus provided a sophisticated philosophical defense of a view that is widespread today, both among intellectuals and in popular culture.

I have argued elsewhere that, despite its enormous appeal, religious pluralism is an incoherent position and simply cannot deliver what it promises.[7] No coherent form of pluralism has yet been formulated—Hick's model itself is riddled with internal inconsistencies and problematic assumptions. Yet the allure of the pluralist vision can be measured by pluralism's remaining so deeply entrenched within the academy despite the many problems that vitiate even its most sophisticated formulations.

Recent Religious Epistemology and Religious Pluralism

Some significant recent developments within philosophy of religion have implications for responding to religious pluralism. While these developments can provide an effective response to the earlier challenges from atheism and agnosticism, they are of limited value, however, in addressing basic issues presented in the current challenge from religious diversity. Such can be illustrated by looking briefly at the work of John Hick, William Alston, and Alvin Plantinga, three of the most influential philosophers of religion of the past fifty years.

First, though, a brief look at the legacy from earlier days provides a backdrop for the current discussion. From the seventeenth through the mid-twentieth centuries it was widely accepted by many Christians and non-Christians alike that orthodox Christian belief was irrational unless Christians could demonstrate that the claims of Christianity were true. An influential tradition responded to this challenge through *natural theology*—the attempt to

---

6. Hick, *A Christian Theology of Religions*, 27.
7. See Netland, *Encountering Religious Pluralism*, chap. 7.

demonstrate truths about God without recourse to special revelation from
God. Natural theology has a distinguished, if controversial, place in Western
intellectual history.[8] Since the question of God's existence was at the heart of
the dispute, natural theology gave special attention to the theistic arguments—
the ontological, cosmological, and teleological arguments. What we might call
classical natural theology, often associated with Thomas Aquinas, typically
relied upon deductions drawn from clearly evident premises in an attempt to
derive conclusions about God, thereby creating valid arguments that are
necessarily truth preserving. If successful, such an argument logically guarantees
the truth of its conclusion, decisively refuting the skeptic's challenge. The
prospect of coming up with a definitive "knockdown" argument for Christian
theism accounts for the enduring attraction for some of classical natural
theology.

But classical natural theology fell upon hard times, and by the early twentieth century it was difficult to find anyone—apart from Roman Catholic
Thomists—advocating its agenda. Writing in 1961, Ninian Smart stated, "Natural theology is the Sick Man of Europe. In view of the subtle and exhaustive
objections adduced by Hume, Kant and modern empiricists against the traditional arguments for God's existence, it is no longer reasonable to rely upon
these particular supports for theistic belief."[9] Smart's views on natural theology will be revisited later.

Yet, in one of the great ironies of modern intellectual history, by the 1980s
logical positivism, which had led the assault upon metaphysics and thereby
classical natural theology as well, was itself a thoroughly discredited philosophical movement, and one of the most flourishing branches of philosophy
was indeed philosophical theology.[10] One of the more remarkable developments in the 1980s and 1990s was the emergence of Reformed epistemology,
largely under the leadership of Alvin Plantinga.[11] Plantinga and others pro-

8. For a discussion of the historical legacy of natural theology, as well as its prospects in the
    contemporary intellectual context, see the essays in *Prospects for Natural Theology,* ed.
    Eugene Thomas Long (Washington D.C.: Catholic University of America Press, 1992).
9. Ninian Smart, "Revelation, Reason and Religions," in *Prospect for Metaphysics: Essays of
    Metaphysical Exploration,* ed. Ian Ramsey (London: George Allen and Unwin; New York:
    Philosophical Library, 1961), 80.
10. The literature on logical positivism is enormous, but a helpful introduction to the issues
    related to Christian theism can be found in Malcolm L. Diamond and Thomas V.
    Litzenburg Jr., eds., *The Logic of God: Theology and Verification* (Indianapolis: Bobbs-
    Merrill, 1975).
11. Plantinga's views can be found in Alvin Plantinga, "Reason and Belief in God," in *Faith
    and Rationality: Reason and Belief in God,* ed. Alvin Plantinga and Nicholas Wolterstorff

vided a trenchant critique of what he called "classical evidentialism," a set of assumptions that was said to provide the epistemological framework for both earlier critics and defenders of Christian belief. In contrast to classical evidentialism, Reformed epistemology insists that there is no need to provide "sufficient reasons" for the Christian faith. As Plantinga famously put it, it can be "entirely right, rational, reasonable, and proper to believe in God without any evidence or argument at all."[12] Reformed epistemology and its response to religious pluralism will also be revisited shortly.

But first brief attention must be given to two significant developments in recent philosophy of religion, these having important implications for consideration of Christianity and other religions. The first is a shift away from the expectations of classical natural theology and attempts to demonstrate the truth of Christian theism in favor of the more modest agenda of showing that it can be *rational* for a Christian, in the appropriate circumstances, to hold Christian beliefs. The second is a shift away from relying upon the classical theistic arguments in favor of an appeal to *religious experience* as grounds for the rationality of Christian belief. In considering these changes, it is especially instructive to note the prominence in the discussion of the themes of religious diversity, religious disagreement, religious ambiguity, and religious skepticism. For these are factors that tend for many to reinforce the plausibility of religious pluralism.

In order to appreciate the first development—the shift away from focusing on the truth of Christian theism to showing that Christian belief can be rational—a couple of distinctions are necessary. The first distinction is that between truth and rationality. Although the two concepts are related, rationality is not the same thing as truth. Truth is a property of statements or propositions such that a statement is true if, and only if, the state of affairs to which that statement refers is as the statement asserts it to be; otherwise, it is false.[13]

(Notre Dame: University of Notre Dame Press, 1983), 16–93; and idem, "Justification and Theism," in *Faith and Philosophy* 4 (October 1987): 403–26. Plantinga's general epistemological framework is found in idem, *Warrant: The Current Debate* (Oxford: Oxford University Press, 1993); and idem, *Warrant and Proper Function* (Oxford: Oxford University Press, 1993). For the application of his epistemological views to the question of Christian faith, see Alvin Plantinga, *Warranted Christian Belief* (Oxford: Oxford University Press, 2000).

12. Plantinga, "Reason and Belief in God," 17.
13. On truth in religion, see Netland, *Encountering Religious Pluralism*, chap. 6. For a helpful discussion of the concept of truth itself, see William P. Alston, *A Realist Conception of Truth* (Ithaca, N.Y.: Cornell University Press, 1996).

Rationality, by contrast, is a property of persons when they accept beliefs in appropriate circumstances or for appropriate reasons. Although a correlation exists between rationality and truth—that is, what is rational to believe is also generally true—in principle it can be rational to believe something that, in fact, is false.

Second, we can distinguish stronger and weaker notions of rationality. A strong notion of rationality carries with it norms and expectations that make acceptance of the relevant belief obligatory. To fail to accept the belief is then irrational. Belief in the reality of the external world, for example, is usually regarded as eminently rational, while failure to accept this belief indicates cognitive malfunctioning or irrationality of some sort. We are not merely *permitted*, then, to believe in the reality of the external world; rather, the expectation is that people whose cognitive faculties are operating properly, and who are rational, *will* do so.

But a weaker sense of rationality allows that it can be rational for a person—in a particular set of circumstances and with particular background beliefs—to believe a proposition *p* even if others, in their particular set of circumstances, can also be rational in not believing *p*. This sense of rationality is thus person relative and context dependent. Whereas the stronger notion of rationality involves what we might call epistemic obligation, the weaker sense involves epistemic permission. Thus one, given a relevant set of conditions, can be rational in believing *p*, even if others are not necessarily obligated also to believe *p* in order for them to be rational. In this weaker sense, given appropriate circumstances and background beliefs, it can be rational for two people to believe different propositions that are, in fact, mutually contradictory.

Demonstrating the truth of the statement "God exists," however, is a far more ambitious and difficult task than simply showing that belief in God can be reasonable, especially in the weaker sense of rationality. It is not surprising that the latter task is considerably more popular today than the former. But the focus upon the rationality of Christian belief, rather than the truth of Christian claims, introduces its own questions.[14] What degree of epistemic confidence should accompany my commitment to Christian theism? What are the epistemic implications of radical religious diversity and disagreement for someone who holds that his or her own religion is distinctively true? To what extent should awareness of religious diversity be a factor in the calculation of the rationality of one's own religious commitments? Does focusing on

---

14. Some of these questions are explored in Paul J. Griffiths, *Problems of Religious Diversity* (Oxford: Blackwell, 2001).

rationality create a sense that Buddhists or Muslims, once they become aware of the credentials for Christianity, should abandon their respective beliefs and embrace Christian beliefs if they are to remain rational? Does awareness of radical religious disagreement actually undermine the claims of *all* religions, so that religious agnosticism is really the most appropriate posture to adopt? And so on.

We can illustrate the two shifts in religious epistemology by looking at the work of John Hick. In his 1957 work *Faith and Knowledge,*[15] for example, Hick rejected the agenda of classical natural theology and acknowledged that the traditional theistic arguments are either clearly unsound or at best inconclusive. Rather than try to demonstrate the *truth* of Christian theism, he argued that it could be entirely *reasonable* or *rational* for a Christian in appropriate circumstances to believe in God. Moreover, Hick argued that this more modest way of justifying Christian belief is grounded in certain kinds of experience, that is, what the Christian takes to be experiences of the presence and activity of God:

> We become conscious of the existence of other objects in the universe, whether things or persons, either by experiencing them for ourselves or by inferring their existence from evidences within our experience. The awareness of God reported by the ordinary religious believer is of the former kind. He professes, not to have inferred that there is a God, but that God as a living being has entered into his own experience. He claims to enjoy something which he describes as an experience of God.[16]

While this concept is widely adopted today, it was a novel approach for an analytic philosopher in 1957.

In *Faith and Knowledge* Hick also introduced the notions of *"experiencing-as"*—or the inherently interpretive nature of all experience—and the *religious ambiguity* of the world. Both themes have been influential in subsequent philosophy of religion and are integral to his later model of religious pluralism. Hick distinguished three dimensions of reality implicit in our experiences: the natural or physical, the human and ethical, and the divine or religious realms. He argued that in each dimension exists an irreducible element of interpretation involved in our experience—and hence the need for interpretation—with

---

15.   John Hick, *Faith and Knowledge* (Ithaca, N.Y.: Cornell University Press, 1957). A second revised edition appeared in 1966, also published by Cornell University Press.
16.   Ibid., 95.

the religious dimension having the greatest degree of epistemological ambiguity. Not only is all of our experience interpretive but it is accompanied by an irreducible religious ambiguity such that the world can be experienced rationally in either religious or nonreligious ways. Strong arguments can be offered for Christian theism as well as for naturalism, asserts Hick, and the evidence is not such that a conclusive case can be made for either position. Given such ambiguity, the determinative factor in rational assessment is the nature of one's own experience. The person who experiences God interprets the totality of life theistically; the one who fails to experience God interprets life naturalistically. Either response *can* be rational, depending upon one's particular set of circumstances and experiences.

Faith and Knowledge was written by Hick in an attempt to defend the reasonableness of Christian belief in the face of atheistic critiques in the 1950s. Yet two decades later Hick had abandoned Christian orthodoxy and was an apologist for religious pluralism. But in spite of his change in theological outlook, his basic epistemological framework has remained intact. In his later work, however, some of the earlier epistemological assumptions, which had been used so effectively in defending Christian belief against attacks from atheism, are also used, when modified slightly, to argue, based upon the religious experiences of those within other religious traditions, for the rationality of non-Christian religious beliefs.

The adaptability of these arguments was recognized by Hick as early as 1971, in the final chapter of his *Arguments for the Existence of God:*

> The principle which I have used to justify as rational the faith of a Christian who on the basis of his own religious experience cannot help but believing in the reality of "the God and Father of our Lord Jesus Christ," also operates to justify as rational the faith of a Muslim who on the basis of *his* religious experience cannot help believing in the reality of Allah and his providence; and the faith of the Buddhist who on the basis of *his* religious experience cannot help accepting the Buddhist picture of the universe; and so on.[17]

Given Hick's premises it becomes very difficult indeed to maintain that Christianity is uniquely true or that Christian belief is rationally superior to other religions. Hick, of course, later rejected the notion that Christianity is

---

17. John Hick, *Arguments for the Existence of God* (New York: Herder & Herder, 1971), 117–18. Emphasis in the original.

distinctively true or rational and embraced a theory of radical religious plu-ralism. But in doing so he was, among other things, working out the implica-tions of a set of basic epistemological assumptions he had made much earlier in *Faith and Knowledge.*

Perhaps the most influential recent attempt to ground the rationality of religious belief in religious experience is William P. Alston's *Perceiving God.*[18] It is significant that Alston credits Hick's *Faith and Knowledge* with being a formative influence upon his own approach to religious epistemology.[19] Alston examines what are called "doxastic practices," or belief-forming practices. His argument rests upon an analogy between practices relying upon sense percep-tion—which provide access to the physical world around us and result in be-liefs about the physical world—and religious practices that provide the believer with experiences or "perceptions" of God, thereby producing beliefs about God. Both sense-perception and perception-of-God beliefs are formed by en-gaging in certain doxastic practices, or socially established practices, that re-sult in formation of appropriate beliefs. In neither case is it possible to justify the reliability of the doxastic practices in a strictly noncircular manner. Yet both cases produce established procedures for distinguishing appropriate from inappropriate beliefs. Thus, Alston argues, beliefs formed through the relevant doxastic practices can be granted *prima facie* justification, and if confronted with no sufficient "overriders" (factors that would rebut or undermine the beliefs) then those beliefs can be considered "unqualifiedly justified." So the Christian can be rationally justified in believing in God based upon her or his experience or perception of God.

Alston himself recognizes, however, that religious diversity presents a two-fold challenge to his thesis. First, while Alston's argument supports the ratio-nality of Christian beliefs, based upon Christian experiences of God, it also in principle supports the rationality of the beliefs of practitioners of other reli-gions, based upon *their* respective religious experiences. So, in and of itself, Alston's theory offers little help in answering the question, *Why should some-one be a Christian instead of a Hindu or Buddhist?*

The second challenge is that religious diversity itself actually seems to undermine Alston's thesis about the general reliability of religious doxastic practices for religious belief formation. And in the efficacy of forming religious

---

18. William P. Alston, *Perceiving God: The Epistemology of Religious Experience* (Ithaca, N.Y.: Cornell University Press, 1991).
19. See William P. Alston, "John Hick: Faith and Knowledge," in *God, Truth, and Reality: Essays in Honour of John Hick*, ed. Arvind Sharma (New York: St. Martin's Press, 1993), 25.

belief, the differences between sense perception and religious perception are important. While the doxastic practices for sense perception produce similar beliefs about the external world among diverse peoples (water is wet for Buddhists and Christians alike), the doxastic practices of different religious communities result in strikingly different, even incompatible, beliefs. Thus, religious diversity seems to call into question the reliability of any single doxastic practice, including that of the Christian community. For even if one form of practice is uniquely reliable in religious belief formation, we have no way of determining which one that is. While acknowledging the force of this objection, Alston maintains, however, that it still can be rational for the Christian to "sit tight with the practice of which I am a master and which serves me so well in guiding my activity in the world" and to continue to hold Christian beliefs on the basis of experiences of God.[20]

In responding to Alston, however, John Hick argues that if a Christian is justified in believing that Christianity is uniquely true on the basis of his or her experience of God, then it follows that the Christian should also conclude that the beliefs of adherents of other religions, based upon their respective experiences, are actually false. But if this is so, then it also follows that most of the religious beliefs based upon religious experience worldwide are, in fact, false. And thus, for one particular religious community to assume that *its* doxastic practices are reliable and that *its* beliefs are justified, when those of the other religious communities are not, is simply arbitrary unless this assumption can be somehow justified on independent grounds.[21] Hick is likely correct on this point, and thus resorting to some form of natural theology for those grounds is unavoidable. More on this in a moment.

Evangelicals in particular have been attracted to Reformed epistemology, and thus its contribution to the issues raised by religious diversity should be addressed here briefly. It is interesting that, although Plantinga does address the subject of religious pluralism,[22] he does not directly consider the question of why one should be a Christian rather than, say, a Buddhist or Muslim. Rather, his response grows out of Reformed epistemology's twin convictions that (1) a Christian can be entirely rational in believing as he or she does without ap-

---

20. Alston, *Perceiving God*, 274.
21. John Hick, "The Epistemological Challenge of Religious Pluralism," *Faith and Philosophy* 14, no. 3 (1997): 278.
22. See Alvin Plantinga, "Pluralism: A Defense of Religious Exclusivism," in *The Rationality of Belief and the Plurality of Faith: Essays in Honor of William P. Alston*, ed. Thomas D. Senor (Ithaca, N.Y.: Cornell University Press, 1995), 191–215; and Plantinga, *Warranted Christian Belief*, 422–57.

pealing to evidence or reasons to justify those beliefs, and (2) that belief in God can, in appropriate circumstances, be included within the set of properly basic beliefs. In light of this, Plantinga insists that, even with awareness of radical religious diversity and disagreement, a Christian can be rational in continuing to believe in the exclusive truth of Christianity without necessarily justifying this belief through argument or evidence.

In order to appreciate Plantinga's point here, it is necessary to elaborate upon what is meant by a basic belief and a properly basic belief.[23] A *basic belief* is that which someone holds but which is not inferred from, or held based upon, the evidential basis of other beliefs. Acceptance of the belief is immediate and noninferential, and the belief is "basic" to one's noetic structure in that it forms part of the basis from which other beliefs are derived. But, in fact, not all beliefs that function as basic beliefs *should* be accepted as basic beliefs. A basic belief that one is justified in holding is a *properly basic belief;* its function as a basic belief for someone in certain circumstances violates no relevant epistemic norms, so that one is "within her or his epistemic rights" in accepting it as a basic belief. The distinction between basic beliefs and properly basic beliefs is itself not particularly controversial, although no clear consensus has been reached in regard to criteria for identifying properly basic beliefs. What is controversial, however, is Reformed epistemology's insistence that, for the Christian in appropriate circumstances, belief in God can be properly basic.[24]

Let it be assumed that Reformed epistemologists are correct in saying that it can be entirely reasonable in appropriate circumstances for belief in God to be properly basic. If so, Philip Quinn, among others, notes that this assumption comes with a price, for "this is a game any number can play. Followers of Muhammad, followers of Buddha, and even followers of the Reverend Moon can join the fun."[25] Quinn's point is important. It is difficult to see why belief in God can be accepted as properly basic by Christians but

---

23. See Plantinga, *Warranted Christian Belief,* 83–85, 175–78, 186–90.

24. For helpful discussions of Reformed epistemology, see Michael Peterson, William Hasker, Bruce Reichenbach, and David Basinger, *Reason and Religious Belief: An Introduction to the Philosophy of Religion,* 2d ed. (Oxford: Oxford University Press, 1998), chap. 7; Kelly James Clark, *Return to Reason: A Critique of Enlightenment Evidentialism and a Defense of Reason and Belief in God* (Grand Rapids: Eerdmans, 1990); and idem, *Rational Faith: Catholic Responses to Reformed Epistemology,* ed. Linda Zagzebski (Notre Dame, Ind.: University of Notre Dame Press, 1993).

25. Philip Quinn, "In Search of the Foundations of Theism," *Faith and Philosophy* 2, no. 4 (1985): 473. See also William Wainwright, *Philosophy of Religion,* 2d ed. (Belmont, Calif.: Wadsworth, 1999),167–70.

fundamental beliefs of other religions cannot also be properly basic for their adherents.[26] The central insights of Zen Buddhism, for example,—including the belief that ultimate reality is *Sunyata,* or Emptiness—are said to be perceived directly in the experience of *satori,* or enlightenment. Such insights are not the product of rational argument; indeed, evidence and argument actually are counterproductive in attaining enlightenment. Moreover, the experience of *satori* grounds the relevant claims. Thus, belief in emptiness as the ultimate reality is a basic belief for Zen Buddhists. Is it also properly basic for Buddhists? Nothing that I have seen shows why this could not be the case. Nor will it help matters to appeal to Plantinga's discussion of "proper function"[27] at this point, for the dispute then simply shifts to the question of what constitutes proper function of the cognitive faculties. Buddhists, for example, maintain that belief in a personal creator God is both false and the product of malfunctioning cognitive faculties. The issue, then, between the Christian and Buddhist is not merely a disagreement over what beliefs can be properly basic. It also concerns what constitutes proper function of the cognitive faculties. And settling *that* question requires determining the truth value of some of the central claims of the Christian or Buddhist traditions.

The implications of the general approach to religious epistemology illustrated through the work of Hick, Alston, and Plantinga have been forcefully presented in a significant recent work by Robert McKim, *Religious Ambiguity and Religious Diversity.*[28] McKim is not a religious pluralist. Moreover, he agrees that it can be rational for a Christian to believe in the truth of Christianity even in contexts of religious diversity. The fact of radical religious disagreement, however, prompts McKim to follow Hick in maintaining the irreducibly religiously ambiguous nature of the world:

26. See Netland, *Encountering Religious Pluralism,* 269–75.
27. One's cognitive faculties can be said to be functioning properly when they are "subject to no disorder or dysfunction—construed as including absence of impedance as well as pathology." For Plantinga, a belief has "warrant" (that quality or quantity that distinguishes knowledge from merely true belief) only if it is produced by cognitive faculties that are functioning properly. The notion of proper function is intimately linked to that of "design plan," the way the noetic structure and cognitive faculties are supposed to work. "There is a way in which a human organ or system works when it works properly, works as it is supposed to work; and this way of working is given by its design plan." Plantinga, *Warranted Christian Belief,* 153–54.
28. Robert McKim, *Religious Ambiguity and Religious Diversity* (Oxford: Oxford University Press, 2001).

To say that the world is religiously ambiguous is to say that it is open to being read in various ways, both religious and secular, by intelligent, honest people. . . . The presence of disagreement suggests that the matters about which there is disagreement are ambiguous. In particular, disagreement in the area of religion suggests that this is an area in which the available evidence does not point clearly in one direction rather than another, and it suggests that the matters about which religions purport to speak are matters about which it is unclear what we ought to believe. [29]

McKim makes special reference to the work of Plantinga and Alston, pointing out the implications of their general approach to the rationality of Christian belief for adherents of other religions:

In general, many of the phenomena to which appeal is made by those who accept a particular religious position have their counterparts in the case of the other traditions. Two small pieces of evidence that this is so: the basic belief apologetic as developed by Alvin Plantinga, can be deployed as readily by members of non-Christian traditions as by Christians. And the same goes for the doxastic practice apologetic of William P. Alston, as Alston acknowledges. These are two of the best games in town; and many teams are equally capable of playing them.[30]

McKim claims that in light of religious ambiguity and religious diversity we ought to adopt a moderate skepticism and tentativeness in our beliefs.

Given the religiously ambiguous nature of the world, certain sorts of belief rather than others probably are appropriate. It is unlikely that certainty about the details of the doctrine of any particular religion about God is either obligatory or appropriate, and it is likely that tentative belief, at most, is appropriate. . . . The sort of belief that is appropriate, given our circumstances, will not be dogmatic. It will view different accounts of the nature or purposes of God, especially the details of those accounts, as equally likely to be true, as stabs in the right direction of something about which it is difficult to be certain. The implication is that theists ought to be skeptical of many of the

29. Ibid., 24, 181–82.
30. Ibid., 182

claims about God that are made by the dominant theistic traditions, including their own.[31]

Is this, indeed, the appropriate response to religious diversity? If not, how are McKim's conclusions to be avoided?

NATURAL THEOLOGY AND RELIGIOUS DIVERSITY

It seems clear that the adequacy of a Christian response to the issues raised by religious pluralism will be in part a function of its capacity to answer the question, *Given pervasive religious diversity and disagreement, why should one accept the Christian worldview as true rather than other alternatives?* As has been seen, attempts to defend Christian belief by appealing to religious experience and a weak notion of rationality are inconclusive. While allowing for the rationality of Christians' believing as we do, this approach also in principle admits the rationality of Muslims or Buddhists or Mormons believing as they do. Moreover, it provides no reason for the secularist, who does not have religious experiences, to embrace any particular religion. Indeed, given religious diversity and conflicting claims, it would seem most rational for the agnostic to continue to withhold judgment on the question of religious truth. Thus, what is required is an approach to religious diversity that goes beyond appeal merely to religious experience and reliance upon a weaker notion of rationality.

It is interesting that, at the same time Hick wrote *Faith and Knowledge,* another Christian analytic philosopher was well ahead of his time, calling attention to the need to take seriously the questions raised by religious diversity. In 1960 Ninian Smart, an acknowledged authority on Hindu and Buddhist thought, challenged Christians to address the question, "Why be a Christian rather than a Buddhist?"[32] In the same 1961 essay in which he referred to natural theology as the "Sick Man of Europe," Smart also argued,

> Any appeal to religious experience (whether intuitive or otherwise) must inevitably lead to a consideration of the experience not merely of Christians but of Buddhists and others, and thereby to an examination of the way experience is linked to different sorts of doctrines. Through this investigation one is bound to ask what the criteria are for choosing between different formulations of religious belief. And

31. Ibid., 123–24.
32. Ninian Smart, *A Dialogue of Religions* (London: SCM, 1960), 11.

from the apologetic point of view it is necessary to give reasons for accepting one's own faith rather than some other.[33]

While rejecting the methodology and expectations of classical natural theology, Smart acknowledged the need for formulating a fresh kind of natural theology that spoke to the challenges of our pluralistic world. He spoke of this project as "soft natural theology," and although in later years he became increasingly preoccupied with the phenomenology of comparative religion, up until his death in 2001 Smart continued to call for a responsible formulation for analyzing worldviews.[34]

What, though, might this soft natural theology involve? First, it must challenge the reigning assumption that our world is "religiously ambiguous" in the sense that rational reflection cannot adequately resolve at least some questions about the relative acceptability of religious worldviews. This assumption is almost axiomatic in religious studies today. To be sure, increased awareness of religious diversity and disagreement does suggest that the issues are not so clear-cut as some previously thought. But is it really the case that the proposition "God exists" has no greater evidential or rational support than does its denial? Is it really true that the central claims of Theravada Buddhism or Mormonism have the same degree of rational support as those of orthodox Christianity? Moreover, why should it be assumed that disagreement, or lack of public consensus, on a question indicates that rational considerations are inconclusive in responding to it? While consensus is desirable and the epistemic significance of disagreement should not be dismissed, it must also be remembered that a crucial distinction exists between rejecting a belief and refuting it, and that widespread agreement can conceal unwarranted assumptions as well as indicate sound judgment. History reveals that on occasion truth defies consensus and rests with the minority.

Those who embrace the assumption about religious ambiguity typically

---

33. Smart, "Revelation, Reason and Religions," 92.
34. See Ninian Smart, *Reasons and Faiths: An Investigation of Religious Discourse, Christian and Non-Christian* (London: Routledge and Kegan Paul, 1958); idem, *Philosophers and Religious Truth* (New York: Macmillan, 1968); Ninian Smart and Steven Konstantine, *Christian Systematic Theology in a World Context* (Minneapolis: Fortress, 1991), chap. 4; Ninian Smart, "Soft Natural Theology," in *Prospects for Natural Theology*, 198–206; idem, "The Philosophy of Worldviews, or the Philosophy of Religion Transformed," in *Religious Pluralism and Truth: Essays on Cross-cultural Philosophy of Religion*, ed. Thomas Dean (Albany: State University of New York Press, 1995), 17–31; and idem, *Worldviews: Cross-cultural Explorations of Human Beliefs*, 2d ed. (Englewood Cliffs, N.J.: Prentice-Hall, 1995).

regard as doomed to fail any attempt to show that one religious worldview is rationally preferable to others. Some argue there are no nonarbitrary or nonquestion-begging criteria for worldview assessment, so any such attempt is necessarily biased or question-begging. Others hold that there are some very general principles that can be applied in such evaluation, but when applied to specific worldviews and issues the criteria prove to be of no real value. There is no reason, however, to accept either assertion.[35] Unqualified acceptance of either claim results in relativism. Furthermore, philosophers such as Ninian Smart, William Wainwright, Paul Griffiths, and Keith Yandell—each a distinguished philosopher well versed in other religions—recognize the existence of some nonarbitrary criteria that can be used in assessing rival religious worldviews, although their actual application to particular questions can be a complicated and controversial matter.[36] Such assessment requires not only philosophical competence but also a sophisticated understanding of the religious worldviews under evaluation. But there is no reason to suppose that such assessment, when done responsibly, cannot show the rational superiority of one perspective over others.

Second, a soft natural theology should be appropriate to contemporary intellectual and cultural contexts and should be somewhat modest in expectations. There is no reason to expect that an appropriate natural theology in contexts of religious diversity requires a simple algorithmic procedure for testing worldviews or even that it should seek a conclusive deductive argument for theism. Nor should we suppose that soft natural theology commits us to the view that all reasonable persons, when presented with the relevant evidence, will be readily convinced. Few issues of any significance meet these expectations.

Rather, what seems the most promising approach involves what is often called a cumulative case argument, or a comprehensive argument based upon inference from the best explanation.[37] This approach maintains that a strong

35. For more on this point, see Netland, *Encountering Religious Pluralism*, chap. 9.
36. See Ninian Smart, "Truth, Criteria, and Dialogue Between Religions," in *Religious Pluralism and Truth*, 67–71; William Wainwright, "Doctrinal Schemes, Metaphysics and Propositional Truth," in *Religious Pluralism and Truth*, 73–85; idem, "Worldviews, Criteria, and Epistemic Circularity," in *Interreligious Models and Criteria*, ed. J. Kellenberger (New York: St. Martin's Press, 1993), 87–105; idem, *Philosophy of Religion*, chap. 7; Keith Yandell, *Christianity and Philosophy* (Grand Rapids: Eerdmans, 1984), chap. 8; idem, *Philosophy of Religion: A Contemporary Introduction* (London: Routledge, 1999), chaps. 9–13; and Paul Griffiths, *An Apology for Apologetics* (Maryknoll, N.Y.: Orbis, 1991), chaps. 2–4.
37. On cumulative case arguments, see Basil Mitchell, *The Justification of Religious Belief* (Oxford: Oxford University Press, 1981); and William J. Abraham, "Cumulative Case Arguments for Christian Theism," in *The Rationality of Religious Belief: Essays in Honour of*

case for the truth of Christian theism can be established through the careful accumulation and analysis of a wide variety of data from various dimensions of our experience and the world. While none of these phenomena, either individually or collectively, entail the truth of Christian theism, the argument claims that Christian theism provides a more plausible explanation for the data than do other alternatives. An inescapable measure of personal judgment is, of course, involved in such an argument, but such judgments are not necessarily arbitrary. As William Abraham puts it, "Personal judgment simply means the ability to weigh evidence without using some sort of formal calculus."[38]

Third, formulating a model of soft natural theology involves a cumulative case argument that gives special attention to three issues. Given the nontheistic nature of many religions, a major issue will be the question of God's existence. Certainly discussion of the classical theistic arguments will continue to be important.[39] But in light of the perhaps impossibly high expectations that accompany deductive arguments, it might be more productive to take the central insights of such arguments—such as the notion of contingency from the cosmological argument—and present them as part of the phenomena demanding adequate explanation in a cumulative case argument.

A second issue to be given attention in a cumulative case argument involves the growing emphasis upon moral issues and agendas in interreligious dialogue and debates over pluralism. A potentially fruitful line of inquiry concerns the implications of moral awareness for worldviews. Not all religious worldviews acknowledge an ultimate distinction between good and evil, nor can all provide a satisfying reason for our commitment to the dignity of persons and human rights. It can well be argued that the best explanation for certain irreducible features of moral obligation, which George Mavrodes has called the "queerness of morality," is that the world was created by a God who is himself an inherently moral being.[40]

Basil Mitchell, ed. William J. Abraham and Steven W. Holtzer (Oxford: Clarendon, 1989), 17–37. Perhaps the most rigorous and influential recent example of a cumulative case argument for theism is Richard Swinburne's defense of the rationality of Christian theism. See especially Richard Swinburne, *The Existence of God,* 2d ed. (Oxford: Oxford University Press, 1991); and idem, *Is There a God?* (Oxford: Oxford University Press, 1996).

38. Abraham, "Cumulative Case Arguments for Christian Theism," 34.
39. For a discussion of the classical theistic arguments, see Stephen T. Davis, *God, Reason and Theistic Proofs* (Grand Rapids: Eerdmans, 1997).
40. See George Mavrodes, "The Queerness of Morality," in *Philosophy of Religion: Selected Readings,* ed. William L. Rowe and William J. Wainwright, 3d ed. (New York: Harcourt Brace, 1998), 197–207.

A third issue related to a cumulative case argument concerns the epistemology of religious experience and the assumption of a parity across traditions with respect to rationality in religious experiences. Is it just as rational to accept as veridical purported experiences of nirguna Brahman or Emptiness as it is to accept purported experiences of the personal God of Christian theism? Keith Yandell, among others, has rigorously and persuasively argued that certain introspective enlightenment experiences at the heart of Advaita Vedanta Hinduism and Buddhism logically *cannot* be veridical.[41] This argument has, of course, significant implications for religious perspectives that are based upon precisely such experiences.

That rational considerations of this sort can be significant in a person's abandoning a non-Christian worldview and embracing Christian theism is illustrated in the recent conversion of Paul Williams from Buddhism to Roman Catholicism. Williams is professor of Indian and Tibetan philosophy and head of the Department of Theology and Religious Studies at the University of Bristol. He was for twenty years a practicing Buddhist, served as president of the U.K. Association of Buddhist Studies, and has written four highly respected books on Buddhism. But Williams recently converted to Roman Catholicism, and he has shared his spiritual and intellectual journey in the most remarkable book *The Unexpected Way: On Converting from Buddhism to Catholicism.*[42] Among the factors involved in his eventual rejection of Buddhism were (1) his conviction about the incoherence of the allegedly nondualistic introspective experiences at the heart of Buddhism, (2) the inability of Buddhism to account for the integrity of the human person, and (3) the inability of Buddhism to account for the contingency of the universe. In particular, it was Buddhism's failure to address satisfactorily the question, *Why is there something instead of nothing?* that prompted Williams to look again at theism. As Williams puts it, "I have come to believe that there is a gap in the Buddhist explanation of things which for me can only be filled by God, the sort of God spoken of in a Christian tradition such as that of St. Thomas Aquinas."[43]

The issue of contingency was critical for Williams, and he is worth quoting at length on this point:

---

41. See Keith Yandell, *Philosophy of Religion*, chaps. 12–13; and idem, *The Epistemology of Religious Experience* (New York: Cambridge University Press, 1993), chaps. 8–9, 13–14.
42. Paul Williams, *The Unexpected Way: On Converting from Buddhism to Catholicism* (Edinburgh and New York: T. & T. Clark, 2002).
43. Ibid., 27.

Why is there something rather than nothing? Why is there anything at all? And why is there a world in which, among other things, the processes (causation, etc.) detected by the Buddha are the case? Why is it that this way of things *is* the way of things? As the Buddhist scriptures *(sutras)* have it: "Whether Buddhas occur or do not occur, the true way of things (Sanskrit: *dharmata*) remains." Why? Why is it like that? The *dharmata* is not what we call "necessarily existent." That is, there is no logical *contradiction* in a world in which things are not like that. . . . Thus the *dharmata,* the true way of things, is contingent. It could have been otherwise. . . . We have a contingent fact or state of affairs, how things happen to be in the actual world, for which we are entitled to ask the reason. . . .

Any answer to that question—if there is one—would have to be a *necessary* being, a being about which it would make no sense to ask the question why *that* exists rather than not. For the theist God is the answer to this question, and God is needed as the ultimate explanation for existence at any time, keeping things in whatever existence things have.

I think I have to agree with the theist.

For me the question "Why is there something rather than nothing?" has become a bit like what Zen Buddhists call a *koan.* It is a constant niggling question that has worried and goaded me (often, I think, against my will) into a different level of understanding, a different vision, of the world and our place in it.[44]

Furthermore, surely a central piece of the soft natural theology under discussion must be consideration of the distinctiveness of the historical person of Jesus Christ. It is crucial to present the historical data supporting the New Testament claims about Jesus. But in arguing for God's decisive presence and action in Jesus of Nazareth it will also be essential to address the issues concerning the relation between history and religious truth. This is not merely a rehash of Lessing's "Ugly Ditch"; it involves a response to the dominant traditions in Indian, Chinese, and Japanese thought that minimize history and this space-time world, and locate religious truth in an ontologically distinct dimension.

Finally, an adequate soft natural theology must respond to the issues raised

---

44. Ibid., 28–30.

by religious pluralism and take into account the cultural context in which such worldview assessment is done. The plausibility of a soft natural theology with respect to religious diversity depends in part upon its capacity to engage the social and cultural factors underlying the enormous attraction of religious pluralism in the West. Among other things, an appropriate soft natural theology must acknowledge and build upon the very legitimate desire to affirm the growing ethnic, cultural, and religious diversity in the West, without falling victim to a sentimental relativism.

Similarly addressed must be the widespread perception that Christian exclusivism leads to religious intolerance and mistreatment of certain groups. The engine driving the juggernaut of religious pluralism today is concern about how to deal with our very diverse and fragmented societies. The strong push for an undisciplined tolerance that refuses to make negative judgments about other traditions is certainly excessive, but the concern behind it is not without merit. Can Christians, Jews, Muslims, Hindus, Buddhists, Mormons, Bahais, and atheists all live together without resorting to violence? Frankly, the history of religions is not very reassuring. Whether accurate or not—and perhaps it is more accurate than we care to admit—the perception of Christian insensitivity to religious others undermines the plausibility of Christian orthodoxy and reinforces the attraction of pluralism.

It is in this cultural context that the church should seize the opportunity and lead the way, demonstrating how to be both deeply committed to our Christian convictions and also appropriately accepting of diversity. It is not enough to point to the bizarre excesses of multiculturalism or the political correctness movement. We as Christians must demonstrate through our actions and attitudes as well as words that we do accept ethnic and cultural diversity and we will support the right of other religious communities to live and practice in our midst. But at the same time, we cannot abandon our commitment to Jesus Christ as the one Lord and Savior for all humankind. So even as we accept Hindus and Buddhists as fellow citizens, human beings created in God's image, we must urge them to be reconciled to God through Jesus Christ. And when appropriate, we must be prepared to present cogent reasons for their accepting the Christian gospel, rather than other attractive alternatives, as true.

2

Other Religions in Old Testament Theology

DANIEL I. BLOCK

ONOMASTIC EVIDENCE AVAILABLE from both the Old Testament and extrabiblical inscriptions suggests that, throughout Israel's history as a nation, Yahwism was the predominant religion within every stratum and region.[1] The Old Testament as a whole, however, presents a rather different picture. From the nation's founding at Sinai (Exod. 32) to its final demise in 586, the religion practiced by the Israelites apparently followed a variety of forms, some syncretistic, others thoroughly pagan. The course of Israel's history—and indeed the shape of the Old Testament itself—can only be imagined had the people as a whole lived according to the ideals championed by the authors of the Old Testament. As attested to in the Old Testament and in the archaeological record, Israelite faith varied textually, iconographically, and monumentally. The writers of the Old Testament represent only one form of ancient Israelite faith, that of monotheistic and ethical Yahwism, which we refer to hereafter as "orthodox Yahwism."

---

1. For brief discussion and bibliography, see Daniel I. Block, *The Gods of the Nations: Studies in Ancient Near Eastern National Theology,* 2d ed., ETS Studies (Grand Rapids: Baker, 2000), 40–41. J. Tigay (*You Shall Have No Other Gods: Israelite Religion in the Light of Hebrew Inscriptions,* HSM 31 [Atlanta: Scholars Press, 1986], 7–8) estimates that around eleven percent of the names in the Old Testament were probably pagan, bearing elements like "Baal" (Ishbaal) and "Haddu" (Hadoram). The epigraphic evidence is even more one-sided. Based on the evidence available in 1986, Tigay noted that only 35 names bear pagan theophores (5.9%), while 592 are Yahwistic (94.1%). His calculation excludes names containing *'el* or *'ēlî* (p. 15).

Of course, the question of predominant religion involves not just those Old Testament texts that explicitly refer to deviant expressions of faith (from the Yahwistic authors' point of view)—that is, texts that proscribe the worship of other deities, that describe Israel's participation in the worship of other deities, or that denounce Israel for worshiping other deities. The book of Judges illustrates dramatically and graphically the link between spiritual recidivism and ethical degeneration. Many, if not most, of the social ills that afflicted the nation relate directly to the abandonment of the ethical monotheism of orthodox Yahwism in favor of syncretistic henotheism or overtly pagan idolatry. But by its very nature the current subject of biblical faith and other religions in the Old Testament privileges orthodox Yahwism, for the Old Testament represents the perspective of the winners in the centuries-long conflict between Yahwism and other forms of religion. Not only does the Old Testament from beginning to end deride and denounce other expressions of faith and devotion, but the authors also persistently and consistently suppress the voices of those more sympathetic to other forms.

The question is complicated, however, in that the Old Testament knows nothing of faith in the abstract—that is, faith as "a doctrine or system of doctrines, propositions, etc., held to be true,"[2] or faith as "belief in the truths of religion."[3] Indeed, biblical Hebrew lacks a word for "faith" in this sense. The nearest counterpart is *yārē'*, "fear," but as an abstract notion it generally means "fright, awe." When used as an approximate designation for faith it is regularly followed by a divine direct object, that is, "to fear Yahweh," or "to fear another god/other gods." Biblical Hebrew also lacks a word for "religion."[4] Rather, religious devotion is concretized with specific expressions like *hištaḥăwâ lipnê*, "to prostrate oneself before [a deity]"; *hithallēk/hālak lipnê*, "to walk before [a deity]"; *hālak 'aḥărê*, "to walk after, that is, follow [a deity]"; *'ābad*, "to serve, work for [a deity]"; and in Aramaic *pĕlaḥ*, "to serve, worship, revere, minister to [a deity]." Accordingly, an essay that addresses biblical faith and other religions in the Old Testament would be extremely short. But when contemplating this topic, what is really meant is the disposition of biblical Yahwism toward

---

2. *The New International Webster's Comprehensive Dictionary of the English Language*, Deluxe Encyclopedic ed. (Naples, Fla.: Trident Press, 1996), s.v. "faith."

3. *Oxford English Dictionary*, compact ed. (Oxford: Oxford University Press, 1971), s.v. "faith."

4. The word is lacking in all the modern translations of the Old Testament: AV, ASV, RSV, NASB, NIV, NRSV, ESV. In relation to this point, James Barr observes, "But the Bible is not about religion; it is about God and his action, his revelation, and so on." See James Barr, *The Concept of Biblical Theology: An Old Testament Perspective* (Minneapolis: Fortress, 1999), 107.

devotion to and/or the service of other gods in the Old Testament. And on that topic, the Old Testament has a great deal to say. The subject, then, will be examined under three headings:

1. Yahwistic parallels to pagan religious ideas and practices;
2. Yahwistic exploitation of pagan religious ideas and practices;
3. Yahwistic repudiation of pagan religious ideas and practices.

It should be noted at the outset that this discussion will not be balanced, and each of these subtopics will not be given equal treatment. Most readers will recognize immediately that the last of these three subtopics is much more overt in the Old Testament than the first two.

YAHWISTIC PARALLELS TO PAGAN RELIGIOUS IDEAS AND PRACTICES

One need not look far to discover fundamental common denominators between Yahwistic faith and extrabiblical religious perceptions. Shared notions include customs, rituals, sacred objects, architecture, iconography, and religious personnel, but the current discussion will be limited to two areas: shared *belief* and shared *religious practices*.

SHARED BELIEFS

Most ancient Near Easterners believed in a three-tiered universe structured something like this:

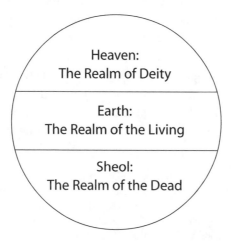

Most ancient Near Easterners would have assumed, too, that the occupants of the heavenly realm antedated the universe—in fact they created the world. It was also assumed that human beings were subservient to the gods. Most ancient Near Easterners were also keenly aware that their behavior, whether ethical or cultic, had angered the gods and that the gods expected some sort of penitential ritual to placate their wrath. All ancient Near Easterners assumed that the gods determined the fates of human beings, this applying not only to the course of historical events in particular, but also to people's prosperity in general. Yahwists also shared with their neighbors the conviction that, in death, people departed to the netherworld, where they continued to exist as "living corpses."

Obvious parallels are also evident in the manner in which gods relate to their subjects. Specifically, in the ancient Near East there was widespread recognition of the tripartite symbiotic relationship involving a patron deity, the land over which the god exercised authority/care, and the human occupants of that land. Just as the god's disposition toward his or her land was influenced by the ethical and cultic conduct of the human subjects, so Yahweh's disposition toward his land and toward his people was determined by the response of the Israelites to him. Persistent human misconduct, in fact, resulted in the deities' abandonment of their respective lands, leaving the people at the mercy of invaders. In Yahwism, this perspective is evident especially in the covenant curses of Leviticus 26 and Deuteronomy 28, and represents the heart of the judgment oracles of later prophets. At the same time, the Israelites shared with some of their pagan neighbors the view that their God would not be angry with them forever. In due course, he would have a change of heart, restore the exiled population to their native land, install a king over the land, and return to the land himself. In this respect Israel's later messianic hope, as expressed for example in Ezekiel, is perfectly at home in the ancient Near Eastern religious world.[5]

Although a previous generation of critical scholars tended to interpret these links in ideology, custom, and design as evidence for Israelite borrowing from other cultures, now we are more prepared to recognize parallel developments and/or Yahwists' adoption of familiar symbols to communicate divine truth.

---

5. I have developed this theme in several places. In addition to my commentary on Ezekiel, see Block, *Gods of the Nations*, 113–47; as well as idem, "Divine Abandonment: Ezekiel's Adaptation of an Ancient Near Eastern Motif," in *The Book of Ezekiel: Theological and Anthropological Perspectives*, ed. M. S. Odell and J. T. Strong, SBL Symposium Series 9 (Atlanta: Society of Biblical Literature, 2000), 15–42.

An evangelical perspective proposes that these common features originate in some pristine revelation that, in the hands of pagans, was garbled almost beyond recognition, but whose purity was secured in Israel through the inspirational work of the Holy Spirit.

SHARED RELIGIOUS PRACTICES

In addition to these shared beliefs, orthodox Yahwists shared many religious practices with their neighbors. For example, they communed with their deity through prayer and sacrifice. The need for both arose not only from a general sense of dependence upon the deity, but also from the deep conviction that the god/gods were angered through human sin. Accordingly, certain offerings were presented to "smooth the face" of the deity;[6] others were presented as food/gifts for the deity and/or eaten in his or her presence as an act of fellowship; still others involved simply purification rites. Most of the categories of sacrifice found in Leviticus 1–5 are, in fact, attested to outside Israel, most notably *zebaḥ*, "sacrifice, sacrificial meal"; *šĕlāmîm*, "peace/well-being offering"; *ʿōlâ*, "whole burnt offering"; *minḥâ*, "gift, grain/cereal offering."[7]

It has long been recognized that, although the blueprint for the temple was revealed by Yahweh to David in writing (1 Chron. 28:11–19), in the actual construction Solomon decorated it with many well-known Phoenician motifs:

---

6. *ḥillâ pĕnê YHWH*, cf. Malachi 1:9.
7. Cognates of *zebaḥ* are attested to in Ugaritic (*"dbḥ," UT* #637), Phoenician/Punic (J. Hoftijzer and K. Jongeling, "*zbḥ*," in *DNWSI* [Leiden: Brill, 1995], 1:301–2), Aramaic *(zbḥ)*, Akkadian (W. von Soden, "*zību*," in *AHw* [Wiesbaden: Harrassowitz, 1965–81], 3:1525; cf. R. E. Averbeck, "זבח," in *NIDOTTE*, ed. W. G. VanGemeren [Grand Rapids: Zondervan, 1997], 1:1066–68). Cognates of *šĕlāmîm*, "peace/well-being offering," are attested to in Ugaritic *(šlm/šlmm, UT* #2424), Punic (Hoftijzer and Jongeling, "*šlm*," in *DNWSI*, 2:1152); in Akkadian this offering is represented by *keldi;* in Hittite by *keldiya* or *tale šulaš* (cf. R. E. Averbeck, "שֶׁלֶם," in *NIDOTTE*, 4:135–36). Cognates of *ʿōlâ*, "whole burnt offering," are apparently attested to in Neo-Punic *(ʿlt)* and perhaps in the Proto-Sinaitic inscriptions (see D. Kellermann, *TDOT*, ed. G. J. Botterweck and H. Ringgren, trans. J. T. Willis, G. W. Bromiley, and D. E. Green [Grand Rapids: Eerdmans, 1974–], 11:97–98), but corresponding designations for this offering elsewhere include *kll* (cf. Hebrew *kālîl*, "whole, complete") in Punic, *šrp* (cf. Hebrew *śārap*, "to burn") in Ugaritic (*UT* #2489), and *ambassi* in Hittite (cf. R. E. Averbeck "עֹלָה," in *NIDOTTE*, 3:405–7). Cognates of *minḥâ*, "gift, grain/ cereal offering," are attested to in Ugaritic (*"mnḥ," UT* #1500), Phoenician and Punic *(mnḥt,)*, and Official Aramaic (Hoftijzer and Jongeling, "*mnḥh*," in *DNWSI*, 2:659; cf. R. E. Averbeck, "מִנְחָה," in *NIDOTTE*, 2:978–79). For a discussion of these and other sacrificial expressions within their ancient Near Eastern context, see M. Weinfeld, "Social and Cultic Institutions in the Priestly Source Against Their Ancient Near Eastern Background," *Proceedings of the Eighth World Congress of Jewish Studies* (1983): 105–11.

cherubim, palm trees, open flowers (1 Kings 7:29–36).[8] Perhaps even more remarkable is the basic structure of both the tabernacle and the temple. Like other ancient Near Eastern temples, both structures were perceived primarily as the residence of God and consisted of two main rooms: the large front hall (Holy Place) and the most sacred room at the back, the *dĕbîr* (Holy of Holies). In pagan temples this room housed the statue of the deity. Although Yahwism was aniconic,[9] conceptually the room served a similar function, housing the ark of the covenant and the *kĕbōd YHWH,* both symbols of the divine presence. The parallels between the Israelite temple and extrabiblical patterns have been dramatically illustrated by John Monson's recent analysis of the Syrian temple at Ain Dara.[10]

YAHWISTIC EXPLOITATION OF PAGAN RELIGIOUS IDEAS AND PRACTICES

One does not need to read far in the biblical text before encountering pagan notions that have been adopted and exploited for Yahwistic purposes, but without the process giving assent to the veracity of those notions.

YAHWEH'S EXPLOITATION OF PAGAN PRACTICES

Included in this category would be Ezekiel's reference to Yahweh's guiding Nebuchadnezzar to attack Jerusalem rather than the Ammonites. The Babylonian king resorted to divination, specifically by manipulating arrows (rhabdomancy), consulting (*šā'al*) the *teraphim,* and examining a sheep liver (hepatoscopy; Ezek. 21:21). Although the Mosaic Torah expressly condemns these kinds of activity as detestable practices of the nations (*tôʿăbôt haggôyim,*

---

8. Cf. O. Keel, *The Symbolism of the Biblical World: Ancient Near Eastern Iconography and the Book of Psalms,* trans. T. J. Hallett (New York: Seabury, 1978), 141–44. For a detailed discussion of the Israelite temple within its ancient Near Eastern context, see Victor (Avigdor) Hurowitz, *I Have Built You an Exalted House: Temple Building in the Bible in the Light of Mesopotamian and Northwest Semitic Writings,* JSOTSup 115 (Sheffield: Sheffield Academic Press, 1992); for a more popular treatment, see Volkmar Fritz, "Temple Architecture: What Can Archaeology Tell Us About Solomon's Temple?" *BAR* 13, no. 4 (July–August 1987): 38–49.
9. For a study of the nature and history of aniconism in Israel against its ancient Near Eastern cultural background, see Tryggve Mettinger, *No Graven Image? Israelite Aniconism in Its Ancient Near Eastern Context,* CBOT 42 (Stockholm: Almqvist & Wiksell, 1995).
10. John Monson, "The New 'Ain Dara Temple: Closest Solomonic Parallel," *BAR* 26, no. 3 (May–June 2000): 20–35, 67.

Deut. 18:9–14), in this case they worked. A pagan king employed strictly forbidden techniques of divination and thereby discovered the will of Yahweh.[11]

Closer to Israel's home we may also cite Saul's consultation of the medium *('ôb)* at Endor on the day before his death (1 Sam. 28:3–25). With his alienation from Samuel, Saul—the most tragic figure in Israel's history—had also lost contact with God. In Saul, a descendant of the wretched Benjamites who had stood up to defend sodomites among them (the people of Gibeah, Judg. 19–21), Yahweh had given the Israelites exactly what they had demanded—"a king like the nations [had]" (1 Sam. 8:5, 19–20). Despite Saul's earlier efforts to eradicate all mediums *('ôbôt* and *yiddě'ōnîm)*, he thoroughly compromised himself spiritually. And when Yahweh refused to respond to his pleas for guidance, either through dreams, or the Urim, or his prophets (28:6), Saul sought out the medium at Endor to bring Samuel back from the netherworld. Again, even though Yahweh was absolutely opposed to such practices, remarkably it worked! From the ground emerged a figure, whom the medium perceived as a divine being *('ělōhîm,* v. 13). But there was no doubt in the writer's mind about the identity of this shrouded figure (vv. 15–16). That this was indeed Samuel is confirmed both by the figure's recollection of his past relationship with Saul (vv. 16b–18) and by the precise fulfillment of his prediction on the following day.[12]

How could this happen? As puzzling as Yahweh's communicating with a pagan in the first instance and a syncretistic Israelite in the second is the fact that he would do so through absolutely forbidden pagan forms. Yahweh obviously retains complete freedom with respect to the means he uses to relate to human beings. When communicating with pagans or paganized Israelites, he speaks in a language they understand. But this is more than mere accommodation; in so doing he also exposes the folly of their perceptions.

YAHWEH'S EXPLOITATION OF PAGAN PERCEPTIONS

Similar phenomena occur elsewhere in the Old Testament. Although Ezekiel's inaugural vision is a complete riddle to most modern readers, within the context of ancient Near Eastern religious iconography all of the elements— the multiheaded creatures, the cherubim, the chariot, the platform bearing a

---

11. On this text, see Daniel I. Block, *The Book of Ezekiel Chapters 1–24*, NICOT (Grand Rapids: Eerdmans, 1997), 681–89.

12. Compare 1 Sam. 28:19 and 31:1–13.

throne, which in turn bears a divine figure—make perfect sense.[13] What Ezekiel sees is not an actual representation, but a reflection of deity. Nevertheless, the redundancy of "a likeness like the appearance of a man" guards the prophet from even contemplating any idolatrous notions. While extra-Israelite motifs have been incorporated into the vision, this strategy does not represent capitulation to pagan thought. On the contrary, with powerful visual rhetoric this vision challenges pagan conceptions at every turn. The glory of Yahweh cannot be reduced to human definition or plastic art. Everything about the vision is in the superlative mode. God is alone above the platform, removed from all creatures, and stunning in his radiance. There is none other beside(s) him. But this does not prevent him from communicating with mortals. Whereas Yahweh had chosen "the lip of Canaan" (Isa. 19:18) as the vehicle of verbal intercourse in an earlier revelatory moment, now he adopts the art of Mesopotamia as his method of ocular communication. And in so doing he beats the pagans and their gods at their own games.

YAHWEH'S EXPLOITATION OF ROLES ATTRIBUTED TO PAGAN GODS

Under the rubric of exploited pagan ideas should also be included those numerous texts that apply to Yahweh roles that non-Yahwists normally associated with pagan gods. In the Old Testament these roles are especially evident in pronouncements of blessing and judgment. With respect to the former, Deuteronomy 7:13–14 provides a striking example of Yahweh assuming fertility functions that Canaanites generally attributed to Baal/Hadad—the storm-god—and other lesser divinities responsible for specific crops. The blessings Moses lists here represent tangible rewards that Yahweh promises to those who pass the test of love through their obedience. Moses begins by cataloguing on the one hand those areas of life upon which people are most dependent for their security, and on the other those areas where the fertility-gods of Canaan were thought to be active (v. 13). "The fruit of your womb and the fruit of your soil" serves as a thesis statement covering all areas of agriculture upon which humans are dependent.[14] Reversing the order, Moses specifies three products that derive directly from the soil (grain, wine, and oil), and a pair that derive from domesticated livestock (calves and lambs).

---

13. For a study of the correlation between Ezekiel's vision and ancient Near Eastern art, see Othmar Keel, *Jahwe-Visionen und Siegelkunst: Eine neue Deutung der Majestätschilderun in Jes 6, Ez 1 und Sach 4*, SBB 84/85 (Stuttgart: Katholisches Bibelwerk, 1977), 125–273. For additional discussion, see Block, *Book of Ezekiel Chapters 1–24*, 95–104.
14. Although, as will be learned from verse 14, "fruit of the womb" also includes children.

Inasmuch as each of the terms Moses uses for these products is linked with the pantheon of Canaanite deities, here an informed reader recognizes a subtle polemic against the idolatry of the land. *Dāgān*, "grain," is cognate to the name for the god of grain, Dagon, known in the Ugaritic texts as the father of Baal (cf. Judg. 16:23; 1 Sam. 8:1–12) and from the Emar and Mari texts as the head of the pantheon in the region of Syria around the great bend of the Euphrates.[15] The rare word *tîrôš*, which Moses uses instead of the more common *yayin* (cf. Deut. 14:26), is cognate to the name of the god Tirshu/Tirash, attested to in the El-Amarna letters and in Ugaritic (as *trṯ*).[16] Another rare word, *yiṣhār*, employed in place of the more common *šemen* (cf. 8:8), for olive oil, may be cognate to the name of the old god of olive oil.[17] The unusual expression, *šĕgar-᾽ĕlāpêkā*,[18] literally "increase of your herds," rather than *῾ēgel*, for calf, is linked to the god Shaggar/Sheger, whose veneration is attested to in Ugaritic, Emar, Deir ῾Allā, and Punic texts, and who in some instances apparently functions as the deity of the full moon.[19] The mythological connection is most obvious, however, in the designation for lambs, *῾aštĕrōt-ṣō᾽nĕkā*, which substitutes for the more common *kebeś* (cf. Exod. 29:39). The veneration of Ishtar/Astarte, the goddess of fertility, was among the most widespread of any divinity in the ancient Near East. Her role in fertility is reflected in an ancient text from Babylon:

> Bow down to your city goddess [Ishtar] that she may grant you off-spring, take thought for your livestock, remember the planting.[20]

The extent to which the Israelites in Moses' audience caught the links between the words he chose to use and the religion of the Canaanites is uncertain. However, his preference for these rare expressions seems to represent a deliberate stab at the jugular of Canaanite religion. Not these pagan deities, but Yahweh, the God of Israel, is Israel's only guarantee of security. In the land

---

15. On *Dāgān*/Dagon, see J. F. Healey, "Dagon," in *DDD*, ed. K. van der Toorn, B. Becking, and P. W. van der Horst (Leiden: Brill, 1995), 216–19; and D. E. Fleming, *The Installation of Baal's High Priestess at Emar*, HSS 42 (Atlanta: Scholars Press, 1992), 240–48.

16. On which see J. F. Healey, "Tirash תירש תידש," in *DDD*, 871–72.

17. Cf. N. Wyatt, "Oil יצהר," in *DDD*, 640.

18. Elsewhere only in Deut. 28:4, 18, 51; Exodus 13:12, substituting for the more common *῾ēgel* (cf. 9:16, 21).

19. Cf. K. van der Toorn, "Sheger שגר," in *DDD*, 760–62; and Fleming, *Installation of Baal's High Priestess at Emar*, 205.

20. Cf. W. G. Lambert, *Babylonian Wisdom Literature* (Oxford: Clarendon, 1960), 108–9. For further information on Astarte, see N. Wyatt, "Astarte," in *DDD*, 109–14.

that he promised on oath to give to the descendants of their ancestors, the blessing of the crops and herds would be in his hands alone.[21]

Much later in the book, Moses concludes his blessing of the Israelite tribes on an exuberant note of praise to Yahweh and congratulations to Israel, so privileged to have him as their God:

> There is none like God, O Jeshurun,
>> who rides through the heavens to your help,
>>> majestic through the skies.
> He subdues the ancient gods,
>> shatters the forces of old;
> he drove out the enemy before you,
>> and said, "Destroy!"
> So Israel lives in safety,
>> untroubled is Jacob's abode
> in a land of grain and wine,
>> where the heavens drop down dew.
> Happy are you, O Israel!
> Who is like you,
>> a people saved by Yahweh,
> the shield of your help,
>> and the sword of your triumph!
> Your enemies shall come fawning to you,
>> and you shall tread on their backs.[22]
>> —Deuteronomy 33:26–29 NRSV, modified

The image of Yahweh riding the heavens/skies recalls Canaanite myths recorded in the tablets found at Ugarit, in which one of Baal's epithets is "Cloudrider" *(rkb ʿrpt).*[23]

The exploitation of Canaanite religious ideas occurs also in several of the

---

21. M. Weinfeld (*Deuteronomy 1–11: A New Translation with Introduction and Commentary,* AB 5 [New York: Doubleday, 1991], 373) notes that the sequence grain, wine, cattle, and sheep is identical to that found in the blessings recorded in a Phoenician inscription by Azitawada (early seventh century B.C.). For the text, see *CIS* 2.148–49 (iii.2–11).
22. In general, our scriptural citations represent adaptations of NRSV.
23. As translated by Mark S. Smith in *Ugaritic Narrative Poetry,* ed. S. B. Parker, SBLWAW 9 (Atlanta: Scholars Press, 1997), 124, passim. For a study of the significance of the epithet, "Cloudrider," see W. Herrmann, "Rider upon the Clouds," in *DDD,* 703–5. On the mythical sea monster Leviathan, see C. Uehlinger, "Leviathan," in *DDD,* 511–15.

psalms, most notably Psalms 29 and 104, which some have argued represent Yahwistic makeovers of originally Egyptian or Canaanite hymns in praise of the storm-god.[24] The storm-god imagery is especially impressive in the opening stanza of the latter:

> Bless Yahweh, O my soul.
> O Yahweh my God, you are very great.
> You are clothed with honor and majesty,
> wrapped in light as with a garment.
> You stretch out the heavens like a tent;
> You set the beams of your chambers on the waters;
> You make the clouds your chariot;
> You ride on the wings of the wind;
> You make the winds your messengers,
> fire and flame your ministers.
> —Psalm 104:1b–4 NRSV, modified

In verses 10–17 the psalmist celebrates Yahweh's role in ensuring the fertility of the earth, and in verses 18–30 he praises Yahweh for his care for the animals, noting specifically Leviathan, the mythical sea monster (Ugaritic *ltn*), whom Yahweh has created to be his pet.[25] In regard to the Canaanite images found in the above psalm, Craigie commented, "External influences on the psalm have undergone thorough adaptation and have been brought into harmony with the general tenor of Hebrew religious thought."[26]

Similar rhetorical exploitation of pagan motifs occurs in Old Testament pronouncements of judgment. Such is evident especially in the way biblical authors speak of the involvement of secondary forces of destruction. Deuteronomy 32:23–25 offers a striking illustration:

---

24. For discussion of these and other psalms of this type, see Oswald Loretz, *Ugarit-Texte und Thronbesteigigungs-psalmen: Die Metamorphose des Regenspenders Baal-Jahwe (Ps 24, 7–10; 29; 47; 93; 95–100 sowie Ps 77, 17–20; 114)*, UBL 7 (Münster: Ugarit-Verlag, 1988), rev. ed. of Psalm 29. *Kanaanäische El- und Baaltraditionen in jüdischer Sicht*, UBL 2 (1984).

25. For more detailed study of the possible foreign cultural roots of this psalm, see Peter C. Craigie, "The Comparison of Hebrew Poetry: Psalm 104 in the Light of Egyptian and Ugaritic Poetry," *Semitics* 4 (1974): 10–21. For a general discussion of the issues and further bibliography, see Leslie C. Allen, *Psalms 101–150*, WBC 21 (Waco, Tex.: Word, 1983), 28–32.

26. Craigie, "Comparison of Hebrew Poetry," 18. For a recent interpretation of the book of Job against the backdrop of ancient Near Eastern mythology, see R. S. Fyall, *Now My Eyes See You: Images of Creation and Evil in the Book of Job*, NSBT 12 (Downers Grove, Ill.: InterVarsity, 2002).

> I will heap disasters *[ra'ôt]* upon them,
>   spend my arrows *[hissay]* against them:
>   wasting hunger *[ra'āb]*,
>   burning consumption *[rešep]*,
>   bitter pestilence *[qeteb]*.
> The teeth of beasts *[běhēmôt]* I will send against them,
> with venom of things crawling in the dust.
> In the street the sword *[hereb]* shall bereave,
> and in the chambers terror *['êmâ]*,
> for young man and woman alike,
> nursing child and old gray head. (NRSV)

This text provides the background for Ezekiel 5:16–17. All three words in Ezekiel's *hissê hārā'āb hārā'îm*, "deadly arrows of famine," appear in the first three lines quoted above. But this raises the question, *How can Ezekiel associate arrows so directly with famine?* The answer may lie in this same Deuteronomy text, which juxtaposes *rā'āb* with *rešep* and *qeteb*. The mythological connotations of the latter two expressions surface elsewhere in the Old Testament. Note especially Habakkuk 3:5, in which Pestilence *(deber)* and Plague *(rešep)* appear as attendants of God as he proceeds from Teman.[27] Remarkably, several extrabiblical texts indicate that the symbol of Resheph was the arrow.[28] Resheph may also serve as background to the *hēs yā'ûp*, "flying arrow," which is conjoined with *deber*, "plague," and *qeteb*, "scourge," in Psalm 91:5–6. The origin of the expression "calamitous arrows of famine" should, therefore, probably be sought in pagan mythology.

---

27. See also Job 5:7; Psalms 76:4; 78:48; and Song of Songs 8:6.
28. *UT* 1001:3, *b'l hz ršp*, "Resheph, lord of the arrow," and *UT* 128:II:6, *ršp zbl*, "Prince Resheph." His ventures are reflected in the legend of Kirta 19: *mḥmšt . yitsp . ršp*, "A fifth was gathered by Resheph." Cf. Smith, *Ugaritic Narrative Poetry*, 12. Note also the reference to *ršp hṣ*, "Resheph of the Arrow," mentioned on a fourth-century B.C. Phoenician inscription (H. Donner and W. Röllig, *KAI*, 2d ed. [Wiesbaden: Harrassowitz, 1966–69], 32:3–4). On this figure, see J. Day, "New Light on the Mythological Background of the Allusion to Resheph in Habakkuk III 5," *VT* 29 (1979): 259–74; Y. Yadin, "New Gleanings on Resheph From Ugarit," *Biblical and Related Studies Presented to Samuel Iwry* (Winona Lake: Eisenbrauns, 1985), 259–74. M. Weinfeld ("Divine Intervention in War in Ancient Israel and in the Ancient Near East," *History, Historiography and Interpretation: Studies in Biblical and Cuneiform Literature* [Jerusalem: Magnes and Hebrew University Press, 1983], 124–31) associates Resheph with the "shooting stars" in Judges 5:20–22. For a discussion of Resheph, see P. Xella, "Resheph," in *DDD*, 700–703.

Similar exploitation may be observed in regard to the figure of Mot, the god of the netherworld in Canaanite mythology. The term *māwet/môt* usually refers to the experience of death. In some poetic texts with mythological backgrounds, however, the word appears to be used as a proper name identifying the chthonic power behind death, Mot of the Ugaritic texts.[29] Especially striking is Hosea 13:14, where Mawet, "Death," is personified as the ruler of the netherworld who sends out his plagues (*Deber*, pl.) as his agents:

> Shall I ransom them from the power of Sheol?
> Shall I redeem them from Death *[māwet]*?
> O Death *[māwet]*, where are your plagues?
> O Sheol, where is your destruction?
> Compassion is hidden from my eyes.

Although critical scholars tend to interpret texts like this as tacit admissions of the existence of such divinities, neither psalmist nor prophet would have countenanced such a notion.[30] On the contrary, orthodox Yahwists thoroughly demythologized all these notions. Yahweh himself assumed the role of Resheph and all other malevolent spirits that might have kept non-Israelites in constant fear. Furthermore, it is not Mot but Yahweh alone who has the keys to the gates of death and the netherworld.[31] In Ezekiel 5:16–17 the arrows pointed at Jerusalem are Yahweh's own. His intention is to intensify the famine in the city until the staff of bread is broken, in fulfillment of the covenant curses of Leviticus 26 and Deuteronomy 28. According to these texts, Yahweh has a host of destructive agents at his disposal: pestilence, disease, foreign armies (the sword), drought, and wild animals. When disaster strikes, it is Yahweh's work,

---

29. Habakkuk 2:5; Job 18:13–14; 28:22; Hosea 13:14; Isaiah 28:15, 18; Psalm 49:15; Song of Songs 8:6; cf. also Psalm 141:7; Proverbs 1:12; 27:20; 30:15–16; Isaiah 5:14. In a few instances *māwet/môt* refers to the place of the dead (Job 38:17; Pss. 6:5[6]; 9:14; 107:18; Prov. 7:27).

30. The comment of Donald E. Gowan with respect to Jeremiah (*Theology of the Prophetic Books: The Death and Resurrection of Israel* [Louisville: Westminster/John Knox, 1998], 104–5) is typical: "Like his predecessors since the time of Amos, he [Jeremiah] does not speak of a theoretical monotheism, but he is a 'practical monotheist'; that is, it matters not whether other gods may exist; for Israel, Yahweh is the only God." Support for this interpretation is found in the first commandment, "You shall have no other gods before [or besides] me" (Exod. 20:3).

31. On this image of Sheol, see Isaiah 38:10 ("the gates of Sheol") and Job 38:17; Psalms 9:13; 107:18 ("the gates of death"). Cf. also Revelation 1:18.

not the effects of malevolent spirits dispatched by Mot, the supposed king of the netherworld.[32]

YAHWEH'S EXPLOITATION OF DIVINE EPITHETS

Biblical authors exploit pagan mythological motifs for rhetorical purposes, either to expose the folly of Israelite syncretism or to declare the supremacy of Yahweh. Such is the function of epithetic expressions like "God of gods," which appears four times in the Old Testament: Deuteronomy 10:17; Psalm 136:2; Daniel 2:47; 11:36. Interpreted literally, this phrase suggests the existence of other gods, and is undoubtedly how Nebuchadnezzar, a non-Israelite, used the expression in Daniel 2:47, to which we return in a moment.

Moses' use of the expression in Deuteronomy 10:17, however, should be interpreted in the light of earlier unequivocally monotheistic statements such as those found in 4:32–40.[33] In 10:17 Moses declares Yahweh's supremacy through a single verbless clause with three predicates: "For Yahweh your God, he is God of gods, Lord of lords, the El." Each epithet is loaded with meaning. Like "heaven of heavens" in verse 14, "God of gods" (ʾĕlōhê hāʾĕlōhîm) and "Lord of lords" (ʾădōnê hāʾădōnîm) express the superlative degree. Both epithets appear in hymnic liturgical formulae in later texts. Note especially, Psalm 136:1–2, the only place where these two epithets appear together:

> Give thanks to the God of gods, for his *ḥesed* endures forever.
> Give thanks to the Lord of lords, for his *ḥesed* endures forever.

---

32. In contrast to the peoples around Israel, who lived in constant dread of malevolent spirits, Old Testament Yahwism has no place for such divine or semi-divine beings. The nearest equivalent is the "evil spirit" that Yahweh sends upon people to create disaster (cf. Judg. 9:23; 1 Sam. 16:14). The epilogue in Job expressly attributes to Yahweh the calamities *(rāʿâ)* by which Job's adversary *(hassāṭān)* had robbed this saint of all he possessed (42:11).

33. Whether they treat this chapter as a unity or a literary conglomerate, critical scholars are virtually unanimous in interpreting it as a late, if not the latest, insertion into the book of Deuteronomy, composed during the exile to give hope to a community that had lost its way spiritually and whose election as the people of Yahweh seemed jeopardized. See Georg Braulik, "Wisdom, Divine Presence and Law: Reflections on the Kerygma of Deut 4:5–8," in *The Theology of Deuteronomy: Collected Essays of Georg Braulik, O.S.B.*, trans. U. Lindblad, Bibal Collected Essays 2 (N. Richmond Hills, Tex.: Bibal, 1994), 1–25; M. Rose, *5. Mose, vol. 2, 5. Mose 1–11 und 26–34 Rahmenstücke zum Gesetzkorpus,* Zürcher Bibelkommentar, AT 5.2 (Zurich: Theologischer Verlag, 1994), 488–503; and Weinfeld, *Deuteronomy 1–11,* 229–30.

The expression "God of gods" declares Yahweh's superiority over all divine and semi-divine beings. It expresses a truth that became especially important as the collapse of Judah and Jerusalem approached in the sixth century B.C. In the ancient world it was generally assumed that the outcomes of military battles on earth were actually determined by the relative strengths of the patron deities of the respective nations at war. And even as Nebuchadnezzar's battering rams were being set up against the walls of Jerusalem, the inhabitants remained convinced that their God, who had entered into an irrevocable covenant with them, was superior to Marduk, the god of the Babylonians, and that he would protect his temple, his city, and his people. When Jerusalem finally fell, the faith of many of its citizens was devastated. Just as in an earlier era Yahweh had demonstrated in the plagues and the Exodus (Exod. 12:12; Num. 33:4) his superiority over the gods of Egypt, so Marduk had apparently demonstrated his superiority over Yahweh in this context.

It is scarcely coincidental that the only other occurrences of the expression "God of gods" occurs in the book of Daniel, one of whose major themes is the supremacy—despite all appearances to the contrary—of Yahweh over all gods. In fact, in 2:47 we hear from the lips of the king of Babylon himself, "Truly, your God is God of gods and Lord of kings." The expression recurs in 11:36, where Daniel predicts the appearance of a hostile king who will "exalt and magnify himself above every god and will say unheard-of things against the God of gods." If Moses speaks of Yahweh as "God of gods," he is not thereby assenting to the existence of other gods alongside Yahweh (cf. Deut. 4:35, 39); his statement is purely rhetorical.[34]

The third title Moses ascribes to Yahweh, the God of Israel, is "the El" (*hāʾēl;* cf. also 7:9). Strictly speaking *ʾēl/ʾêl* is a common noun meaning "god, divine

---

34. If "God of gods" declares Yahweh's supremacy over all spiritual and heavenly powers, then "Lord of lords" speaks to his supremacy over earthly rulers. This expression occurs in the Old Testament only here and in Psalm 136:3. Elsewhere supreme earthly rulers are referred to as "king of kings" (*melek mĕlākîm;* Ezra 7:12; Ezek. 26:7; Dan. 2:37) and "lord of kings" (*mārēʾ malekîn;* Dan. 2:47), which probably explains why the Aramaic Targums and the Syriac Peshitta translate *melek mĕlākîm* as *mrʾ mlkyn,* "lord of kings." Similar epithets for supreme rulers occur also in extrabiblical texts: a Philistine king refers to Pharaoh in Aramaic as *mrʾ mlky,* "lord of kings" (Donner and Röllig, *KAI,* 266:1, 6); Eshhmunazzar king of Sidon refers to his Persian overlord as *ʾdn mlkm,* "lord of kings" (ibid., 14:18); Akkadian equivalents include *bēl bēle,* "lord of lords"; *bēl šarrāni,* "lord of kings"; *šar šarrāni,* "king of kings." On the Akkadian epithets, see M.J. Seux, *Épithèts royals Akkadiennes et Sumériennes* (Paris: Letouzey er Ané, 1967), 55–56, 318–19. In the New Testament the divine epithet "King of kings" always accompanies "God of gods" (1 Tim. 6:15; Rev. 17:14; 19:16).

being," a fact confirmed by the Old Testament usage of the singular,[35] as well as the plural *ʾēlîm/ʾêlîm*, which may denote either gods in general[36] or the heavenly angelic assembly in particular.[37] Moses' attachment of the article to "El" may bear a double significance. On the one hand, within the context of Deuteronomy, Moses hereby declares that Yahweh is the one and only God, and on the other hand, he declares that Yahweh is "the [one and only] El" who presides over heavenly and earthly affairs. As is well-known, in Canaanite mythology El was the name of the head of the pantheon, the husband of Asherah and father of seventy gods of second rank, including Baal, Mot, and Yamm. In the Ugaritic texts El's epithets include "Holy One"*(qdš),* "Father" *(ab),* "Father of Years" *(ab šnm),* "Father of Humanity" *(ab adm),* "Creator of Creatures" (the common understanding of *bny bnwt),* "the benevolent, good natured El" *(ltpn il dpid),* and "the Bull El" *(tril).*[38] But the myths portray this El inconsistently: on the one hand, he is a lusty figure, who brazenly boasts of his sexual prowess[39] and on the other hand, he is a gray-bearded old man who presides rather ineptly over an extremely unruly and dysfunctional pantheon.

In Moses' portrayal of Yahweh as *hāʾēl,* "the El," we should probably recognize an intentional polemic against Canaanite perceptions of El. In Deuteronomy 7:9–10 Moses challenges Israel:

> Know therefore that Yahweh your God is God, the faithful El who maintains covenant loyalty with those who love him and keep his commandments, to a thousand generations, and who repays in their own

---

35. Exodus 34:6; Deuteronomy 3:24; 32:12, 21(//*hăbālîm,* "idols"); Psalms 44:20; 77:13; 81:9; Isaiah 31:3; 43:10; 44:10, 15, 17 (making images of a god); 45:20 (//*pesel,* "image/idol"); 46:6; 48:2; and Malachi 2:11.
36. Exodus 15:11 asks, "Who is like you among the gods *(bāʾēlim)?*" Daniel 11:36 speaks of the monstrous king who will exalt himself above every God *(kol ʾēl)* and speak horrible things against "the God of gods." Here *ʾēl ʾēlîm* is best interpreted as equivalent to *ʾēlōhê hāʾĕlōîm.* Cf. J. Goldingay, *Daniel,* WBC (Dallas: Word, 1989), 30:280.
37. Psalms 29:1; 89:7 (both *bĕnê ʾēlîm*); and Job 41:17. Cf. the similar use of the singular in Psalm 82:1.
38. For discussion of these epithets, see W. Herrmann, "El," in *DDD,* 274–20.
39. See especially CAT 1.23, conveniently published in original text and translated by T. J. Lewis in *Ugaritic Narrative Poetry,* ed. S. B. Parker, SBLWAW 9 (Atlanta: Scholars Press, 1997), 208–14. Lewis's comments on this text are very helpful (205–7). Translation and even more detailed commentary are also provided by D. Pardee, "Dawn and Dusk (The Birth of the Gracious and Beautiful Gods)," Text 1.87 in *The Context of Scripture,* vol. 1 of *Canonical Compositions from the Biblical World,* ed. W. W. Hallo (Leiden/New York: Brill, 1997), 274–83; and N. Wyatt, *Religious Texts from Ugarit: The Words of Ilimilku and His Colleagues,* Biblical Seminar 53 (Sheffield: Sheffield Academic Press, 1998), 324–35.

person those who reject him. He does not delay but repays in their own person those who reject him.[40]

Moses is even more specific in 10:14–18, wherein he highlights what is distinctive about Yahweh, the God of Israel, alternating transcendent (vv. 14, 17a) and immanent (vv. 15, 17b–18) qualities. With respect to God's transcendence, first with the skillful use of parallelism, merismus ("heaven and earth"), and the superlative degree ("heaven of heavens"),[41] Moses declares that Yahweh, the God of Israel, owns the entire cosmos: "To Yahweh your God belong the heavens and the heavens of heavens: the earth and all that is in it" (v. 14).

As has already been observed, the ancient Israelites shared with their Near Eastern neighbors the perception of the universe as a three-tiered structure consisting of Sheol (the realm of the dead), earth (the realm of the living), and heaven (the realm of God/the gods and semi-divine beings). Here, Moses claims that all those realms that others ascribed to other gods were under the exclusive authority of Yahweh, the God of Israel. Furthermore, Yahweh is the "great"

---

40. Hebrew: וְיָדַעְתָּ כִּי־יְהוָה אֱלֹהֶיךָ הוּא הָאֱלֹהִים הָאֵל הַנֶּאֱמָן שֹׁמֵר הַבְּרִית וְהַחֶסֶד לְאֹהֲבָיו וּלְשֹׁמְרֵי מִצְוֹתוֹ לְאֶלֶף דּוֹר:

וּמְשַׁלֵּם לְשֹׂנְאָיו אֶל־פָּנָיו לְהַאֲבִידוֹ לֹא יְאַחֵר לְשֹׂנְאוֹ אֶל־פָּנָיו יְשַׁלֶּם־לוֹ:

41. In general, ancient Near Easterners, the Israelites included, perceived the universe as a multitiered structure consisting of Sheol (the realm of the dead), earth (the realm of the living), and heaven (the realm of God/the gods and semi-divine beings). Some, however, imagined these tiers to be subdivided further. Some Mesopotamian texts, for example, know of three heavens, occupied from top to bottom by 300 Igigi, Mel/Marduk, and the stars/constellations, respectively. For discussion, see W. G. Lambert, "The Cosmology of Sumer and Babylon," in *Ancient Cosmologies,* ed. C. Blacker and M. Loewe (London: George Allen & Unwin, 1975), 58–59; and idem, "Himmel," *Reallexikon der Assyriologie,* 4:411–12. A series of medical incantation texts speak of "seven heavens, seven earths," or "earth seven, heaven seven." These probably do not refer to the number of heavens, but like the Hebrew expression, "heaven of heavens," refer to the totality of the cosmos. Thus J. E. Wright, *The Early History of Heaven* (New York: Oxford, 2000), 40–41. Jewish tradition speaks of as many as seven heavens (see L. I. Rabinowitz, "Cosmology," in *EncJud* [Jerusalem: Encyclopedia Judaica; New York: Macmillan], 5:982), and even in the New Testament we read of multiple heavens generally (Eph. 4:11; Heb 4:14) and the third heaven specifically (1 Cor. 12:2). For discussion, see Wright, *Early History of Heaven,* 145–50. These perceptions apparently derive from geocentric Pythagorean Greek models. According to Plato, each of the seven celestial bodies traveled alone in its orbital space around the earth. For full discussion, see Wright, *Early History of Heaven,* 98–104. In the present context this is obviously a figure of speech whereby Moses declares that whatever cosmic entity one may imagine to exist out there, or however far one may travel in space, it all belongs to Yahweh, the God of Israel.

(gādôl), "strong" *(gibbōr),*[42] and "awesome" *(nôrāʾ)* El.[43] If this triad of expressions does not express the superlative degree, it is certainly emphatic—Yahweh is the supreme God.[44] This statement builds on Moses' earlier semi-catechetical declaration in 7:21: "For Yahweh your God in your midst is El, great and glorious."[45]

With respect to Yahweh's immanence, Moses declares, first, that Yahweh hand-picked Israel's ancestors as the object of his affection *(ḥāšaq),* to love *(ʾāhab)* them and—out of all the families on earth from which to choose *(bāḥar)*—their descendants after them. This statement serves as a summary of Deuteronomy 4:32–34, where Moses affirms Yahweh's absolute uniqueness vis-à-vis all other gods as demonstrated by his rescue of Israel from Egypt, an extraordinary act based upon his love for the ancestors. Second, Moses declares that Yahweh governs his people fairly by executing justice for the marginalized, and demonstrates his covenant commitment *(ʾāhab)* to aliens by providing them with food and clothing. This concern for human beings contrasts sharply with Canaanite myths, which portray El as preoccupied with pantheonic affairs.[46] It is Moses' custom to exploit pagan notions by alluding to pagan divinities and then ascribing many of their titles and functions/spheres of influence to Yahweh.

YAHWISTIC REPUDIATION OF PAGAN RELIGIOUS IDEAS AND PRACTICES

The last, and probably most fascinating part of this discussion concerns explicit Yahwistic rejection of pagan religious ideas. Hostility toward idols and

---

42. Cf. the title *El Gibbor* in Isaiah 9:6. In Deuteronomy 3:24 Moses had referred to Yahweh's actions on behalf of Israel as *gĕbûrôt,* "mighty acts."

43. Nehemiah 9:32 employs these expressions liturgically, adding, "who keeps his covenant and steadfast love *(ḥesed),*" from Deuteronomy 7:9 and 12.

44. Cf. Exodus 34:7, according to which Yahweh forgives iniquity *(ʿāwôn),* rebellion *(pešaʿ),* and sin *(ḥaṭṭāʾ),* that is, every kind of sin; and Deuteronomy 6:5, according to which Israelites are to love Yahweh with all their hearts *(kol lēb),* their entire person *(kol nepeš),* and all their substance *(kol mĕʾōd),* that is, without any reservation whatsoever.

45. Which in turn, builds on 6:15, but note the differences in the syntax of the three verses:
(6:15)   *kî ʾēl qannāʾ yhwh ʾĕlōhêkā bĕqirbekā*
          For Yahweh your God in your midst is a passionate God.
(7:21)   *kî yhwh ʾĕlōhêkā bĕqirbekā ʾēl gādôl wĕnôrāʾ*
          For Yahweh your God in your midst is El, great and awesome.
(10:17) *kî yhwh ʾĕlōhêkā hûʾ ... hāʾēl haggādōl haggibbōr wĕhannôrāʾ*
          For Yahweh your God is . . . the El, great, strong, and awesome.

46. As in Psalm 8, where the psalmist's reflection on the cosmos as the handiwork of God leads to an expression of utter amazement at his interest in humankind, Moses' doxology of 14 sets the stage for his election of Israel.

the worship of other gods is expressed in four principal ways: (1) pejorative designations for idols and the gods they represent; (2) explicit prohibitions of idolatry; (3) hostile actions against idols; (4) polemical portrayals of idols and idolaters. Each shall be examined in turn.

PEJORATIVE DESIGNATIONS FOR IDOLS AND THE GODS THEY REPRESENT

Even though, or perhaps precisely because, orthodox Yahwists denied the existence of other gods or the validity of their worship, the Old Testament attests to a remarkably extensive vocabulary referring to idols. The most common expression for an idol or the divinity behind the idol is, of course, *'ĕlōhîm*, "god." When referring to smaller household idols, *'ĕlōhîm* was occasionally interchanged with *tĕrāpîm*. The etymology of *'ĕlōhîm* remains uncertain, but a derivation from Hittite *tarpi/tarpiš*, which designates a spirit that can on some occasions be regarded as protective and on others malevolent, seems most likely.[47]

Some designations for idols/divine images are actually neutral in value, but they reflect the view expressed by Moses in Deuteronomy 4:28 that these gods are no more and no less than the products of human effort, mere objects of wood and stone. Accordingly, an idol/pagan deity is often referred to generally as the "work of human hands" *(ma 'ăśēh yĕdê 'ādām)*,[48] but more specifically as a *ṣelem*, "image, replica";[49] a *pesel*, a divine image carved from wood, sculpted from stone, or cast in metal (Deut. 4:16, 23, 25); a *semel*, a sculpture of a divine image (Ezek. 8:3, 5; 2 Chron. 33:7 (//pesel); a *tĕmûnâ*, "likeness, representation, form" (Deut. 4:16, 23, 25); a *maśkît*, "monument, image" (Ezek. 8:12); a *tabnît*, "construction, model, copy" (Ezek. 8:10); a *nesek*, "molten image";[50] an *'āṣāb*, "effigy."[51]

---

47. Cf. T. J. Lewis, "Teraphim תרפים," in *DDD*, 844–50, for discussion. For references, see Genesis 31:19, 34–35; Judges 17:5; 18:14, 17–18, 20; 1 Samuel 15:23; 19:13, 16; 2 Kings 23:24; Ezekiel 21:21; Hosea 3:4; and Zechariah 10:2.

48. Deuteronomy 4:28; 27:15; 2 Kings 19:18 = Isaiah 37:19 = 2 Chronicles 32:19; Psalms 115:4; 135:15; Isaiah 2:8; Jeremiah 1:16; 10:3, 9; 25:6–7; 44:8; Hosea 14:4; Micah 5:12; and 2 Chronicles 34:25.

49. Numbers 33:52; Ezekiel 7:20; and Amos 5:26.

50. Isaiah 41:29; 48:5; Jeremiah 10:14; 51:17. Cf. *nāsîk*, Daniel 11:8; *măsēkâ*, Exodus 32:4, 8; 34:17; Leviticus 19:4; Numbers 33:15; Deuteronomy 9:12, 16; 18:17–18; 27:15; Judges 17:3–4; 1 Kings 14:9; 2 Kings 17:16; 2 Chronicles 28:2; 34:3–4; Nehemiah 9:18; Psalm 106:19; Isaiah 30:22; 42:17; Hosea 13:2; Nahum 1:14; and Habakkuk 2:18.

51. First Samuel 31:9; 2 Samuel 5:21; 1 Chronicles 10:9; Psalms 106:36, 38; 115:4; 135:15; Isaiah 2:8; 10:11; 46:21; Jeremiah 50:2; Hosea 8:4; 13:2; 14:9; Micah 1:7; and Zechariah 13:2.

The occasional vocalization of the last word as ʿōṣeb (Isa. 48:5; Ps. 139:24), in imitation of bōšet ("shame"), leads us into another vast category of designations, that is, derogatory expressions for idols/pagan gods: ʾĕlîlîm, "nonentities, nothings";[52] ʾāwen, "nothingness";[53] habĕlê šāw, "empty trivialities, worthless things";[54] hebel, "vanity," or as my teacher Thomas McComiskey used to say, "soap bubbles";[55] kĕzābîm, lies;[56] rîq, "emptiness" (Ps. 4:2; cf. Isa. 30:7; 49:4); šeqer, "illusions, tricks, lies";[57] ʾêmâ, "frightful and horrifying objects" (Jer. 50:38); gillûlîm, "dung pellets, round things," as in sheep droppings;[58] šiqquṣîm, "monstrosities, abhorrent/detestable objects";[59] tôʿēbâ, "abhorred/abominable object".[60] Yahwists, then, presented their neighbors with an irony: they dismissed that which can be seen as nothing, and that which cannot be seen accepted as the ultimate reality. The nations worship gods of wood and stone that have eyes but see not, ears but hear not, and hands that can lend no aid at all (Deut. 4:28).

EXPLICIT PROHIBITIONS OF IDOLATRY AND THE WORSHIP OF OTHER GODS

The Old Testament frequently expresses the hostility of orthodox Yahwists toward the worship of other gods and explicitly prohibits worship of any deities other than Yahweh. Based on his exclusive claims to Israel's devotion (Deut. 6:4–5), his covenantal passion (qinʾâ; Exod. 34:14; Deut. 4:24; 5:9; 6:15), and his repudiation of the existence of any other gods (Deut. 4:35, 39), reverential acts of submission and homage before beings or objects in the place of the one true God are absolutely forbidden in Israel's constitution. So fundamental is this prohibition that it is built into the covenant itself, involving the first two principles of covenant relationship as expressed in the Decalogue:

---

52. Leviticus 19:4; 26:1; 1 Chronicles 16:26; Psalms 96:5; 97:7; Isaiah 2:8, 18, 20; 10:10–11; 19:1, 3; 31:7; and Habakkuk 2:18.
53. Isaiah 66:3; cf. 41:29; 1 Samuel 15:23; Isaiah 1:13; Hosea 4:15; 10:8; 12:12; 66:3; and Zechariah 10:2.
54. Psalm 31:7; Jonah 2:9; cf. Psalm 24:4; and Jeremiah 18:15.
55. Deuteronomy 32:21; 1 Kings 16:13, 26; 2 Kings 17:5; Psalm 31:7; Jeremiah 2:5; 8:19; 10:8, 15; 14:22, 51:18; 14:22; and Jonah 2:9.
56. Psalms 4:3; 40:5; and Amos 2:4.
57. Isaiah 44:20; Jeremiah 10:14; 16:19; and 51:17.
58. Leviticus 26:30; Deuteronomy 29:19; 1 Kings 15:12; 21:26; 2 Kings 17:12; 21:11, 21; and Ezekiel (38 times!).
59. Deuteronomy 29:16; 2 Kings 23:24; 2 Chronicles 15:8; Isaiah 66:3; Jeremiah 4:1; 7:30; 13:27; 16:18; 32:34; Ezekiel 5:11; 7:20; 11:18, 21; 20:7–8, 30; and 37:23.
60. Deuteronomy 32:16; Isaiah 44:19; cf. Deuteronomy 13:15; 17:4 (the worship of foreign gods).

You shall have no other gods before me. You shall not make for yourself
an idol, whether in the form of anything that is in heaven above, or that
is on the earth beneath, or that is in the water under the earth. You shall
not bow down to them or worship them; for I Yahweh your God am an
impassioned God, punishing children for the iniquity of parents, to the
third and the fourth generation of those who reject me, but showing
steadfast love to the thousandth generation of those who love me and
keep my commandments (Exod. 20:3–6; Deut. 5:7–10).[61]

The exclusivity of Israel's devotion to Yahweh is highlighted in the Shemaʿ,
which orthodox Jews recite twice a day to this day: *šĕmaʿ yiśrāʾēl YHWH
ʾĕlōhênû YHWH ʾeḥād*. This declaration should be interpreted as "Hear O Israel, our God is Yahweh, Yahweh alone."[62] Admittedly this interpretation goes
against the grain of longstanding tradition, but in context this is the correct
interpretation, for as R. W. L. Moberly affirms, "What 'Yahweh is one' means
must be something that makes appropriate the total and unreserved 'love' that
is immediately specified" in verse 5,[63] that is, covenant commitment with one's
whole heart, person, and substance. Surely this involves having only Yahweh as
one's God. Indeed, in Deuteronomy Moses treats this as *hammiṣwâ*, "the commandment" par excellence, and he labels spiritual apostasy and/or the division of allegiance with other gods "the [supreme] evil" *(hāraʿ)* in the eyes of
Yahweh (cf. 4:25; 13:5).[64]

In Deuteronomy 4:24–27 and 11:16–18, Moses spells out the consequences
of violating this prohibition in principle and, in his recitation of the covenant
curses in chapter 28, he develops this theme in great detail. In short, if the

---

61. The prohibition is reiterated repeatedly in the Sinaitic revelation and Mosaic preaching:
Exodus 20:23; 34:11–17; Leviticus 19:4; 26:1; Deuteronomy 4:15–24, 25–31; 6:14–15; 7:3–
5; 13:1–18; 16:21–22; 27:15.

62. For detailed discussion of the Shema and a defense of this translation, see my essay, "How
Many is God? An Investigation into the Meaning of Deuteronomy 6:4–5," *Jets* 47 (2004):
193–212.

63. "Toward an Interpretation of the Shema," C. Seitz and K. Greene-McCreight, eds., in
Theological Exegesis: Essays in Honor of Brevard S. Childs (Grand Rapids: Eerdmans, 1999),
132–33, modifying the position taken in an earlier essay (J. A. Emerton, ed., "Yahweh Is
One: The Translation of the Shema," in *Studies in the Pentateuch*, VTSup 41 [Leiden: Brill,
1990], 209–15).

64. The article on *raʿ* suggests a particular kind of evil, in this instance violation of the first
two principles of covenant relationship: no other gods, and no physical representations
of God. This formula will be repeated seven times in the book of Judges, "The sons of
Israel did 'the evil' in the eyes of Yahweh" (2:11; 3:7, 12; 4:1; 6:1; 10:6; 13:1).

Israelites behave like the Canaanites and go after other gods, rejecting the one who had rescued them from Egypt, then Yahweh will treat them like Canaanites (7:25–26; 8:19–20). Whereas these texts all highlight Yahweh's personal expression of fury in the face of Israelite idolatry, in Deuteronomy 13 Moses places the responsibility squarely on the community for maintaining exclusive devotion to Yahweh by all the members. If a prophet, or a member of one's own family, or any scoundrel (*'ănāšîm běnê bělîya 'al*) attempts to entice any Israelite to worship other gods, both leaders and followers in the crime will be executed.

The prophets follow in the tradition of Deuteronomy, denouncing with the strongest language the veneration of deities other than Yahweh. Idolatrous practices are treated as spiritual harlotry,[65] an abomination,[66] detestable,[67] foolishness,[68] and utterly disgusting.[69] According to the orthodox Yahwists, the God of Israel would brook no rivals.[70] In this respect the Old Testament's view of

---

65. Judges 2:17; 8:27, 33, and many more. Cf. *BDB*, 275–76.
66. *Tô'ēbôt*, Deuteronomy 13:15, and many more. Cf. *BDB*, 1072–73. On the expression, see E. Gerstenberger, "*t'b*. To abhor," *TLOT* 3:1428–31 (English translation of *THAT* 2:1051–55).
67. *šiqquṣ*," Deuteronomy 29:16, etc. Cf. *BDB* (Oxford: Oxford University Press, 1907), 1054–55; and M. A. Grisanti, "שׁקץ," in *NIDOTTE*, 5:243–46.
68. Note the satirical attacks of the prophets in Isaiah 40:18–20; 41:6–7; 44:9–20; 46:1–2; and Jeremiah 10:1–10. Cf. also Psalm 115:1–8. See further below.
69. *gillûlîm*, Ezekiel. 8:10 + 37 times in Ezekiel. Cf. *BDB*, 165, "dungy things"; L. Koehler, W. Baumgartner, and J. J. Stamm, *HALOT*, trans. and ed. under the supervision of M. E. J. Richardson (Leiden: Brill, 1994–), 1:192, "droppings." This seems to have been an artificially created word derived from the root *gll*, "to roll," to which was added the vowels of *šiqquṣîm*. Cf. H. D. Preuss, "גּ *gillulim*," in *TDOT*, 3:1–5. Ezekiel's adoption of this expression for idolatry may have been prompted by the pellet-like shape and size of sheep feces. One can hardly imagine a more caustic remark about idolatry. Cf. Block, *Book of Ezekiel Chapters 1–24*, 226.
70. On the issue of monotheism in Israel, see W. F. Albright, *Yahweh and the Gods of Canaan: A Historical Analysis of Two Contrasting Faiths* (Garden City: Doubleday, 1968), 153–64; idem, *From Stone Age to Christianity: Monotheism and the Historical Process*, 2d ed. (Garden City: Doubleday, 1957), 257–72; D. Baly, "The Geography of Monotheism," in *Translating and Understanding the Old Testament: Essays in Honor of Herbert Gordon May*, ed. H. T. Frank and W. L. Reed (Nashville: Abingdon, 1970), 253–78; H. Ringgren, "Monotheism," in *The Interpreter's Dictionary of the Bible*, ed. K. Crim, supplementary vol. (Nashville: Abingdon, 1978), 602–4; F. Stolz, "Monotheismus in Israel," in *Monotheismus im alten Israel und seiner Umwelt*, ed. O. Keel, Biblische Beiträge 14 (Fribourg: Schweizerisches Katholisches Biblewerk, 1980), 163–74; M. S. Smith, *The Early History of God: Yahweh and Other Deities in Ancient Israel* (San Francisco: Harper & Row, 1987), 147–57; R. Albertz, *A History of Israelite Religion in the Old Testament Period*, trans. J. Bowden, 2 vols., OTL (Louisville: Westminster/John Knox, 1994), esp. 1:82–91, 146–56.

Israel's relationship to its patron deity differed fundamentally from the perceptions of all other surrounding nations.

The orthodox Yahwism of the Old Testament is unequivocal in its prohibition of Israelites' worshiping any other gods besides, in addition to, or in place of Yahweh. But what stance does the Old Testament take on the worship of other gods by outsiders? A related issue addresses the openness of Yahweh to the acceptance of other gods for other nations. Does the Old Testament contemplate two ways to relationship with God, one way for the Israelites and another way for non-Israelites?

There is no doubt that characters in the narratives of the Old Testament accepted a more open stance. While Jephthah may have gotten his facts wrong, according to his response to the Ammonites in Judges 11:24, he seems to recognize the actual involvement of Chemosh in Ammonite affairs, as on a par with Yahweh's activity in Israel's: "Should you not possess what your god Chemosh gives you to possess? And should we not be the ones to possess everything that Yahweh our God has conquered for our benefit?" It should be remembered, however, that Jephthah embodies all that is wrong with Israel at this time. With his self-interested perspective on his own office and in particular his sacrificing of his daughter in fulfillment of a stupid vow to secure the favor of Yahweh, Jephthah's syncretism is typical of the recidivist Israelites in the dark days of the judges. Consider, too, David's response to Saul in 1 Samuel 26:19, when he tells him to "Go, serve other gods." Surely David's faith and religious commitment at this point is impeccable. The problem evaporates, however, when it is recognized that David is quoting cursed men who have been trying to drive him away from Yahweh.

Aside from the way characters in the narratives treat other religious commitments, the Old Testament seems to reflect on this issue at several levels. At the literary level, prophets and poets refer freely to the Moabites as the people of Chemosh (Num. 21:29; Jer. 48:46), and the Ammonites as the people of Milcom (Jer. 49:1), and of these and other gods as active participants in the affairs of their respective peoples.[71] These references are recognized, however, as poetic and exploiting rhetorical license, for the same prophets who speak of

---

71. In Jeremiah 49:1, Yahweh himself asks, "Why has Milcom dispossessed Gad, and his people settled in its cities?" Cf. also 49:3, where Jeremiah predicts that "Milcom shall go into exile, along with his priests and his officials." In 48:7 he makes a similar comment about Chemosh. Elsewhere Jeremiah speaks of Bel being put to shame and Merodach (i.e., Marduk) being dismayed (50:2), and of Yahweh punishing Bel in Babylon as if she were a real entity (51:44). In a similar vein Isaiah speaks of Bel bowing down and Nebo (i.e., Nabu) stooping, and their images being carried off (Isa. 46:1).

other gods in this way explicitly deny their objective reality, as in Jeremiah's sarcastic comment in 2:11:

> Has a nation ever changed its gods (even though they are not gods)?
> But my people have exchanged my glory for "The Useless One."[72]

In fact, Jeremiah goes beyond sarcasm and speaks of idolatry as a crime for which the nations will experience the sword (50:35–40; cf. 12:14–17).

But how are we to understand Moses' declaration in Deuteronomy 4:19?: "And when you look up to the heavens and see the sun, the moon, and the stars, all the host of heaven, do not be seduced and bow down to them and serve them, objects that Yahweh your God has allotted to all the peoples everywhere under heaven." Most of this verse is clear and sensible in the present context. Having warned his people not to attempt to reduce Yahweh to physical definition (after all, he had not revealed himself in any form, vv. 15–18), in verse 19a Moses cautions against a second kind of twisted religious thinking: turning to the sun and moon and stars as if they were representations of Yahweh or divinities in their own right, thereby rejecting not only Yahweh, their redeemer, but also Yahweh's definition of himself (cf. Job 31:24–28). But the last clause is arguably the most difficult theologically in the entire book of Deuteronomy, especially in the light of Moses' later absolute rejection of the existence of any other gods besides Yahweh (Deut. 4:35, 39). How is the statement—the sun, the moon, the stars, and all the other heavenly objects have been allotted to all the peoples under the whole heaven—to be understood? Did Yahweh really allot *(ḥālaq)* these to the other nations as objects of worship, while reserving himself for Israel's worship?[73]

72. Treating *bělô' yô'îl* as a proper name, a play on the name *Baal*, with J. A. Thompson, *The Book of Jeremiah*, NICOT (Grand Rapids: Eerdmans, 1980), 166, 170. The reading "my glory" follows the note in *BHS*, ed. K. Elliger and W. Rudolph (Stuttgart: Deutsche Bibelgesellschaft, 1983), indicating the third masculine suffix in place of the first common suffix as a case of *Tiqqun Sopherim*. On Isaiah's parodies on idolatry in 44:6–20, see below. Cf. Jeremiah 2:9–13; 5:7; 16:20; also Hosea 8:6; Psalm 96:5 (= 1 Chron. 16:26). Critical scholars generally dismiss these categorical rejections of the existence of other gods as insertions deriving from a later stage in the evolution of Israelite monotheistic thinking. For a recent discussion of this issue, see J. Barr, *The Concept of Biblical Theology: An Old Testament Perspective* (Minneapolis: Fortress, 1999), 85–99. This conclusion is possible, however, only if one dates Deuteronomy as a whole to a late preexilic period and the hortatory sections of chapters 4 and 10 to the postexilic period, a procedure that relies on suspiciously circular argumentation.

73. In 32:8–9 Moses sings of Elyon allocating (*nḥl* in hiphil) the grants of land to the nations; at that time he divided the human population on the basis of the number of *bĕnê 'ēlîm*

Interpreting this verse within a henotheistic framework, most critical scholars answer the question in the affirmative. Moshe Weinfeld's comment is typical of many: "The heavenly bodies as objects of worship were assigned to the nations by God himself. The stars were considered divine beings."[74] This interpretation may be questioned, however, on several counts. First, and most obvious, it is impossible to square with Moses' own unequivocal denial of the existence of any other gods (vv. 35, 39). Second, this interpretation flies in the face of the Old Testament's consistent antipathy toward idols of any kind. Third, this interpretation reads too much into this verse. The last clause translates simply, "and you serve what Yahweh assigned to all the peoples under the whole heavens."[75] While Moses clearly affirms Yahweh's role in allocating the hosts of heaven to all the peoples under the whole heaven, the assumed purpose, "as objects of worship," must be supplied from outside. The text is in fact silent on the purpose for the allotment. Fourth, this interpretation excludes Israel from "all the peoples under the whole heavens," and assumes this nation has no relationship to (let alone dependence upon) the heavenly bodies. Fifth, this interpretation misses the links between this passage and the account of creation in Genesis 1. Having borrowed from Genesis 1:20–23 the categories of creatures—which are listed in verses 17–18 and are the products of days five and six of creation—with his references

---

available to function as intermediary patrons on his behalf (following LXX and a Qumran fragment; see my discussion in *Gods of the Nations*, 25–32). But Yahweh reserved Israel for a direct relationship with him as his *ḥēleq*, "allotment," and his *naḥălâ*, "reserved property." The verb *ḥālaq* is used elsewhere of apportioning the land of Canaan among the tribes of Israel (Josh. 14:1; 18:2) or distributing the spoils of their enemies (Josh. 22:8).

74. Weinfeld, *Deuteronomy 1–11*, 206. J. Tigay explains the issue as follows: "The view of polytheism reflects the assumption that if the rest of mankind does not worship the true God, that must be God's will. For this reason it is no sin for other nations to worship idols and the heavenly bodies; it is considered sinful only when done by Israel, to whom God revealed Himself and forbade the worship of these objects" (*Deuteronomy*, Jewish Publication Society Torah Commentary [Philadelphia: Jewish Publication Society, 1996], 435). This compares with S. R. Driver's comment: "The God of Israel is supreme: He assigns to every nation its objects of worship; and the veneration of the heavenly bodies by the nations (other than Israel) forms part of His providential order of the world. Natural religion, though it may become depraved (Rom 1:21ff.), is a witness to some of the deepest needs and instincts of humanity: in default of a purer and higher faith, the yearnings of mankind after a power higher than themselves find legitimate satisfaction in it" (*A Critical and Exegetical Commentary on Deuteronomy*, ICC [Edinburgh: T. & T. Clark, 1902], 70–71).

75. So also C. J. H. Wright, *Deuteronomy*, NIBC (Peabody: Hendrickson, 1996), 52.

to the heavenly bodies, Moses appears to be backing up to day four, which involved the creation of these objects. His comment that they were apportioned "to all the peoples under the whole heaven" represents a legitimate interpretation of Genesis 1:14–19. These objects were created and placed in the sky not as objects to be worshiped but as instruments of divine providence, governing *(māšal)* the world and guaranteeing the annual rhythm of life for the sake of its inhabitants. In other words, by means of these objects Yahweh exercised general providential care over all the peoples. Sixth, this interpretation sidetracks the primary agenda of this passage, which is to highlight Israel's special covenant relationship with God. As the following verse indicates, and verses 32–40 will develop in detail, only Israel is the special object of Yahweh's redemptive action. For Israel to cast Yahweh in physical form is blasphemous because it inevitably underestimates the infinite nature of divinity and in any case rejects Yahweh's own self-definition (vv. 15–18). For Israel to worship the sun, moon, and stars in place of Yahweh is blasphemous because it rejects his gracious actions on Israel's behalf (v. 20). While God exercises his general providential care over all peoples, through these intermediaries only Israel has been singled out for a specific and special covenant relationship with him. The first principle of covenant relationship calls for a direct response to the preamble of the covenant document: "I am Yahweh your God who brought you out of the land of Egypt, out of the house of slavery" (Exod. 20:2; Deut. 5:6).

HOSTILE ACTIONS AGAINST IDOLS AND IDOLATERS

The historical narratives of the Old Testament include a series of accounts in which the preceding prohibitions were actually enforced. It is evident from these accounts that the danger of spiritual recidivism haunted the Israelites from their birth as a nation until their final demise in 586 B.C. Despite Yahweh's dramatic revelation of his power and his person in the deliverance of Israel from Egypt, and his verbal revelation at Sinai, and despite their threefold declaration in Exodus 19 and 24 of fidelity to Yahweh and his covenant, within a matter of days they apostatized, creating for themselves a golden calf and celebrating its role in their deliverance. Moses' response was decisive: "He took the calf that they had made, burned it with fire, ground it to powder, scattered it on the water, and made the Israelites drink it" (Exod. 32:20). He then ordered those who had participated in the rebellion to be executed by sword, which resulted in the deaths of about three thousand persons (v. 28).

In Judges 6:25–27 we find a description of Gideon's demolition of the altar of Baal and the Asherah in his father's back yard. It is ironic that when the perpetrator of this act was exposed, the townsfolk demanded that he be killed, which was precisely the punishment the Torah had prescribed for those who might promote idolatry in Israel (Deut. 13). This prescription undoubtedly underlies Elijah's treatment of the altar of Baal and its prophets at Mount Carmel. After Yahweh's dramatic demonstration of his superiority over Baal, at Elijah's order the prophets of Baal were seized and dragged to the Wadi Kishon and killed (1 Kings 18:40). Following his anointing by Elisha, Jehu engaged in a purge of Baalism in the northern kingdom of Israel, slaughtering all of Baal's followers, whom he had deceitfully invited to a celebration at a Baalistic shrine, burning the idolatrous images and turning the temple of Baal into a latrine (2 Kings 10:18–28). More than a century later, as part of Hezekiah's reforms in Judah, he demolished the pagan shrines, tearing down the *maṣṣēbôt* (phallic symbols of Baal) and cutting down the Asherah (wooden symbols of the fertility goddess). Apparently because the people were treating the bronze serpent that Moses had made centuries earlier (Num. 21:8–9) as an idolatrous relic, Hezekiah even had this reminder of Yahweh's past grace destroyed (2 Kings 18:1–5; cf. 2 Chron. 31:1).

At the end of the seventh century B.C. Josiah's religious reforms seem to have been even more thorough than those of Hezekiah almost a hundred years earlier (2 Kings 23:1–25; cf. 2 Chron. 34:33). Extending his purge into what had formerly been the northern kingdom, he eradicated the idolatrous priests, desecrated the pagan and syncretistic cult sites, and demolished the cult images and other appurtenances. His treatment of the latter recalls Moses' actions with respect to the golden calf: combustible items (like the Asherah) he burned outside the city near the garbage dump (the Kidron), and incombustible items (like the sacred pillars of Baal) he smashed. The remains of both he ground to dust and desecrated by carrying them off to Bethel (2 Kings 23:4), scattering them over the graves of the common people (v. 6), or throwing them into the Kidron brook (v. 12). The sacred sites themselves he desecrated by replacing the cult images with the bones of the victims of his purge (v. 14). But it was too little and too late. Yahweh had already sealed the fate of the city, and in 586 B.C. his agents, the Babylonians, performed the ultimate purge by destroying the temple, razing Jerusalem, and either slaughtering or deporting the population. The covenant curses for persistent rebellion expressed in going after other gods were fulfilled.

POLEMICAL PORTRAYALS OF IDOLS AND IDOLATERS

Within the narratives of the Old Testament subtle attacks on pagan beliefs are often observed. Almost thirty years ago Gerhard Hasel argued convincingly that the account of creation in Genesis 1:1–2:4a deliberately challenges pagan perceptions of God and the nature of the cosmos.[76] But this polemic is not restricted to the Genesis 1 account. The Old Testament understanding of creation generally makes a decisive break with typical ancient Near Eastern creation theology. Concerning this matter E. W. Nicholson asserts, "God is not continuous with his creation, does not permeate it, is not to be identified with, or represented by, anything within it, but stands outside his creation confronting it with his righteous will."[77]

Anti-pagan/idolatrous polemics are also recognized in Genesis 31:30–35—the comical episode of Laban looking for his stolen gods/household idols (ʾĕlōhîm/tĕrāpîm). Here, the narrator spoofs not only Laban's powerlessness vis-à-vis Jacob, but also the gods' powerlessness to defend themselves against theft in the first instance and ritual contamination in the second; Rachel is sitting on them while having her menstrual period. The impotence of Baal is surely an important motif in the account of Gideon's destruction of Baal in Judges 6:25–32. Joash's comment in defense of his son, "If Baal is a god let him defend himself because someone has torn down his altar" (v. 31), represents a damning admission that the idolatrous cult he has been sponsoring in his own back yard is precisely what the designations for idols listed above had declared—a vain and empty lie.

Elijah's contest with the prophets of Baal on Mount Carmel as described in 1 Kings 18 represents the most striking and caustic attack on idolatry in all the historiographic writings. The point of Elijah's victory over the pagan prophets was to demonstrate Yahweh's supremacy over the gods of Canaan. Elijah takes advantage of the occasion, however, to mock the prophets of Baal and their futile confidence in their god. Many have recognized his taunt of the prophets in verse 27 to be laced with Canaanite mythological coloring, now familiar to all who have read the religious texts from Ugarit. In the face of Baal's silence the fearless

76. G. Hasel, "The Polemic Nature of the Genesis Cosmology," *EvQ* 46 (1974): 81–102; cf. A. Heidel, *The Babylonian Genesis,* 2d ed. (Chicago: Chicago University Press, 1954), 91, passim.
77. E. W. Nicholson, "Prophecy and Covenant," in *God and His People: Covenant Theology in the Old Testament* (Oxford: Clarendon, 1986), 207–8.

prophet of Yahweh challenges the prophets of Baal to cry louder, for Baal is a god, and as such he does not respond to casual entreaties. His devotees must be serious in seeking his attention, for, like ordinary mortals, Baal is often preoccupied: either he is defecating/urinating *(śîaḥ* and *śîg lô)*, or he is on a journey *(derek lô)*, or he is asleep *(yāšēn)*.[78] That Elijah's scurrilous derision of his opposition betrays thorough knowledge of Baal mythology, has become evident from the mythological texts discovered at Ras Shamra/Ugarit. These and other examples suggest that biblical narrators took great delight in exposing through satire and parody the futility and stupidity of idolatry.[79]

In the later prophets, this strategy is employed with even greater force. The rhetorical tradition may be traced back to Moses, who dismisses foreign gods as "the work of human hands, objects of wood and stone that neither see nor eat nor smell" (Deut. 4:28), in contrast to Yahweh's personal unprecedented and unparalleled deliverance of Israel from Egypt, thereby demonstrating that Yahweh alone is God in heaven above and on earth below; there is no other (4:31–40). Later prophets display a particular penchant for satirizing the manufacture and care of idols. We witness this in Hosea (8:4–6; 13:2–3), Micah (5:12–13), Habakkuk (2:18–19), Jeremiah (10:1–6), and Zephaniah (2:10–11).[80] No one, however, satirizes idolatry more effectively than Isaiah, whose utterances become increasingly pointed in 40:19–20; 41:5–14; and 44:6–20.

In the light of recent research by Michael Dick and Christopher Walker on the manufacture of cult images in Mesopotamia, these texts take on much greater significance than when they are interpreted in cultural isolation.[81]

---

78. *śîaḥ* and *śîg lô* apparently function as a hendiadys, that is, the use of two words to express a single idea. Our interpretation is supported by G. A. Rendsburg, "The Mock of Baal in 1 Kgs 18:27," *CBQ* 50 (1988): 414–17. For another interpretation, see H. D. Preuss, *Die Verspottung fremder Religionen im Alten Testament*, BZAW, n.s. 12 (Stuttgart: Kohlhammer, 1971), 86.

79. See Exodus 32:1–6, 21–24; Judges 17–18; 1 Samuel 5:1–5; 1 Kings 12:25–13:6; and 2 Kings 5:15–19. Leah Bronner has argued convincingly that the entire Elijah–Elisha cycle of narratives is driven by an anti-Baalistic polemic. See L. Bronner, *The Stories of Elijah and Elisha as Polemics Against Baal Worship* (Leiden: Brill, 1968).

80. Zephaniah 2:10–11 speaks of starving all the gods of the earth, on which see now D. Rudman, "When Gods Go Hungry: Mesopotamian Rite Clarifies Puzzling Prophecy," *BR* 18, no. 3 (June 2002): 37–39.

81. See C. Walker and M. B. Dick, "The Induction of the Cult Image in Ancient Mesopotamia: The Mesopotamian *mīs pî* Ritual," in *Born in Heaven, Made on Earth: The Making of the Cult Image in the Ancient Near East*, ed. M. B. Dick (Winona Lake: Eisenbrauns, 1999), 55–121. For a more popular presentation, see M. B. Dick, "Worshiping Idols: What Isaiah Didn't Know," *Bible Review* 18, no. 2 (April 2002): 30–37.

Because earthly and godly artisans produced the cult statue, the creation of a god represented a supremely synergic act between heavenly and earthly "hands." The procedure whereby an ordinary piece of wood or stone was transformed into a legitimate object of worship, animated by the spirit of the god whom it represented, was complex and various, but the process in general may be summarized as follows:

1. The artisans who were to create the cult statue were carefully chosen and subjected to purification rituals that prepared them to enter the *bīt mummi*, the temple workshop, where statues and ornaments of the gods and other sacred objects used in temple worship were made and animated or restored and reanimated.

2. Using the materials available (wood, stone, clay), the artisans crafted the image.

3. Based upon the calendar and special rites of divination, "a propitious day in a favorable month" was chosen for the "birth of the god."

4. By special incantations and a ritual known either as *pit pî* ("the opening of the mouth") or *mīs pî* ("the washing of the mouth") the god was "born," that is, transformed from a merely physical object into an animated representative of the deity. In one attested instance the statue was brought to an orchard next to a canal. It was purified with holy water from a sacred basin, and its mouth was opened/washed four times with honey, ghee (specially prepared soap), cedar, and cypress.[82] Without this ritual the statue remained the dead product of human hands, incapable of smelling incense, drinking water, or eating food (all provided by the devotees and priests), let alone hearing the pleas and praise of a supplicant or speaking a word of reassurance or hope.

5. Special rituals were performed to dissociate the cult images from the human hands that made them and reinforce the conviction that they were actually the products of divine creation. While they were swearing that not they but the craft-deities had made the image, the artisans'

---

82. This part of the ritual apparently alludes to the actions of a midwife who cleans and opens the breathing passage of a newborn at birth. This enables the spirit of the god, whom it represents, to enter the statue and animate it. Therefore, the cult image was ultimately not the product of a human craftsman but was "born of the gods." This interpretation is reinforced by the perceived role of the birth-goddess, Belet-ili, and her brick (a structure on which a woman lay/sat for her labor [cf. Exod. 1:16]). By this process of "theogony" ("birth of a god") the new god becomes the child of the Mother Goddess.

hands were cut off with a tamarisk sword. The tools used to make the image were wrapped in the carcass of a sheep, which had been sacrificed, and thrown into the river, thereby returning them to Nudimmud (Ea) the craft-god. Accordingly, despite being the work of human hands, the cult image was in fact perceived as "the work of the god."

6. The god could then be transported to and installed in the cella, the "holy of holies" of the temple constructed as its official residence.

7. Since the welfare of the people depended upon the happiness of the god, special priestly orders were appointed to take care of the material needs of the gods. After all, the welfare of the devotees depended upon the happiness, that is, the smile (favorable disposition) of the god. Animal and vegetarian sacrifices were regarded as literal means of satisfying the gods' appetites, and aromatic incense was waved in front of the statue's nose as a soothing aroma/narcotic. These were prepared in the temple kitchens and the food was eaten by the temple staff. The cult statue had to be constantly bathed, dressed in the finest garments, taken to bed in the god's ornately decorated bed-chamber, and treated to festivities and entertainment, including music.

Although the specific customs involved in making gods would have varied from place to place, some such procedures lie behind Isaiah's scathing critique of idolatry. Following a powerful and poetic affirmation of Yahweh's incomparability and unrivaled status as the only God, in 44:6–20 Isaiah provides his own colorful but realistic prose description of the process whereby idols are fabricated:

All who make idols are nothing, and the things they delight in do not profit; their witnesses neither see nor know. And so they will be put to shame. Who would fashion a god or cast an image that can do no good? Look, all its devotees shall be put to shame; the artisans too are merely human. Let them all assemble, let them stand up; they shall be terrified, they shall all be put to shame. The ironsmith fashions it and works it over the coals, shaping it with hammers, and forging it with his strong arm; he becomes hungry and his strength fails, he drinks no water and is faint. The carpenter stretches a line, marks it out with a stylus, fashions it with planes, and marks it with a compass; he makes it in human form, with human beauty, to be set up in a shrine. He cuts down cedars or chooses a holm tree or an oak and lets it grow strong among the trees of the forest. He plants a cedar and the rain nourishes it. Then it can be used as fuel. Part of it he takes and warms himself; he kindles a fire and bakes bread. Then he makes a god and worships it, makes it a carved image and bows down before it. Half of it he burns in the fire; over this half he roasts meat, eats it and is satisfied. He also warms himself and says, "Ah, I am warm, I can feel the fire!" The rest of it he makes into a god, his idol, bows down to it and worships it; he prays to it and says, "Save me, for you are my god!" They do not know, nor do they comprehend; for their eyes are shut, so that they cannot see, and their minds as well, so that they cannot understand. No one considers, nor is there knowledge or discernment to say, "Half of it I burned in the fire; I also baked bread on its coals, I roasted meat and have eaten. Now shall I make the rest of it an abomination? Shall I fall down before a block of wood?" He feeds on ashes; a deluded mind has led him astray, and he cannot save himself or say, "Is not this thing in my right hand a fraud?"

But such critiques of idolatry were not distinctive to prophets and historians. Similar dispositions are expressed by psalmists in 115:1–8 and 135, especially verses 15–18. Even Job, a non-Israelite, recognized the worship of the sun, moon, and stars as incompatible with true devotion to God (31:24–28).

Conclusion

It is appropriate here to consider one final question: If this was how orthodox Yahwists viewed the worship of other gods, how did they perceive the place of their own religion within the broader cultural environment? Specifically, how did they think non-Israelites perceived their religion? One's immediate response is to cite the familiar references in Isaiah to Israel as a light to the nations:

I am Yahweh, I have called you in righteousness, I have taken you by the hand and kept you; I have given you as a covenant to the people, a light to the nations to open the eyes that are blind, to bring out the prisoners from the dungeon, from the prison those who sit in darkness. I am Yahweh, that is my name; my glory I give to no other, nor my praise to idols. (Isa. 42:6–8)

He [Yahweh] says, "It is too light a thing that you should be my servant to raise up the tribes of Jacob and to restore the survivors of
Israel; I will give you as a light to the nations, that my salvation may
reach to the end of the earth." Thus says Yahweh, the Redeemer of
Israel and his Holy One, to one deeply despised, abhorred by the
nations, the slave of rulers, "Kings shall see and stand up, princes,
and they shall prostrate themselves, because of Yahweh, who is faithful, the Holy One of Israel, who has chosen you." (Isa. 49:6–7)

But Isaiah was not the first to recognize the privilege the Israelites enjoyed
in view of Yahweh's gracious redemption, his gracious call to covenant relationship with him, and his gracious revelation to them of a pattern of religious expression that would actually solve the problem of human alienation
from god/the gods and make them the envy of the whole world. In the previous millennium, Moses had already reflected on the significance of Israel's
experience with Yahweh. In Deuteronomy 4:5–8 he declared,

See, just as Yahweh my God has charged me, I now teach you statutes
and ordinances for you to observe in the land that you are about to
enter and occupy. You must observe them diligently, for this will show
your wisdom and discernment to the peoples, who, when they hear all
these statutes, will say, "Surely this great nation is a wise and discerning people!" For what other great nation has a god so near to it as
Yahweh our God is whenever we call to him? And what other great
nation has statutes and ordinances as just as this entire law that I am
setting before you today?

It is difficult for American evangelicals—whose disposition toward the Old
Testament tends to be determined by Paul's critical statements concerning the
law taken out of context—to grasp the significance of this statement. Perhaps
appeal to an ancient text, written in Sumerian and discovered in the library of
Ashurbanipal, will help.

A Prayer to Every God[83]

May the fury of my lord's heart be quieted toward me.[84]
May the god who is not known be quieted toward me;
May the goddess who is not known be quieted toward me.
May the god whom I know or do not know be quieted toward me;
May the goddess whom I know or do not know be quieted toward me.
May the heart of my god be quieted toward me;
May the heart of my goddess be quieted toward me.
May my god and goddess be quieted toward me.
May the god [who has become angry with me][85] be quieted toward me;
May the goddess [who has become angry with me] be quieted toward me.
    (10) (lines 11–18 cannot be restored with certainty)
In ignorance I have eaten that forbidden of my god;
In ignorance I have set foot on that prohibited by my goddess. (20)

---

83. Adapted from J. B. Pritchard, ed., *Ancient Near Eastern Texts Relating to the Old Testament*, 3d ed. (Princeton: Princeton University Press, 1969), 391–92. Bibliography is provided. In the preamble to his translation, F. J. Stephens wrote,

> This prayer is addressed to no particular god, but to all gods in general, even those who may be unknown. The purpose of the prayer is to claim relief from suffering, which the writer understands is the result of some infraction of divine law. He bases his claim on the fact that his transgressions have been committed unwittingly, and that he does not even know what god he may have offended. Moreover, he claims, the whole human race is by nature ignorant of the divine will, and consequently is constantly committing sin. He therefore ought not to be singled out for punishment. The text is written in the Emesal dialect of Sumerian, furnished with an interlinear Akkadian translation. The colophon of the tablet indicates that it was part of a series of prayers, the next tablet of which began with the line "By his word he has commanded my well-being." The tablet comes from the library of Ashurbanipal, 668–633 B.C., and was copied from an older original. There are, however, numerous features of the Sumerian text that are characteristic of the late period, and it is probable that the original composition of the text is not much older than Ashurbanipal.

84. According to Stephens, "literally the Sumerian says, 'of my lord, may his angry heart return to its place for me.'" The phrase "return to its place" is figurative language meaning "to settle down"; the imagery may be that of a raging storm or of the contents of a boiling kettle. The scribe indicates that each of the next nine lines ends with the same phrase, although he actually writes only the first word of the phrase after having written it once fully.

85. Stephens restores the line on the basis of line 32, after Langdon.

O Lord, my transgressions are many; great are my sins.
O my god, (my) transgressions are many; great are (my) sins.
O my goddess, (my) transgressions are many; great are (my) sins.
O god whom I know or do not know,
(my) transgressions are many; great are (my) sins;
O goddess whom I know or do not know,
(my) transgressions are many; great are (my) sins.
The transgression which I have committed, indeed I do not know;
The sin which I have done, indeed I do not know.
The forbidden thing which I have eaten, indeed I do not know;
The prohibited (place) on which I have set foot, indeed I do not know.
The lord in the anger of his heart looked at me; (30)
The god in the rage of his heart confronted me;
When the goddess was angry with me, she made me become ill.
The god whom I know or do not know has oppressed me;
The goddess whom I know or do not know has placed suffering upon me.
Although I am constantly looking for help, no one takes me by the hand;
When I weep they do not come to my side.
I utter laments, but no one hears me;
I am troubled; I am overwhelmed; I can not see.
O my god, merciful one, I address to you the prayer,
"Ever incline to me";
I kiss the feet of my goddess; I crawl before you. (40)
(lines 41–49 are mostly broken and cannot be restored with certainty)
How long, O my goddess, whom I know or do not know,
ere your hostile heart will be quieted? (50)
Man is dumb; he knows nothing;
Mankind, everyone that exists,—what does he know?
Whether he is committing sin or doing good, he does not even know.
O my lord, do not cast your servant down;
He is plunged into the waters of a swamp; take him by the hand.
The sin that I have done, turn into goodness;
The transgression that I have committed, let the wind carry away;
My many misdeeds strip off like a garment.
O my god, (my) transgressions are seven times seven;
remove my transgressions;
O my goddess, (my) transgressions are seven times seven;
remove my transgressions; (60)

O god whom I know or do not know,
(my) transgressions are seven times seven;
remove my transgressions;
O goddess whom I know or do not know,
    (my) transgressions are seven times seven;
    remove my transgressions.
Remove my transgressions (and) I will sing your praise.
May your heart, like the heart of a real mother, be quieted toward me;
Like a real mother (and) a real father may it be quieted toward me.

Is this not a pathetic piece? And what an indictment this prayer is on the religious systems of the world around ancient Israel! To be sure, with his keen sense of sin and his awareness of ultimate accountability before deity, this person expresses greater enlightenment than many in our own day. But he is faced with three insurmountable problems: first, he does not know which god he has offended; second, he does not know what the offense is; third, he does not know what it will take to satisfy the god/gods. It is against this backdrop that we must interpret Moses' statements. With their clear knowledge of the will of Yahweh, the faithful in Israel perceived themselves as incredibly privileged and the envy of the nations. Unlike other peoples, whose gods of wood and stone crafted by human hands neither saw nor heard nor smelled (Deut. 4:28; cf. Ps. 135:15–17), Yahweh hears his people when they call upon him (Deut. 4:7). And unlike the nations, whose idols have mouths but they do not speak (Ps. 135:16), Israel's God has spoken. By his grace he has given his people statutes and judgments that are perfect in righteousness (Deut. 4:8), perfect because (1) they reveal with perfect clarity who he is, (2) they reveal with perfect clarity what sin is, and (3) they reveal with perfect clarity how that sin may be removed and a relationship of peace and confidence with him established. Why would anyone give up this sparkling spring of water that leads to life for the broken cisterns of idolatry that can yield only death (cf. Jer. 2:9–13)? This is a question that the people of God must answer in every age. May the Lord deliver us from our idolatries,[86] and may we, the twenty-first-century people of God, delight in the revelation and life that God offers in Jesus Christ. And may we radiate this light to all who still languish in the darkness of their futile idolatries.

---

86. For an insightful series of analyses of contemporary evangelical idolatry, see O. Guinness and J. Seel, eds., *No God but God: Breaking with the Idols of Our Age* (Chicago: Moody, 1992).

3

Other Religions in
New Testament Theology

GREGORY K. BEALE

MANY EVANGELICALS WHO DISCUSS the relationship between the theology of New Testament writers and their surrounding culture often point out the uniqueness of the Christian gospel in comparison to the surrounding pagan beliefs of the first century. In this respect, many underscore the notion that salvation comes exclusively through Christ and no other god or religion. Thus, the relationships drawn between the New Testament's theological claims and those of pagan religion tend to be drawn in more general terms. The New Testament writers typically do not make reference to specific pagan religions, philosophies, and their belief systems. Some of the well-known exceptions are 1 Corinthians 15:33; Titus 1:12; Acts 14:11–18; and, above all, Paul's address to the Athenians in Acts 17:16–34.

In more recent years, however, more and more work has been done on possible parallels and specific allusions and references regarding pagan religion and philosophy in the New Testament. Two works on the background of Ephesians[1] and Colossians by Clinton E. Arnold are notable.[2] The *Thesaurus Linguae Graecae* has been available for years, but recently it has become more

---

1. Clinton E. Arnold, *Power and Magic: The Concept of Power in Ephesians* (Grand Rapids: Baker, 1992).
2. Clinton E. Arnold, *The Colossian Syncretism: The Interface between Christianity and Folk Belief at Colossae* (Grand Rapids: Baker, 1996).

"user friendly," and an increasing number of scholars have been making use of its resources in studying the Hellenistic background to the New Testament. Reviving the old Wettstein tradition is an ongoing project of the New Wettstein, represented by numerous articles usually published in the journal *Novum Testamentum*. In 1995, the *Hellenistic Commentary to the New Testament* appeared.[3] Most recently, the new volumes called the *Neuer Wettstein* have been released, edited by Georg Strecker and Udo Schnelle;[4] only the synoptic Gospels remain to be done. These last two projects, however, only list texts, without evaluating whether they are material or formal parallels. At the same time, other scholars with more awareness of Old Testament backgrounds are detecting Old Testament allusions in the very same contexts where Greco-Roman experts perceive pagan literary references. It is of interest that those perceiving Old Testament background do not pay much attention to the Hellenistic influence, and those detecting Hellenistic influence do not address the Old Testament influence to any significant degree.

This current essay takes sample passages wherein both backgrounds are in mind and focus upon both in order to see how they might be related, and it will be proposed that New Testament authors allude to specific competing religious claims that confront them in the pagan religious or philosophical environment. These allusions to pagan religion then set off a spark in the biblical writers' minds, leading them back to particular relevant sections of the Old Testament that are similar or almost identical to the pagan claims. The Christian writer appeals to these various parts of the Old Testament to demonstrate that the divine attributes with which pagans depict their own gods are true only of the God of Israel, who has revealed himself in Christ.

THE COMBINATION OF REFERENCES TO PAGAN RELIGION AND THE OLD TESTAMENT

PAUL'S AREOPAGUS SPEECH IN ATHENS

It is an intimidating task to comment upon Paul's speech in Athens since, as one commentator put it, "Probably no ten verses in the Acts of the Apostles

---

3.   M. E. Boring, K. Berger, and C. Colpe, eds., *Hellenistic Commentary to the New Testament* (Nashville: Abingdon, 1995).

4.   Udo Schnelle, ed., *Neuer Wettstein, Texte zum Neuen Testament aus Griechentum und Hellenismus,* vol. 1.2 (Berlin: W. de Gruyter, 2001); Georg Strecker and Udo Schnelle, eds., *Neuer Wettstein,* vol. 2.1 (Berlin: W. de Gruyter, 1996); and idem, *Neuer Wettstein,* vol. 2.2 (Berlin: W. de Gruyter, 1996).

have formed the text for such an abundance of commentary as has gathered round Paul's Areopagitica."[5] The following analysis is not intended to represent an exhaustive survey of past study, especially with respect to proposals about Greek religious and philosophical backgrounds, but focuses only on the issue of how certain aspects of Hellenistic influence might be related to Old Testament influence.

Martin Dibelius said of Paul's speech,

> This is what the author considered, at the end of the first Christian century, to be a suitable example of the sort of sermon which ought to be preached to cultured Gentiles! All this has very little to do with the Paul of the epistles, but a great deal to do with the exponents of a Christian philosophical system in the second century, namely the Apologists. What is seen here, very clearly, but already with considerable predilection, is the manner of constructing a Christian theology not on biblical, but on philosophical, especially Stoic ideas. The true parallels to this speech are found not in Paul but in Cicero and Seneca and their Greek predecessors.[6]

W. C. Van Unnik says, too, that Paul's address "reveals a natural theology of a completely un-Pauline character."[7] E. R. Goodenough concurs: "No one in the Galatian or Corinthian churches would have recognized in the pages of Acts the Paul they had heard preach or had read in his letters."[8]

In an article over thirty years ago, Edward Fudge noted these above one-sided perspectives on Acts, and then argued for a predominate Old Testament background for Paul's speech, with barely any attempt to assess the role of pagan philosophy and religion.[9]

What, then, do we have in Paul's speech? In Acts 17:24–25 Paul conducts a polemic against pagan temples and idols, especially epitomized at the Acropolis

5. F. F. Bruce, *The Book of Acts,* NICNT (Grand Rapids: Eerdmans, 1954), 353, which is likewise quoted in N. C. Croy, "Hellenistic Philosophies and the Preaching of the Resurrection (Acts 17:18, 32)," *NovT* 39 (1997): 21.
6. Martin Dibelius, *Studies in the Acts of the Apostles* (New York: Charles Scribner's Sons, 1956), 82.
7. W. C. Van Unnik, "Luke–Acts: A Storm Center in Contemporary Scholarship," in *Studies in Luke–Acts: Festschrift in Honor of Paul Schubert,* ed. L. E. Keck and J. L. Martyn (London: SPCK, 1968), 26.
8. E. R. Goodenough, "The Perspective of Acts," in *Studies in Luke–Acts,* 58.
9. Edward Fudge, "Paul's Apostolic Self-Consciousness at Athens," *JETS* 14 (1971): 193–98.

in Athens. In verse 28 Paul quotes two pagan writers, Epimenides and Aratus, who describe the attributes of Zeus, and then applies these descriptions to the true God. Why does he do this? Paul also weaves into his argument several Old Testament allusions. Again, why does he do so, and how do such allusions relate to his quotations from pagan authors about Zeus? An examination of the context reveals how the apostle is weaving in these pagan quotations.

First, Paul explains that in the present age people are not to fulfill the true God's intentions for humanity by building material temple structures and finding him there:

> The God who made the world and all things in it, since He is Lord of heaven and earth, does not dwell in temples made with hands; neither is He served by human hands, as though He needed anything, since He Himself gives to all life and breath and all things. (vv. 24–25)[10]

Verse 24 begins with a clear echo of Old Testament statements about God creating the world: Genesis 1:1; Exodus 20:11; Isaiah 42:5; 1QH 1,13–15 (e.g., Exod. 20:11, "the LORD made the heaven and the earth . . . all things in them").[11] Paul says that "temples made with hands" are inadequate to house permanently the transcendent divine presence (Acts 17:24). The apostle applies to pagan temples what Stephen has already said about the idolatrous Jewish temple in 7:48:[12] "The Most High does not dwell in houses made by human hands."[13] Further, such cultic structures imply that God needs to be "served by human hands." This is an impossibility, since God is the self-sufficient Creator of everything (v. 25). Furthermore, one would be quite mistaken to think that the true God's presence is to be found behind idols of "gold or silver or stone, an image formed by the art and thought of man" (v. 29). This is so because humans were created to be God's sons (i.e., "the offspring of God" in v. 28b), that

---

10. English translations of biblical references are from the NASB; differences from that version reflect my own translation.

11. Following C. K. Barrett, *A Critical and Exegetical Commentary on the Acts of the Apostles,* ICC (Edinburgh: T. & T. Clark, 1998), 2:839–40.

12. See G. K. Beale, *Eden, the Temple, and the Mission of the Church,* NSBT (Leicester: InterVarsity, 2004), chapter 6, for Stephen's assessment of the temple as an idolatrous institution.

13. See C. J. Hemer, *The Book of Acts in the Setting of Hellenistic History* (Winona Lake, Ind.: Eisenbrauns, 1990), 190, who notes that Stephen's critique of God dwelling in "temples made with hands" (Acts 7:48) influenced Paul's virtually identical critique of pagan temples (Acts 17:24).

is, just as children reflect the image of their parents, so God's children should reflect him, which they do by reflecting the glorious attributes of his "divine nature" (as Gen. 1:26–27 has said), not by reflecting the unspiritual nature of handmade idols. Paul's logic is simple: "If like begets like, it is illogical to suppose that the divine nature who created living human beings is like an image made of an inanimate substance."[14]

If it is not to worship idols, what, then, is God's intention for humanity? Acts 17:26–31 presents a fitting summary:

> And He made from one, every nation of mankind to live on all the face of the earth, having determined their appointed times, and the boundaries of their habitation, that they should seek God, if perhaps they might grope for Him and find Him, though He is not far from each one of us; for in Him we live and move and exist, as even some of your own poets have said, "For we also are His offspring." Being then the offspring of God we ought not to think that the Divine Nature is like gold or silver or stone, an image formed by the art and thought of man. Therefore having overlooked the times of ignorance, God is now declaring to men that all everywhere should repent, because He has fixed a day in which He will judge the world in righteousness through a Man whom He has appointed, having furnished proof to all men by raising Him from the dead.

Paul says in verses 26–27 that God has caused humanity to spread out in order "that they should seek God," and in verse 30 he affirms that since the coming of Christ they may "seek" and "find" him by repenting and trusting in the resurrected Christ. To "repent" is the main point and goal of the Areopagus speech up through verse 31. Therefore, if people do not "repent," verse 31 says, God will judge them.

The commission God gave to Adam in Genesis 1:28 appears to be echoed in the background of verses 26–27. Verse 26 begins with "he made from one [not 'one blood']"[15] . . . to live on the face of the earth," which refers specifically to Adam, from whom all humanity came.[16] That the universal commission to

---

14. W. J. Larkin, *Acts*, IVPNTC (Downers Grove, Ill.: InterVarsity, 1995), 259.
15. For preference of the shorter reading, see B. M. Metzger, *A Textual Commentary on the Greek New Testament* (London/New York: UBS, 1971), 456: and Barrett, *Acts*, 2:842.
16. For example, see D. L. Balch, "The Areopagus Speech," in *Greeks, Romans, and Christians,* ed. D. L. Balch et al. (Minneapolis: Fortress, 1990), 57, who affirms that Christians familiar with the Septuagint would have perceived a reference to Adam. He then speculates

Adam is in mind receives confirmation from at least two observations.[17] First, verse 24 ("the God who made the world and all things in it") echoes Genesis 1:1 and subsequent repetitions of Genesis 1:1 in the Old Testament and Judaism (e.g., Isa. 42:5; 1QH 1,13–15). Among the later paraphrases of Genesis 1:1 is Isaiah 42:5, the context of which mentions the commission of humanity, spearheaded by Israel, to spread out over the earth (likewise 1QH 1,13–15), and it may be Isaiah 42 that is uppermost in mind—even more than Genesis 1:1 and Exodus 20:11. Isaiah 42 and the parallels in Acts 17 read as follows:

Isaiah 42:5	Acts 17:24–25
ὁ θεὸς ὁ ποιήσας τὸν οὐρανὸν καὶ πήξας αὐτόν ὁ στερεώσας τὴν γῆν καὶ τὰ ἐν αὐτῇ καὶ διδους πνοὴν τῷ λαῷ τῷ ἐπ' αὐτῆς καὶ πνεῦμα τοῖς πατοῦσιν αὐτήν *The God who made the heaven* and the earth and established it, who strengthened *the earth and the things in it,* and *who has given breath* to the people who are upon on it *and spirit* to the ones treading on it [author's trans].	verse 24: ὁ θεὸς ὁ ποιήσας τὸν κόσμον καὶ πάντα τὰ ἐν αὐτῷ, οὗτος οὐρανοῦ καὶ γῆς ὑπάρχων κύριος οὐκ ἐν χειροποιήτοις ναοῖς κατοικει verse 25: οὐδὲ ὑπὸ χειρῶν ἀνθρωπίνων θεραπεύεται προσδεόμενός τινος, αὐτὸς διδοὺς πᾶσι ζωὴν καὶ πνοὴν καὶ τὰ πάντα· verse 24: *The God who made the world and* all *things in it,* since he exists as Lord of *heaven and earth,* does not dwell in temples made by hands, verse 25: neither is he served by the hands of men, as though he needed anything, since he himself *gives* all *life and breath* and all things [author's trans].

---

that some who were aware of Stoic creation mythologies might have called to mind the belief that Zeus generated all things from "one seed for the entire world" (on which see Dio Chrysostom, *Orations* 36.56).

17. See L. T. Johnson, *The Acts of the Apostles,* Sacra Pagina (Collegeville: Liturgical Press, 1992), 315, who sees the phrase "he made from one to live on the face of the earth" referring to Genesis 1:27–28 and 2:7.

The very next two verses of Isaiah 42 are the commission given to Israel to be "a light of the Gentiles, to open the eyes of the blind, to lead out from imprisonment the ones bound and from the prison house the ones sitting in darkness" (vv. 6–7 LXX). Isaiah 42:7 and 16 is alluded to in Acts 26:18 to describe Paul's commission to the Gentiles, and Isaiah 49:6—an explicit parallel to Isaiah 42:6—has already been quoted in Acts 13:47 by Paul as part of his self-understanding of his commission to the Gentiles (indeed, Luke 2:32 alludes to both Isa. 42:6 and 49:6 in describing Christ's commission to Israel and the Gentiles). On the basis of this use of Isaiah 42/49 elsewhere in Acts and the use of Isaiah 42 in Acts 17, E. Fudge makes the following conclusion:

> Paul's ministry in Athens ought to be regarded, so far as Paul is concerned, in the light of the prophetic role of Jesus . . . the Servant of Yahweh of Isaiah 42/49; . . . [because] Paul consistently viewed his own apostleship to the Gentiles in terms of the Isaiah passages, via his personal commission from the risen Jesus . . . the speech of Acts 17 finds its motivation in this special self-consciousness of the Apostle Paul.[18]

That Isaiah is in mind is further supported by noting that the phrase in Acts 17:24 "made with hands" (χειροποιήτοις), referring to idolatrous temples, occurs nine times in the canonical part of the LXX, seven of which appear in Isaiah. David Pao has, in fact, attempted to show that throughout Acts 17:24–30 are allusions to Isaiah, underscoring an "anti-idol polemic" based on that Old Testament book.[19] It should be kept in mind, however, that Isaiah 42 is itself an allusion to Genesis 1 and Exodus 20, and that other allusions to Genesis 1 and 2 occur in connection with the original Adamic commission.

Another indication that Paul has in mind the commission to Adam and his seed to cover the earth occurs in Acts 17:25: "He Himself gives to all life and breath and all things." Commentators have concluded that this alludes to Genesis 1:29 and 2:7 (see Greek Old Testament): "I [God] have given to you every seed-bearing herb" (Gen. 1:29), and God "breathed upon his face the breath of life" (Gen. 2:7),[20] although the wording of Isaiah 42:5 still rings in Paul's phrase

---

18. Fudge, "Paul's Apostolic Self-Consciousness at Athens," who alerted me to the full significance of Isaiah 42. Subsequently, D. W. Pao, *Acts and the Isaianic New Exodus,* WUNT 2 Reihe, 130 (Tubingen: Mohr Siebeck, 2000), 194–95, independently has seen the same allusion to Isaiah 42.

19. Pao, *Acts and the Isaianic New Exodus,* 193–97.

20. The allusion of Acts 17:25 may include Genesis 9:3, where the restatement of Adam's commission to Noah in Genesis 9:1–7 includes the expression, "I have given all things to

"life and breath." Both of these Genesis passages appear to elaborate upon Genesis 1:28. W. J. Larkin, in his recent *Acts* commentary, sees Acts 17:26 to be alluding to "God's design . . . for various cultures . . . to cover the face of the earth . . .," citing Genesis 1:28; 9:1, 7; 10:5, 20, 31–32 as background for this passage. Larkin says further that the implication in Paul's mind is apparently that if "all men everywhere should repent," then the Adamic commission would finally be fulfilled.[21] That is, the earth would finally be "filled" with humans reflecting the glorious image of their Creator, who collectively are his vice-regents, ruling over the earth.

In line with this vision of God's purposes is Acts 17:26–27a: "He made from one every nation of mankind to dwell on all the face of the earth, having determined their appointed times, and the boundaries of their habitation, that they should seek God." Ben Witherington sees the second part of Acts 17:26 as an echo of the Tower of Babel event and an allusion to Deuteronomy 32:8: "When the Most High gave the nations their inheritance, when he separated the sons of Adam, he set the boundaries of the peoples according to the number of the sons of Israel."[22] Deuteronomy 32:8 of the Palestinian Targum (Etheridge ed.) explicitly alludes to the scattering of the nations after the Babel episode. These allusions to significant redemptive-historical passages from the Old Testament suggest that Paul has in mind not merely the truths of natural or general revelation, as many commentators highlight, but God's redemptive purposes for the earth.

That Paul has in mind both revelation and redemption is indicated further by Paul's unique wording to indicate that "mankind" should be aware not merely of God's presence in "general revelation" but also of, what we may term somewhat awkwardly, his "special revelatory saving presence": the combination of the words "men" and "all nations" who "seek God [or the Lord]" (and Greek equivalents) occurs in Acts only in 15:17 and 17:26–27. The Acts 15 passage is part of a quotation of Amos 9:11–12: "that the remnant of *men* may *seek* the LORD, and *all the nations* that are called by My name." This text clearly refers to the work of Christ's fulfilling Amos's prophecy that "all the nations"

---

you," and occurs as part of the means by which the commission is to be carried out (v. 3), being introduced (v. 1) and concluded (v. 7) by "be fruitful and multiply, and fill [populate] the earth." Larkin, *Acts*, 257, cites Genesis 1:29; 2:7; and 9:3 as parallels. Ben Witherington, *The Acts of the Apostles* (Grand Rapids: Eerdmans, 1998), 526, also sees allusion to Genesis 1:27–28 and 2:7 in Acts 17:25, while Barrett, *Acts*, 841, sees Genesis 2:7 as a significant parallel.

21. Larkin, *Acts, 257.*
22. Witherington, *Acts of the Apostles*, 527.

would "seek the LORD" and be saved. And, moreover, Acts 15:16–17 portrays the Gentiles' "seeking the Lord" at his rebuilt, new eschatological "tabernacle"— temple—that Luke likely sees standing in contrast to Israel's and the pagans' idolatrous temples![23]

These allusions associated with the commission of Adam in Genesis 1 and 2, and which (Acts 17:25) are then followed by allusions to the human diaspora after the Tower of Babel (17:26–27), are likely not coincidental. Humanity had resisted God's mandate to Adam, which was repeated to Noah (Gen. 9:1, 6–7), to spread throughout the earth. In judgment, God confused their tongues and forced them to spread out. Nevertheless, blessing was mixed with this judgment, since among the nations spreading out was found the family from which Abraham came, out of which he was chosen to accomplish what Adam had been commissioned to do. Thus, Adam's commission in Genesis 1:28 is reapplied to the patriarchs and Israel.[24]

Hence, Paul says in Acts 17:26–27 that the ultimate reason for causing the nations to spread over the globe after Babel was "that they should seek God, if perhaps they might grope for him and find him, though he is not far." When this would be accomplished, so would be accomplished the commission to Adam and his progeny to fill the earth, so that God's glorious presence might finally be manifested throughout the creation by his "offspring," who reflect his image (v. 28).

In verse 28 Paul gives two reasons for his preceding statement that God had caused humanity to disperse throughout the earth "in order that they would seek" him. First, he says, "For in Him we live and move and exist." While some disagree, most still concur that, although we have only the fragmentary text and not much of the context of the original poem, the phrase is from Epimenides and is a description of the god Zeus.[25] As was observed briefly above, Paul is saying that what pagans believed about Zeus is really true only

---

23. See R. Bauckham, "James and the Jerusalem Church," in *The Book of Acts in Its Palestinian Setting*, vol. 4 of *The Book of Acts in Its First Century Setting*, ed. R. Bauckham (Grand Rapids: Eerdmans, 1995), 4:452–58, for the argument that James's use of Amos in Acts 15:16 refers to the end-time temple built by Christ at his first coming.

24. For example, see N. T. Wright, *Climax of the Covenant* (Minneapolis: Fortress, 1991), 21–26; and Beale, *Eden, the Temple, and the Mission of the Church*.

25. Barrett, *Acts*, 2:847, on the basis of an article by Pohlenz and Hommel in *ZNW*, doubts the reference to Epimenides and prefers instead that the saying comes from Posidonius, with background also in Plato. Bruce, *The Book of Acts*, 359; and M. L Soards, *The Speeches in Acts* (Louisville: Westminster/John Knox, 1994), 98, both prefer a reference to Epimenides. Cf. also P. Colacides, "Acts 17,28A and Bacchae 506," *Vigiliae Christianae* 27 (1973): 161–64, for discussion of the source of Acts 17:28a.

of the God of the Old Testament, who has revealed himself through Christ. Thus, Paul's first reason that humanity is to "seek" God is because he is present throughout the creation and one need not travel a far distance to find him, underscoring that God "is not far from each one of us." David Pao contends that Isaiah 55:6 stands behind Acts 17:27: "Seek the LORD while he may be found; call upon him while he is near."[26] If Paul has this Isaiah text partly in mind, then the conclusion herein is further confirmed that he is thinking of the "special revelation" of God's salvation to the nations and not merely saying that the truths of "natural" or "general revelation"—which pagans attribute to Zeus—are applicable only to the God of Jesus Christ.

The second reason for seeking God is found in the phrase "as even some of your own poets have said, 'For we also are His offspring'" (Acts 17:28), which is a quotation from the Greek poet Aratus (*Phenomena* 5), again, about Zeus (there may also be allusion to the similar phrase in Cleanthes, thus accounting for the introductory formula "as even some of your own poets have said").[27] Again, Paul's point is that what Greeks believe about Zeus is true only of the Christian God: humanity is the creation of the God of biblical history. But more of the context surrounding this statement of Aratus is extant than is that of Epimenides. The immediate context of Aratus's statement is strikingly similar to the goal of Adam's commission, namely that God's presence through his image bearers would fill the entire cosmos. The directly preceding context of Aratus's quotation is, "All ways are full of Zeus and all meeting-places of men; the sea and the harbours are full of him. In every direction we all have to do with Zeus."[28] The reason that humans are surrounded by Zeus's presence everywhere is, according to Aratus, "because we also are his offspring." Apparently, the point is that Zeus's presence is everywhere his created offspring dwell because he does not absent himself from his creation.

Paul has taken a pagan affirmation about a false god and applied it to the true God, whom it truly describes, and applied it as well, it would appear, to his original universal intentions.[29] One might think Paul only wants to at-

26. Pao, *Acts and the Isaianic New Exodus,* 196.
27. W. Neil, *Acts,* NCBC (Grand Rapids: Eerdmans, 1973), 191. See the citations of the two quotations by Aratus and Cleanthes in Boring, Berger, and Colpe, eds., *Hellenistic Commentary to the New Testament,* 326–28.
28. Citing Bruce's translation, *The Book of Acts,* 360, instead of Loeb.
29. The Aratus quotation probably pertains to the divine omnipresence of Zeus, but in the light of the Genesis 1 allusions in the immediate context of Acts 17, Paul may well have also transformed the universal descriptions about Zeus in terms of God's ultimate intentions to fill the earth with his glorious rule.

tribute to God the attribute of omnipresence that pagans had attributed to Zeus. The Genesis 1–2, Deuteronomy 32, and Isaiah 42 allusions, however, indicate that Paul has redemptive history uppermost on his mind and not merely the divine attribute of omnipresence. Further, he inserts the Aratus quotation concerning Zeus's omnipresence into a statement about the eschatological, "special revelatory and saving omnipresence" of Israel's God, which is the goal of redemptive history: that God's glorious presence through his "offspring" covers the earth as the waters cover the sea (Hab. 2:14), that is, God created his human "offspring" to subdue the earth as his image bearers,[30] reflecting his glorious presence in every nook and cranny of the creation. After the Fall, God was certainly omnipresent in creation, but not in a salvific sense, which was the original intention he had for his creation, which was to be accomplished by his human offspring.

In this respect, Luke Timothy Johnson is certainly correct: "Luke does not construct or canonize a 'natural theology' [based upon pagan religion]; he simply shows Paul picking up the inchoate longings of this 'exceptionally religious' people and directing them to their proper object."[31] This "proper object" is the special revelation of Jesus Christ, the "man" who has begun to fulfill Adam's commission and will consummate it through judging the world at the end of history (it is perhaps not coincidental that many commentators see the reference to Christ as the "man" in v. 31 to be an echo of the "Son of Man" from Dan. 7:13, i.e., the "Son of Adam").

This redemptive-historical understanding of Paul's speech versus a "common-grace" or "natural theology" perspective receives confirmation from Wolfgang Nauck.[32] Nauck has shown that the address reflects Hellenistic Jewish and Christian mission material, typically consisting of the following elements: (1) allusions to God's creation of the world and of people in his image; (2) mention of borders and times in connection with God's preservation of his creation and unredeemed humanity's "foggy" knowledge about the Creator; (3) repentance, judgment, and salvation.[33] The Jewish form of this literature has precedents the Old Testament texts (Pss. 33:4–18; 74:12–17; 148:3–10),

---

30. See also Johnson, *Acts of the Apostles,* 316, who sees that "it is probable that Luke understood this kinship *[genos]* along the lines of being created in God's image (Gen. 1:26)."
31. Ibid., 319. See Bruce, *The Book of Acts,* 363, for a similar assessment.
32. W. Nauck, "Die tradition und Composition der Arepagrede," *ZTK* 53 (1956): 11–52.
33. In this respect, among the significant sources that he discusses are Wisdom 11–14; Joseph and Asenath 11–13; Romans 1:18–2:10; Acts 14:15–17; 1 Clement 19:2ff. and 33:2ff.; *Apostolic Constitutions* 7:34 and 8:12; *Epistula Apostolorum* 3; the first two of the Eighteen Benedictions; Prayer of Manasses; *Sibylline Oracles* Fragment 1 and 3.

which exhibit a briefer threefold pattern of "creation-preservation-salvation," although Nauck does not comment on these precedents to any significant degree. Accordingly, the quotation of Aratus replaces the first element of the pattern concerning creation in God's image.[34]

Thus, biblical writers "plunder the Egyptians"[35] in this manner. It is remarkable to find the Acts 17 passage combining allusions to the Genesis commission for Adam, to Deuteronomy about Babel, to Isaiah, and to pagan religious claims about Zeus. It appears that Paul has the context of the Aratus quotation in mind, just as it is his habit to quote in context the Old Testament. Also significant is the inclusion of Old Testament allusions in the midst of allusions to pagan religion. Acts 17 appears, in fact, to contain a pastiche of Old Testament allusions. Although when viewed in isolation, some of the proposed allusions could be questioned, their cumulative effect points to the validity of their being used as most commentators suggest. Thus, it is possible that the Acts 17 passage addresses not only Old Testament themes but, more probably, addresses such themes with several specific Old Testament allusions in mind. What Paul meets in his pagan religious environment seems to be the influence leading him back to particular relevant parts of the Old Testament. Consequently, Paul's polemic against pagan religions appears to include not merely applying pagan claims about Zeus to God, but backing up the polemic with similar Old Testament claims about Yahweh. Moreover, in the case of Acts 17, the Old Testament allusions also convey truths about God's "special" redemptive revelation. This combination of claims and truths regarding Yahweh can be found repeatedly in the New Testament writings, as will be seen in the remainder of this study.

Although there is not space here to investigate Acts 14, it is notable to recall the Lycaonians' belief that Barnabas and Paul were Zeus and Hermes. In response, Paul quotes and alludes to several Old Testament passages to prove that mortal humans and idols cannot represent the true God. In this respect, Exodus 20:11 is the most explicit Old Testament reference that Paul makes, which, as has been seen, is also echoed in Acts 17:24. Again, the Old Testament is appealed to in arguing against pagan religion.

Outside of these two passages in Acts and a handful of others, however, the

---

34. For a convenient summary of Nauck's article, see Balch, "The Areopagus Speech," 72–73.
35. This phrase has become proverbial in referring to those times when Christians benefit from the unbelieving world's labors, which are accomplished under the beneficent hand of God.

assessment of Andreas Köstenberger about the General Epistles and Revelation may be generally true elsewhere in the New Testament. He says that

> the presence of other worldviews and religious beliefs is presupposed rather than addressed directly. To what extent can one therefore speak of a contribution made by these [New Testament] books to a biblical theology of religions? Foremost of all, one should avoid overstating one's case by claiming that they reflect a consciously worked out Christian theology and response to religious pluralism in their day—in the opinion of this writer, they do not. Conflicting truth claims are rather brought to the fore by religious persecution and the challenge of formulating a believing approach to it. The New Testament data should not be intellectualized, and one should not claim a greater degree of deliberateness or sophistication than the evidence bears out. Moreover, owing to the occasional nature of these writings, much of the relevant material is incidental rather than systematic, so that many insights can be gained on the level of inference or implication rather than by explicit reference or direct injunction.[36]

Köstenberger concludes that all one can do is gather material "on the unique person and work of Christ, on Christians' identity in the world, and on the church's relationship to the world, particularly with reference to mission" and how these three topics relate to Christians "interacting with other faiths."[37]

While this assessment may be generally correct, the material in the New Testament needs further investigation. Many more direct allusions to pagan sources may be found than has been formerly thought, although one must be wary of being infected in the process with the illness of "parallelomania." More sources are becoming available, and more work needs to be done in analyzing potential parallels to Hellenism in the New Testament. In particular, the tool of the *Thesaurus Linguae Graecae* will certainly be of help.

In this respect, the book of Revelation deserves further reflection. There is more in the book than meets the eye at first glance, although this data still must remain, to repeat Köstenberger's words, at "the level of inference or

---

36. A. Köstenberger, "The Contribution of the General Epistles and Revelation to a Biblical Theology of Religions," in *Christianity and the Religions*, ed. E. Rommen and H. Netland, Evangelical Missiological Society series, no. 2 (Pasadena, Calif.: William Carey Library, 1995), 113–14.
37. Ibid., 114.

implication." While the evidence to be examined could still be categorized as inferential in nature, it is a different kind of evidence and inference than that which Köstenberger discusses. He looks at the unique aspects of Christian faith, and then asks how this could relate to ancient and modern pagan religion. The study below shows the possibility—even, at times, the probability—that John makes specific and direct reference to pagan religion and that he does so—following Old Testament prophetic precedence—for polemical reasons. The study also proposes that John uses the Old Testament to emphasize the polemical force.

THE LETTER TO THYATIRA IN THE BOOK OF REVELATION

Revelation 2:18 appears to be an example of combining Hellenistic and Old Testament background. There, Jesus introduces himself to the church of Thyatira as "the Son of God, who has eyes like a flame of fire, and His feet are like burnished bronze." Colin Hemer, in his book on the letters to the seven churches of Revelation,[38] discusses the use of χαλκολίβανος, "burnished bronze," in 1:15 and 2:18. Hemer says, "A Thyatiran reading 1:15 would on our view recognize χαλκολίβανος as a local product, though the explicit association of the word with this city does not occur before 2:18."[39] Hemer adduces primary ancient sources that lead him to a conjectural identification of χαλκολίβανος as a fairly unique local product of Thyatira and as a trade term, likely associated with a local guild, whose meaning was familiar in Thyatira.[40] On the basis of the cumulative evidence that Hemer then brings forward, this identification is attractive and is likely correct.

Some commentators, however, have concluded that at this point in Revelation 2:18 Daniel 10:6 [Theod.]provides an allusion: a "son of man" reveals himself to Daniel with "his face as the appearance of lightning, and his eyes like lamps of fire, and his arms and legs as the appearance of shining bronze." But Hemer concludes that the contextual use of χαλκος in Daniel 10:6 is unimportant in determining the meaning in Revelation 1:15 and 2:18. Rather the word is to be understood only against the historical background of the local industry and, therefore, of the local patron-god of the industry, Apollo Tyrimnaeus.

---

38. Colin Hemer, *The Letters to the Seven Churches of Asia in Their Local Setting*, JSNTSup 11 (Sheffield: JSOT Press, 1986), 111–17, 127.
39. Ibid., 17.
40. Ibid., 111–17, 127.

The interpretative point, then, is that the picture of Christ in this letter was meant as a polemic against Apollo Tyrimnaeus, as well as against the mixture of local and imperial religion, since Apollo Tyrimnaeus also appears on imperial coins and on coins from Thyatira, the latter depicting the god together with the Roman emperor.[41] This point may be corroborated further from coins commemorating the deification of Domitian's son, who died in A.D. 83, "coins which show the child seated on a globe surrounded by seven stars."[42] Against this background, the appearance of Christ surrounded by seven stars in Revelation 1:16; 1:20; and 2:1 would seem not to be a haphazard image. Therefore, John's reference to Jesus as the "Son of God" in this letter is likely polemical: it is he who is the true "Son of God," not Apollo Tyrimnaeus nor Caesar's son (cf. Ps. 2:7). That Revelation 2:18 is the only place in the whole book where this christological title *Son of God* occurs points further to a polemical intention.[43]

Hemer's analysis is fairly convincing and helpful, but does it exclude the idea that John also had in mind the Old Testament? John alludes to numerous Old Testament texts in Revelation 1 in order to indicate that Christ has begun to fulfill Old Testament prophetic hopes. The clearest of these references is from Daniel (e.g., Rev. 1:1; 1:7; 1:13–14; 1:19; cf. Isa. 11:4 and 49:2 in Rev. 1:16; and Zech. 12:10ff. in Rev. 1:7). Some of the descriptions of Christ from chapter 1, along with some of the same Old Testament allusions, occur again in Revelation 2–3 in Christ's self-introduction to the churches. Jesus is presented in Revelation 1:13–15, for example, as having begun to fulfill the Daniel 7:13 "Son of man" prophecy. And, indeed, the portrayal of the Son of man in Revelation 1:15 as having "feet like burnished bronze" is quite contextually related to Daniel 10:6, since there it refers to his "legs as the appearance of shining bronze," this description of a heavenly figure in Daniel 10:16 being identified only by Theodotion as ὡς ὁμοίωσις υἱοῦς ἀνθρώπου. John is apparently following Theodotion's identification of the heavenly being in Daniel 10 as that of the "Son of man" from Daniel 7:13.[44]

---

41. Ibid., 116; see also W. M. Ramsay, *The Letters to the Seven Churches of Asia and Their Place in the Plan of the Apocalypse* (London: Hodder and Stoughton, 1904), 318–22. Emperors were often venerated in the temples of traditional gods in the Asia Minor region, even though such veneration was usually not equal to that given the local gods (S. R. F. Price, *Rituals and Power* [Cambridge: University Press, 1984], 155, 164–65, 232).

42. Hemer, *Letters to the Seven Churches of Asia in Their Local Setting,* 116.

43. Cf. ibid., 111–17, 127.

44. That Daniel 10 is in mind is apparent further from noting that Daniel 3 may also be secondarily in mind. In this respect, I argued in my commentary that, at Revelation 1:15, the phrase ὡς φλὸξ πυρός ("as a flame of fire"), together with χαλκολιβάνῳ ("bronze"), echoes the "furnace" in which Daniel's three friends were thrown (cf. Dan. 3:26, 49, 93,

The Daniel 7 context contributes to the idea in Revelation 1 that the end-
time kingdom has finally been inaugurated through Jesus' death and resurrection, and that he is now "Ruler of the kings of the earth" (Rev 1:5). The phrase
ὁ υἱὸς τοῦ θεοῦ ("the son of God") in 2:18 is not found in chapter 1. "Son of
God" in Revelation 2:18 appears to be substituted for "Son of man" from Revelation 1:13–15, which is consistent with equivalent expressions for Son of
man in Judaism and the Gospels, where "Son of man" (or other closely related
phrases in Judaism) and "Son of God" are virtually interchangeable.[45]

Daniel 10	Revelation
10:6: οἱ ὀφθαλμοὶ αὐτοῦ ὡσεὶ λαμπάδες πυρός ... καὶ οἱ πόδες ὡσεὶ χαλκὸς (LXX)	1:13–15: ὅμοιον υἱὸν ἀνθρώπου ... καὶ οἱ ὀφθαλμοὶ αὐτοῦ ὡς φλὸξ πυρὸς ... καὶ οἱ πόδες αὐτοῦ ὅμοιοι χαλκολιβάνῳ
10:16: ὡς ὁμοίωσις υἱοῦ ἀνθρώπου (Theod.)	2:18: ὁ υἱὸς τοῦ θεοῦ, ὁ ἔχων τοὺς ὀφθαλμοὺς αὐτοῦ ὡς φλόγα πυρὸς καὶ οἱ πόδες αὐτοῦ ὅμοιοι χαλκολιβάνῳ

That "Son of God" in 2:18 is an interpretative rendering of υἱὸν ἀνθρώπου
("Son of man") of 1:13 is further apparent, since the descriptions "eyes like a
flame of fire and His feet like burnished bronze," which directly follow in 2:18,
are also found appended immediately following 1:14–15. If the two expressions are equivalent for John, then 2:18's unity with the Daniel fulfillment
context of Revelation 1 is heightened even more. Jesus as the real universal

---

Theod.) and the heavenly being termed "Son of man" who had "eyes like flaming torches"
and "feet like polished bronze" (Dan. 10:6, 16—see G. K. Beale, *The Book of Revelation*
[NIGTC; Grand Rapids: Eerdmans, 1999], in loc.). And now the added mention of "Son
of God" confirms that Daniel 3 is in mind, since there the three friends are delivered by
"one like a son of God(s)." The phrases "son of the gods" and "flame of fire" occur in the
Bible only in Daniel 3 and Revelation 2:18, although the latter has the singular "God," the
difference in phraseology perhaps being due to a depiction of Nebuchadnezzar's pagan
perspective on the being who appeared in the furnace. Just as that "Son of God" protected
them, even in the midst of persecution, so will Christ do the same spiritually for those in
Thyatira who are faithful.
45. On this, see S. Kim, *The Son of Man as the Son of God* (Tubingen: Mohr, 1983).

sovereign controls the destiny of the churches in Asia, including the persecution that they endure at the hands of Rome or local authorities. Indeed, it is by means of the churches' "perseverance" through such "tribulation" that they reign in an invisible messianic "kingdom" (cf. Rev. 1:6, 9), which had previously been so long awaited.

Thus, while Hemer's hypothesis about the specific historical background of Thyatira is attractive and fairly persuasive he, nevertheless, unnecessarily de-emphasizes the connection with Daniel. Both backgrounds are meaningful for John. As I have argued elsewhere about other passages in the Apocalypse, so here local conditions associated with pagan religion have directed John's mind back to the Old Testament.[46] Jesus as the "Son of man" of Daniel 7 and 10 is the true "Son of God,"[47] who will exercise the Ancient of Days' authority in judging the ungodly nations (Dan. 7:9–13; 4 Ezra 13:1–13, 32, 37, 52), as well as those who identify with them through compromise (Dan. 11:30–38, 45). Neither the local bronze guild god Apollos Tyrimnaeus nor the divine Caesar, both of whom were referred to as sons of the god Zeus, is the true God. It is Jesus Christ who is the true "Son of God," who is sovereign over all the earth and over every trade guild, including the guild of bronze workers, and sovereignty is partly why he represents himself as "the Son of God" in association with "shining bronze." The readers must give their exclusive adoration to Jesus and trust him for their economic welfare, since he alone is the true Son of God. Thus, Christ's description as "Son of God" and having "his feet like bronze" carries dual reference to the same pagan and Old Testament portrayals of a heavenly being.

THE INTRODUCTION TO THE BOOK OF REVELATION

Revelation 1:4

Also significant for our subject is Revelation 1:4: "the one who is and who was and who is coming." The complete threefold clause is a reflection of Exodus 3:14 together with twofold and threefold temporal descriptions of God in Isaiah (cf. 41:4; 43:10; 44:6; 48:12), which themselves may be reflections developed upon the divine name in Exodus 3:14. The name of Exodus 3:14 was also expanded in a twofold and threefold manner by later Jewish tradition: (1) "I am He who is

---

46. Hemer himself observes likewise in other passages of Revelation (e.g., *Letters to the Seven Churches of Asia in Their Local Setting*, 42, 51).

47. Cf. above on the interchangeableness of the titles.

and who will be" (Targ. Ps.-J. Exod. 3:14); (2) "I am now what I always was and always will be" (Exodus Rabbah 3, 6; The Alphabet of Rabbi Akiba; likewise Midr. Ps. 72:1); (3) "I am he who is and who was and I am he who will be" (Targ. Ps.-J. Deut. 32:39; see likewise the gloss to Tg. Neof. Exod. 3:14).[48]

It is unlikely that John is dependent only upon the Deuteronomy 32 reference,[49] since the first and last elements of that formula are not the same. Consequently, he is more likely familiar with the general tradition represented by the above texts that expands Exodus 3:14 (so similarly Delling, 124–126; cf. discussion of the targumic references by McNamara, 105–12).[50] All of these phrases are used in their respective contexts to describe God, not merely as present at the beginning, middle, and end of history, but as the incomparable, sovereign Lord over history, and so able to bring prophecy to fulfillment and deliver his people despite overwhelming odds, whether from Egypt, Babylon, or the nations. In Revelation, the last part of the threefold clause, ὁ ἐρχόμενος, is to be understood eschatologically and as referring to God's sovereign consummation of history in the future, an understanding clearly indicated by the interpretation of the third element in 11:17 and 16:5. The saints can be assured that in the end they will be rewarded for their perseverance (11:17–18), and their persecutors will be punished (16:5–7).

While New Testament commentators acknowledge to varying degrees this Old Testament background, fewer observe the elaboration in Judaism, and even fewer that the threefold name is attested to as a name for pagan gods. Indeed, with respect to the last point, a similar threefold formula is found also in pagan Greek literature as a title of the gods (Stuart I, 16):[51] Pausanius, *Description of Greece*, X., *Phocis, Ozolian Locri*, 12.10, Ζεὺς ἦν, Ζεὺς ἔστιν, Ζεὺς ἔσσεται ("Zeus was, Zeus is, Zeus will be"); likewise Plutarch, *Isis and Osiris*,

---

48. In Mekilta Rab. Ishmael, Tract Shirata 4.25–32, as well as Tract Bahodesh 5.25–31, the similar threefold formula describes the God of the Exodus in direct linkage with Deuteronomy 32:39 (the Shirata reference is also linked to a like threefold formula based on Isa. 41:4; note the threefold formula based on Isa. 44:6 in Midr. Rab. Gen. 81.2, Midr. Rab. Deut 1.10, and Midr. Rab. Songs 1. 9 § 1; for a similar threefold formula for God without reference to a precise Old Testament text, see Jos., *Contra Ap.* 2, 190; *Ant.* 8, 280; Aristobulus 4:5; cf. Rom. 11:36).

49. Against L. P. Trudinger, "Some Observations Concerning the Text of the Old Testament in the Book of Revelation," *JTS* 17 (1966): 87.

50. G. Delling, "Zum Gottesdienstlichen Stil der Johannes-Apokalypse," *NovT* 3 (1959): 124–26; cf. discussion of the targumic sources by M. McNamara, *The New Testament and the Palestinian Targum to the Pentateuch*, Analecta Biblica 27 (Rome: Pontifical Biblical Institute, 1966), 105–12.

51. M. Stuart, *Commentary on the Apocalypse* (Andover: Alien, Morrell and Wardwell; New York: M. H. Newman, 1845), 1:16.

9 ("the statue of Athena, whom they believe to be Isis, bore the inscription: 'I
am all that has been, and is, and shall be'"); Orphica 39; Plato, *Timaeus* 37E
("for we say that it [Eternal Being] 'is' or 'was' or 'will be'"; cf. Irenaeus, *Adv.
Haer.* 3,25,5, citing Plato's formula); an inscription describing the god Aion at
Eleusis on the Greek mainland ("Aion . . . [is] of such a nature that he is and
was and will be").[52]

These references from the Hellenistic world may have sparked John's appeal to the Old Testament-Jewish formulae as constituting an apologetic. Thus,
the title for God in Revelation 1:4 carries dual reference to the same pagan and
Old Testament title for God. It is plausible that what led John back to the
threefold divine formula of the Old Testament and Judaism was his awareness
of the same pagan formula for deity, with which some, if not many, of his
Gentile readers would have been familiar from their pre-Christian past. What
pagans think is true of Zeus and other gods is true only of the Old Testament
God, which the Old Testament itself boldly proclaims and John reiterates in
good prophetic style. Recently converted Gentiles are to receive assurance that
whom they formerly thought was the eternal god, whether Zeus or Aion, is
not the true God, but only the Father of Jesus Christ can bear that divine name.

Revelation 1:8, 17; 21:6; 22:13

John also identifies both God and Jesus with the title "the Alpha and the
Omega" (Τὸ Ἄλφα καὶ τὸ Ὦ; Rev. 1:8; 21:6; 22:13). This name cannot be
found in the Old Testament. David Aune has observed, however, that ΑΩ
functions as a divine name in magical papyri and was an essential constituent
of the divine name ΙΑΩ, also occurring in pagan magical texts.[53] This name
was part of a magical incantation uttered by the human practitioner in order
to manipulate the deity to bring about the desired result. Aune documents in
detail the evidence for this. He sees Revelation to be applying the pagan name

---

52. For the inscription and discussion, see S. M. McDonough, *YHWH at Patmos* (WUNT 2
     Reihe, 107; Tübingen: Mohr Siebeck, 1999), 51–55. J. Moffatt, *The Revelation of St. John
     the Divine*, Expositor's Greek Testament (Grand Rapids: Eerdmans, 1970), 5:21, cites a
     similar formula predicated of the Egyptian god Ani in a papyrus text. For other examples,
     see E. Lohmeyer, *Die Offenbarung des Johannes*, Handbuch zum Neuen Testament 16
     (Tubingen: Mohr [Siebeck], 1970), 168, 179, 181; and McNamara, *New Testament and
     Palestinian Targum*, 102; for early patristic references, see R. H. Charles, A *Critical and
     Exegetical Commentary on the Revelation of St. John* (Edinburgh: T. & T. Clark, 1920),
     2:220–21.
53. David Aune, "The Apocalypse of John and Greco-Roman Revelatory Magic," *NTS* 33
     (1987): 481–501.

to Christ (although sometimes there it likely refers to God) to show that only
Christ is the true God who is beyond manipulation by human magical
practitioners.

Aune mentions no Old Testament background for this name, although he
acknowledges that commentators have seen Isaiah 44:6[54] to be standing behind "the first and the last," which Jesus applies to himself in Revelation 1:17
and 22:13. Not only is it apparent that "Alpha and Omega" and "the first and
the last" are synonymous, but Revelation 22:13 interprets them in this manner, adding also the phrase "the beginning and the end" as a third synonymous name, where all three names are applied to Christ.[55] Aune himself makes
no commitment about any Old Testament background for "first and last," although he says the name could have a Hellenistic background.

It may not be coincidental that "Alpha and Omega" occurs first in 1:8 and
then "the first and the last" in 1:17, and that it also occurs first in 21:6 and
22:13. The initial mention of this phrase in these passages, which is attested to
only in Hellenistic magical incantations, appears to have been a springboard,
leading John back to the most comparable Old Testament background of Isaiah
41–48, where the phrase "the first and the last" occurs repeatedly. This may be
confirmed further from 22:13, where "the first and the last" directly follows
"Alpha and Omega." This combination of Old Testament background with
Hellenism certainly fits the pattern observed earlier elsewhere in Revelation
and the New Testament.

Aune is likely correct in recognizing that John applies the magical incanta-
tional divine name *Alpha and Omega* to Jesus to show that he is not suscep-
tible to the manipulation of pagan magic ritual. In light of the Isaiah
background, however, can even more be said? All three of the "first and last"
phrases in Isaiah have the following things in common: (1) they are polemics
against idols who are believed to predict and control future events; (2) in contrast, Israel's God is able to predict and cause future events. Why does God call
himself "the first and the last" in contrasting himself with idols in Isaiah? Like
Alpha and Omega, the name *the first and the last* is a figure of speech called
merism (a merism states polar opposites in order to highlight everything between the opposites). These merisms express God's control of history, espe-

---

54. Cf. further the Hebrew text of 41:4; 44:6; 48:12; cf. 43:10.
55. On which, see further G. K. Beale, *The Book of Revelation,* 213–14; also see McDonough,
    YHWH at Patmos, 42–45, who observes the threefold formula occurring twice in Hesiod,
    Theogony 30–39, and argues that the first use refers to a description of deity.

cially by bringing it to an end in salvation and judgment. The use of the first and last letter of the alphabet was typical of the ancients, including Jewish tradition, in expressing merisms that used *aleph* and *tau* in the same way (e.g., the Jews could refer to keeping the whole law by saying that it should be kept "from *aleph* to *tau*").[56]

Hence the mention that God is the beginning and end of history stresses his rule over all events in between. The "Alpha-Omega" and "first and last" merisms affirm that God was present and in control of history at its beginning and will be present and in control of history at its ending. John likely understands the names in the same way, as he applies them both to God (1:8; 21:6) and to Christ (1:17; 22:13). God the Father and his divine Son, who transcend time, guide the entire course of history because they stand as sovereign over its beginning and end. The Father and the Son are the true deity who cannot be controlled but, indeed, control the future in contrast to the false gods that the pagans attempted to manipulate through magic. Again, we can observe a combination of Old Testament background with Hellenistic background by which the former has been called up in John's mind because of what initially confronts him in the pagan environment.

Revelation 1:19

Another text from Revelation is pertinent to the current topic. Revelation 1:19 says, "Therefore, write what you have seen, and what is and what is about to come to pass after these things." W. C. Van Unnik asserts that the entire formula of verse 19 refers to all of chapters 1–22, and explains that John is commissioned to prophesy about the totality and meaning of history, whose truths apply not only within history but transcend any one historical time period. He argues for this perspective by adducing numerous examples of comparable threefold prophetic formulae in pagan religious contexts, ranging from the time of Homer to the fourth century A.D.[57]

---

56. See J. Gill, *An Exposition of the New Testament III: The Revelation of St. John the Divine* (Philadelphia: Woodward, 1811), 696, for Jewish references.

57. W. C. Van Unnik, "A Formula Describing Prophecy," *NTS* 9 (1962–63): 86–94; see also idem, *Sparsa-Cottecta 2*, NovTSup 30 (Leiden: Brill, 1980), 183–93; cf. J. P. M. Sweet, *Revelation* (London: SCM, 1979), 73, who adopts Van Unnik's view. Cf. also W. C. Van Unnik, *Het Godspredikaat "Het Begin en het Einde" bij Flavins Josephus en in de Openbaring van Johannes*, Mededelingen der Koninklijke Nederlandse Akademie van Wetenshappen afd. Letterkunde, Nieuwe Reeks-deel 39, no. 1 (New York: Noord, 1976).

As a typical example, although from within Christian tradition, Van Unnik cites from the Gnostic Apocryphon of John 2:15–20, in which the Revealer says to John, "Now I have come to reveal to you that which is, that which has been, and that which will be so, that you may know the things which are seen and the things not seen and to reveal to you about the perfect Man."[58] The purpose of the formula here is not primarily to delineate that the revelation pertains to past, present, and future, but to emphasize that the revelation penetrates to the inner meaning of history and ultimate reality, here centering in "the perfect Man," who is to be identified as Christ. This is a particularly significant reference since it is the earliest interpretation (mid-second century A.D.) of Revelation 1:19 that we have, and it interprets the three clauses not as a tidy chronological outline for the book, but as having the connotation of a transcendent interpretation of all history and of Christ's role in that history.

As a result of surveying these threefold pagan formulae, Van Unnik concludes that the somewhat variously arranged formula "that which was, is and shall be" expresses not only eternal duration but a revelation that transcends historical time and uncovers the meaning of existence and of history in its totality. He argues that pagan prophets employed this formula to authenticate the divine inspiration upon them, thus establishing the truth of the mysteries they were revealing.

Van Unnik's view receives corroboration from the observation that verse 19 could function figuratively as a merism (indicating the totality of polarity) supplemented with a middle element, which heightens the figurative significance. This view is supported by the appearance of a strikingly similar threefold formula that we have just discussed above— ὁ ὤν καὶ ὁ ἦν καὶ ὁ ἐρχόμενος ("the one who is and who was and who is coming," in varied order)—in Revelation 1:4; 1:8; and 4:8 (and, with minor variations, 11:17), which also serves as an example of a merism with a middle element inserted to intensify the figurative significance of *all-inclusiveness*. In functioning as a heightened merism the phrase emphasizes, not a chronology of God's obvious existence, but his transcendence and sovereignty over all events throughout history. A middle element is added in these formulae to emphasize the present reality of God's sovereign transcendence. He acts in and rules over all history, including, and especially, the present. God was present and sovereign not only at the

---

58. This is a significant reference, since the context of 2:1–25 is modeled on Revelation 1:12–19; the threefold formula comes immediately after mention of John seeing an "old man," who is associated with "the Son" and "perfect Man," who lives "forever," who is "incorruptible, and who exhorts him, "be not timid."

beginning of world history, and he will be sovereign and present not only at the end of history, but he is sovereign and present at all points between the beginning and the end. In like manner, Van Unnik contends that verse 19 conveys through a revelation, not a chronology of events, that the hidden meaning of history is centered in Christ: he is the ultimate interpreter of history because he is the transcendent sovereign and omnipresent one who planned and guides history.[59]

It can be granted that formulae of the type described above abound in pagan prophetic literature. It can also be granted that prodigious use of such formulae was for the purpose of attesting to the validity of a pagan prophet's revelation. The question may well be asked, then, why John would bother to use a pagan formula in the first place, a question Van Unnik does not pose.

It could be concluded that John coined his threefold commissioning statement in the form of the threefold pagan, prophetic formula in order to elicit an ironic, polemical association in the mind of his readers. In the letters to the churches, for instance, John shows an awareness of his readers' acquaintance with the ideas and religions in their regions, and selects for polemical purposes Old Testament allusions accordingly as a critique of their pagan societies.[60] John may have been motivated to model his threefold formula after the threefold pagan formulae, in order to show Revelation's pan-historical scope. That is, if a threefold formula validated the messages of the pagan prophets, how much more valid is John's revelation of all human history, because the same Christ who set in motion the latter days is he who commissioned John to record his revelation.

Some possible flaws can be found in Van Unnik's approach, which I have elaborated on elsewhere.[61] Van Unnik's interpretation of Revelation 1:19 (in which the vision relates both to eternal events *and* also provides eternal insight) appears to be an example of semantic overload, of placing too much meaning on a given word or phrase.[62] Van Unnik's threefold phrase can refer to either the time

---

59. In partial confirmation of Van Unnik, C. R. Smith has proposed a similar, yet revised, version of the view (cf. Smith, "Revelation 1:19: An Eschatologically Escalated Prophetic Convention," *JETS* 33 [1990]: 461–66, and summary by Beale, "The Interpretative Problem of Rev. 1:19," *NovT* [1992]: 379–81).

60. In this respect, see further my review of *The Letters to the Seven Churches of Asia in Their Local Setting*, by C. Hemer, *Trinity Journal* 7 (1986): 107–11.

61. See Beale, "The Interpretative Problem of Rev. 1:19," 379–81.

62. In ordinary conversation, words or phrases typically have but one meaning, with the exception of figurative expressions like symbolic pictures, puns, and double entendres; furthermore, in cases of ambiguous meaning of a word, "the best meaning is the least meaning" (M. Silva, *Biblical Words and Their Meaning* [Grand Rapids: Zondervan, 1994], 153, citing M. Joos).

span of the visions (i.e., eternal duration) or the visions' meaning (to uncover the meaning of existence and of history in its totality), but probably not both.[63] Some significant commentators have, nevertheless, found Van Unnik's argument compelling, and they may be correct in finding it so.

It is again intriguing to observe that Revelation 1:19 is clearly part of an Old Testament allusion, this time to Daniel 2. The third part of the formula in verse 19, (ἃ μέλλει γενέσθαι μετὰ ταῦτα),[64] reflects the wording of verse 1 (ἃ δεῖ γενέσθαι ἐν τάχει), which is drawn from Daniel 2:28–29a, 45–47 (ἃ δεῖ γενέσθαι ἐπ' ἐσχάτων τῶν ἡμερῶν).[65] The Daniel 2 references treat μετὰ ταῦτα as synonymous with ἐπ' ἐσχάτων τῶν ἡμερῶν (upon which, see following note and chart), both referring to the general era of the end times.

Daniel 2	Daniel 2
verse 28: ἃ δεῖ γενέσθαι ἐπ ἐσχάτων τῶν ἡμερῶν ("what things must take place *in the latter days*," Theod.)	
verse 29: ὅσα δεῖ γενέσθαι ἐπ' ἐσχάτων τῶν ἡμερῶν ("what must take place *in the latter days*," LXX)[66]	verse 29: τί δεῖ γενέσθαι μετὰ ταῦτα ("what must take place *after these things*," Theod.)
verse 45: τὰ ἐσόμενα ἐπ' ἐσχάτων τῶν ἡμερῶν ("the things which will be *in the latter days*," LXX)	verse 45: ἃ δεῖ γενέσθαι μετὰ ταῦτα ("what must take place *after these things*," Theod.)
	Revelation 1 verse 19: ἃ μέλλει γενέσθαι μετὰ ταῦτα ("what is about to [what must] take place *after these things*")

---

63. The last two criticisms were conveyed to me by my research student Greg Goss.
64. Although μέλλει replaces Daniel's δεῖ in most MSS of verse 19, δεῖ is present in some: compare ℵ {* pc (δεῖ μέλλειν), 2050 pc latt (δεῖ), C (δεῖ μέλλει); compare Josephus, *Ant.* 10.210.
65. The wording most resembles Daniel 2:45 (Theod.) ἃ δεῖ γενέσθαι μετὰ ταῦτα.
66. Cf. also, Daniel 2:28–29 in the Aramaic text.

Like Daniel, John may also be using μετὰ ταῦτα as an eschatological reference, particularly to the general period of the latter days, which had com-
menced, was presently ongoing, and would continue in the future until the
consummation.[67] The phrase μετὰ ταῦτα would not, then, be an exclusively
future reference, but would be consistent with the inaugurated end-time outlook of the Daniel 2 allusion in Revelation 1:1 and of the immediate context
throughout Revelation 1 and the New Testament generally.[68]

Given that Van Unnik believes Revelation 1:19 to be reflective of John's commissioning to write about the totality and meaning of history, it may be difficult to understand of what value an allusion to Daniel's latter days would be,
since formulae of this sort already encompass all of world history. Van Unnik
does not even acknowledge the allusion to Daniel, although most commentators do; on the other hand, commentators do not typically recognize the pagan prophetic background that Van Unnik does. The Daniel allusion may,
however, fit into Van Unnik's perspective. The Old Testament allusion may
indicate that, although the general temporal notion of *time* in the latter days is
included in the formula, the precise point of beginning fulfillment of and
unique *nature* of the latter days prophesied by Daniel would remain hidden
until John had revealed that these latter days had begun and would find their
ultimate meaning in Christ's redemptive work. His death and resurrection are
the keys to unlocking the meaning of all history.

John's use of a formula validating the revelation of pagan prophets is
therefore highly polemical. Following Van Unnik, it may be said that John
is asserting that his prophetic insight ("what you saw") covers not only the
full breadth of everything pagan prophets purportedly grasped ("what is"—

---

67. Proof for this all-important assertion is found in that the MT "after this" (אַחֲרֵי דְנָה) of
Daniel 2:29 is in synonymous parallelism with "in the latter days" of Daniel 2:28, which
strongly implies that the former phrase has eschatological import (cf. C. F. Keil, *Biblical
Commentary on the Book of Daniel* [Grand Rapids: Eerdmans, 1971], 111–12). By using
them to translate the MT, the Greek translations confirm the synonymous nature of these
phrases. Theodotion uses μετὰ ταῦτα for Daniel 2:29, 45, while in the very same verses
the old LXX version reads ἐπ᾽ ἐσχάτων τῶν ἡμερῶν, making more explicit the latter-day
sense implicit in the "after this" (אַחֲרֵי דְנָה) of the Aramaic text (note also that Acts 2:17
renders the אַחֲרֵי־כֵן of Joel 3:1 [= μετὰ ταῦτα in the LXX version] with ἐν ταῖς ἐσχάταις).
Therefore, in Daniel 2 μετὰ ταῦτα is an eschatological expression that is synonymous
with, but not as explicit as, ἐπ᾽ ἐσχάτων τῶν ἡμερῶν. Likewise in Revelation, μετὰ ταῦτα
may be a packed eschatological expression in Revelation 1:19 and 4:1. That is, with reference to Revelation 1:19 and 4:1, μετὰ ταῦτα likely does not function as a simple literary
or general temporal transition marker to the next vision, but is a phrase describing the
end times, the eschatological "after this" of which Daniel spoke.
68. On which, see further Beale, *The Book of Revelation,* 152–70.

historical past-present-and-future) but also the inbreaking Danielic eschatological reality that transcends and supersedes it ("that which must be after this"). In this light, Revelation 1:19 could be paraphrased, "You have a divine mandate to write according to the prophetic insight that has been given to you, about the things of this age and those of the in-breaking age to come."[69] Again, the pagan prophetic formula appears to send John (Jesus) back to Daniel to attest to his prophetic authority.

Other examples in Revelation wherein the interpretation of a phrase may depend upon analysis of both Old Testament background and local historical background are (1) the heavenly temple vision in Revelation 4–5 (cf. Aune for the Greco-Roman background and Beale for the Old Testament backdrop),[70] (2) the "seven seals" (Rev. 5:1ff. [cf. Ezek. 2:9–10 and the legal background of Roman testaments]), (3) "Lord of lords and King of Kings" (Rev. 17:14; 19:16 [cf. Dan. 4:37 of LXX and the divine titles for Domitian on Roman coins]), (4) "ten days" (Rev. 2:10; cf. Dan 1:12, 14),[71] and (5) the "door" imagery of Revelation 3:20 (cf. Cant. 5:2 and Hemer's description of the local setting of Laodicea).[72]

Conclusion

As has been shown, some commentators perceive Old Testament background in some New Testament passages but pay little attention to the Hellenistic influence, while other commentators detect Hellenistic influence in the same texts but do not address to any significant degree the Old Testament influence. Due awareness of both backgrounds, however, demonstrates how they might relate to one another. New Testament writers may well make actual allusions to what they meet in their pagan religious environment. These pagan allusions then become an influence in the writers' minds, leading them back to particular relevant parts of the Old Testament that are similar or nearly identical to the pagan claims. The writers thus show that the divine attributes that pagans attribute to their false gods are true only of the God of the Old Testament and of Jesus Christ.

---

69. See Smith, "Revelation 1:19."
70. In this respect, for Greco-Roman background, see D. Aune, "The Influence of Roman Court Ceremonial on the Apocalypse of John," *Papers of the Chicago Society of Biblical Research* 28 (1983): 5–26; for Old Testament background, see Beale, *The Book of Revelation*.
71. In this regard, see also Hemer, *Letters to the Seven Churches of Asia in Their Local Setting*, 69, 77.
72. Ibid., 201–9.

Can this interpretative approach teach Christians any lessons for dialoguing today with other religious claims? The answer may depend upon how one answers, *Should contemporary Christians reproduce the exegetical method that the New Testament writers used in their interpretation of the Old Testament?* Among scholars, including evangelicals, this question has been answered differently. Although some say *no* with respect to a number of the New Testament's exegetical techniques, I and others have "spilled a lot of ink" in saying *yes*, we should, indeed, model our interpretative methods after those of Jesus and the apostles. Accordingly, there will be debate about the present issue of whether to follow the New Testament's technique in responding to pagan religious claims. If the conclusion is correct that we should model our exegetical methods on the apostolic methods, then we should also conclude that we ought to follow the New Testament writers' lead in the way they responded to other religions. We should evaluate the primary claims of the non-Christian religion or philosophy that is confronting us, and then go to those parts of the Bible that most specifically speak to those claims. While many theologians have recognized that this method is grounded in "apologetics" as a subcategory of "systematic theology," it has been demonstrated herein that this method also has a sound exegetical basis. This hermeneutical conclusion is, of course, a biblical-theological inference, since nowhere does the New Testament explicitly command believers to adopt the exegetical and polemical approaches of the apostles. Nevertheless, it can be considered a legitimate inference.

4

God So Loved the World

Theological Reflections on Religious Plurality
in the History of Christianity

RICHARD J. PLANTINGA

INTRODUCTION: AN ENDURING REALITY

Until rather recently, the majority of people residing in the West—including the West's *literati*—demonstrated a shocking illiteracy in regard to the basics of the world's major religious traditions. Consider the case of Ralph Waldo Emerson, who in a letter dated July 17, 1845, reports the following item of community news: "The only other event is the arrival in Concord of the 'Bhagavat-Geeta,' the much renowned book of Buddhism."[1] Such an astonishing blunder—roughly comparable to today calling Tony Blair the prime minister of Canada—is most instructive, for it seems highly unlikely that a well-educated and well-read person living in 1945 or 1995 would make such a gaffe. During the course of the last century, Westerners have become increasingly knowledgeable about the world's great religious traditions.[2] In turn, recognition of religious plurality has led many devout Christian believers into both existential *Angst* and theological turmoil. Accordingly, theological schol-

---

1. Cited in Eric J. Sharpe, *The Universal Gītā: Western Images of the Bhagavadgītā* (London: Gerald Duckworth & Co., 1985), 22.
2. On some of the factors that have contributed to heightened Western awareness of religious plurality, see Richard J. Plantinga, ed., *Christianity and Plurality: Classic and Contemporary Readings* (Oxford: Blackwell, 1999), 1–3.

arship in the West, particularly in the second half of the twentieth century, has taken as one of its agenda items the project of re-thinking Christianity's relationship to the religions of the world.

The theological problem of religious plurality is, however, by no means new to Christianity. Both Testaments of Christian Scripture reflect times in which Israel and the church, respectively, had to come to terms with the complex religious history of the world. Early Christian history testifies to the struggle that nascent Christianity underwent to distinguish itself sequentially from Judaism and Greco-Roman systems of thought, both religious and philosophical. In subsequent centuries, with varying degrees of intensity, Christianity's encounter with Islam, modernity, postmodernity, and Asian religion occupied Christianity's theologians.

This essay ventures two undertakings. First, it explores in broad thematic terms the history of Christian responses to religious plurality, highlighting the dominant types. Second, it briefly analyzes the theological positions distilled from this historical inquiry, concentrating on the triad now commonly used in theological scholarship: exclusivism, inclusivism, and pluralism. It will be argued that this standard typology is flawed on two counts: first, it is reductionistic; second, it is guilty of theological inflexibility.

HISTORICAL: FROM ATHENS TO ASIA

While it is common to think of the history of Christianity in terms of four periods—the Patristic, the Medieval, the Renaissance and Reformation, and the Modern and Postmodern—it is instructive to divide the history of Christianity into three periods. The tripartite division runs as follows: pre-Christendom, beginning in the second century and extending into the fourth or fifth; Christendom, beginning in the fourth or fifth century and extending a good millennium into at least the early Renaissance and Reformation period; post-Christendom, which begins somewhere in the Renaissance and Reformation period and extends into the present. This three-fold strategy is in some ways less precise than the fourfold division, for the lines that divide the three periods from one another—especially between Christendom and post-Christendom—are not easy to draw. But the strategy of adopting the tripartite division does contain a double advantage. First, it utilizes the number 3, which every serious theologian is obligated to do whenever possible. Second, it illustrates something fundamental about Christian responses to religious plurality: the most sustained and interesting Christian reflection on the status of non-Christian religious and philosophical traditions occurs in the two bookend periods—pre- and post-Christendom—for in these periods Christianity was one religious tradition—and by no means the dominant one— among many, and was in general rather concerned about religious plurality. In the middle period, by contrast, Christianity was the chief religious tradition of the West, largely dominant, and not very cognizant of religious plurality. More comments will be later made about the periods in question as the discussion warrants. For now, however, the discussion will assume the admissibility of this tripartite division.

PRE-CHRISTENDOM

No sooner had the fledgling church graduated from its first and apostolic century—in which it had struggled to distinguish itself from Judaism—than Christianity's early thinkers were forced to come to terms with challenges from the Greco-Roman world. Some of the challenges took brutal form, as in the case of the various persecutions that took place in Christianity's first few centuries; some took subtle form, as in the case of the heresies that plagued Christianity's first steps toward doctrinal self-definition; and some took factual form, as in the case of the sheer presence of non-Christian systems of life and thought. In response to these challenges, there arose a need for defenders and promoters of the Christian cause, that is, apologists. These spokesmen for Christianity marched under two different strategic banners: the mediators, who sought to negotiate between the worlds of pagan antiquity and Christian thought and who emphasized continuity (at least where possible); and the critics of heresy *cum* defenders of orthodoxy, who emphasized discontinuity.

The eminent example of the generally irenic, mediational approach is Justin Martyr (c. 100–c. 165), although Clement of Alexandria (c. 150–c. 215) runs a close second. Born a pagan and in adult life a student of Greek philosophy, Justin was forced by his conversion to Christianity to seek connection between his pagan, philosophical past and his Christian, theological present. This biographical quest would come to expression as he sought to mediate between the worlds of Greek and Christian thought. Justin and other like-minded apologists faced a situation well described by E. K. Rand:

Here then is the problem that confronted the Church. With its new revelation, it must break off from the past, but how could it break from a past that agreed at so many points with its own revelation? The

wider the Church spread, the more intimate its contacts became with
the more cultivated portions of society . . . A new form of defence or
apologetics was required, less attack and more negotiation, a reasoned
endeavor to convince the cultured that the new faith contained something worth their attention.[3]

Accordingly, in his work "The First Apology,"[4] Justin, in order to remove
prejudices against Christianity and find common ground, attempts to make
contact between the claims of the Christian gospel and the ideas of the time.
His general strategy is to argue that, although Christianity is *the* truth, there is
also truth in the non-Christian world. Justin's key argument as to why truth
can be found outside of Christianity focuses on the concept of *logos*. Whereas
Christ is *the* word *(logos)* of God made flesh, the *seed* of the word *(logos
spermatikos)* has been spread throughout time and space. This concept of
seminality represents Justin's philosophical way of expressing the idea of natural
or general revelation. The seed of *logos* (Word, Christ, reason) in the non-
Christian world is thus, according to Justin, a source of revelation; everyone
has a fragmentary knowledge of the *logos*. Glimpses of the truth that are expressed by the philosophers arise from their discovery and contemplation of
some part of the *logos*. But without the full *logos*, such philosophers often end
up in contradictions. These partial truths, Justin argues, really belong to Christians, who have the full truth. Accordingly, Christianity is superior to paganism because only Christians truly love and worship the *logos;* philosophy only
gets you part way to the goal. But philosophy is a preparation for the gospel
and a gift of God.

In one form or another, one finds this rather high estimate of non-Christian
thought and culture many times in the subsequent history of Christianity. In
other words, Justin can well be regarded as a representative of a type.

Justin's view that philosophy is continuous with Christianity was emphatically not shared by that uncompromising North African critic of heresy,
Tertullian (c. 160–c. 225), the eminent representative of the discontinuous
approach to the non-Christian world. Because he regarded philosophy as folly
and the source of heresy, Tertullian's strategy was to go on the offensive with
respect to Greco-Roman thought, attacking non-Christian beliefs and practices in addition to setting forth the truth of what he took to be the Christian

---

3. E. K. Rand, *Founders of the Middle Ages* (New York: Dover, 1957), 37–38.
4. See Justin Martyr, "The First Apology," in *Early Christian Fathers,* Library of Christian
Classics, trans. and ed. C. C. Richardson (Philadelphia: Westminster, 1953), 1:242–89.

position. In the process, Tertullian articulated a classical, indeed typological view of Christianity's relationship to philosophy, reason, and culture, centered on the famed dichotomous choice between Jerusalem and Athens.

It must be noted that a major challenge in Tertullian's time was the practice of Gnosticism. In the absence of official Christian Scriptures and doctrines, and because of its apparent similarities to Christianity, Gnosticism was often confused with Christianity. Tertullian thus attempts to distinguish authentic Christianity from Gnosticism. In so doing, he saw—as did his near-contemporary and co-defender of orthodoxy Irenaeus (c. 130–c. 200)—the need to determine the authoritative sources of Christian faith, in which the key idea of the "rule of faith" *(regula fidei)* figures prominently. Tertullian argues in "The Prescriptions Against the Heretics"[5] that God's saving and final revelation in Christ was foretold in the Old Testament, communicated to the apostles, passed on to the church, and expressed in the church's creeds, doctrines, and preaching. He thus constructs an argument for the authority of tradition. Through the mediation of tradition, once Christian revelation has been received in faith, one need only to believe in order to be saved—no more, no less. Questioning is reserved exclusively, Tertullian concludes, for those who have not yet found the truth for which they seek. He writes:

> I have no use for a Stoic or a Platonic or a dialectic Christianity. After Jesus Christ, we have no need of speculation, after the Gospel no need of research. When we come to believe, we have no desire to believe anything else; for we begin by believing that there is nothing else which we have to believe.[6]

With respect to the pairs of terms *church-world, Christianity-culture, faith-reason,* and *theology-philosophy,* Justin's position is therefore "both-and" and inclusivistic, while Tertullian's is decidedly "either-or" and exclusivistic.

But these two strategies for thinking about Christian approaches to non-Christian systems of life and thought do not exhaust the thinking of patristic Christianity; its crowning thinker was yet to weigh in on this crucial matter. St. Augustine (354–430)—who lived in the period when Christianity rose to dominance, that is, at the beginnings of Christendom—would gather up and ex-

---

5. See Tertullian, "The Prescriptions Against the Heretics," in *Early Latin Theology,* Library of Christian Classics, trans. and ed. S. L. Greenslade (Philadelphia: Westminster, 1953), 5:31–64.

6. Ibid., sec. 7.

press in magisterial fashion the heritage of patristic Christianity. Having become a Christian in his early thirties only after great struggle, he gave the rest of his life to understanding the faith that he now confessed. Augustine maintained that one could not, in fact, understand unless one first believed.[7] For this reason, the Greek philosophers, who loved wisdom (the literal meaning of *philosophia*), could not grasp Christianity or truly understand it. But because of the light of Christian revelation, believers can truly understand and, more important, be saved.

Based on this understanding of the relationship of faith and reason, Augustine argued for the truth of Christianity over against other religious systems. In *The City of God,* he responds to the charge that Christianity was to blame for the sack of Rome in the early fifth century.[8] He seeks to refute those who think that pagan gods should be worshiped, either to gain advantage in this life or salvation in the life to come. For Augustine, worship is owed to the one true God alone. Christian truth, moreover, shows other gods to be false and therefore unable to give this-worldly aid or other-worldly eternal life; the gods lack both the will and the power to benefit human beings. In making his case against paganism, Augustine articulates his anti-constructivist conception of the origin of religion by arguing that "true religion is given to . . . true worshippers by the inspiration and teaching of the one true God, the giver of eternal life."[9]

Although Augustine's view of the gods in non-Christian religions was obviously not a high one, he did not apply the same degree of criticism to the conception of divinity as depicted by philosophy, which subject he also addresses in *The City of God.* Philosophical theism represented for Augustine a higher kind of paganism, for it was closer to the truth than nonphilosophical polytheism. Augustine's argument proceeds as follows: if God and wisdom are identified with one another, a philosopher, a lover of wisdom, must be a seeker of God. In dealing with the theological speculation of the philosophers, Augustine salutes these thinkers for their view that God exists and is concerned with human affairs. But he criticizes them for failing to recognize that the "worship of one unchangeable God is sufficient for the attainment of a life of blessedness even after death" and for supposing "that for this end many gods

---

7. See St. Augustine, "On the Profit of Believing," in *The Nicene and Post-Nicene Fathers of the Christian Church,* trans. C. L. Cornish, ed. P. Schaff (Grand Rapids: Eerdmans, 1993), 3:347–66.
8. St. Augustine, *The City of God,* trans. H. Bettenson (Harmondsworth: Penguin, 1972).
9. St. Augustine, *The City of God,* book 6.4. See also St. Augustine, *Of True Religion,* trans. J. H. S. Burleigh (South Bend, Ind.: Regnery/Gateway, 1959).

are to be worshipped, gods who were created and established by him."[10] Noting, as many of the church fathers did, that Greek philosophy came eerily close to many revealed truths of Christianity, Augustine points out in particular that the Platonists rightly taught that the one God created the world and transcends what has been created. Augustine, therefore, shares some of Justin's admiration for Greek philosophy, and so could be considered to have inclusivist leanings; but he also shares Tertullian's stern critique of paganism as well as his view that salvation is to be found in Christ alone, and so demonstrates clear exclusivist leanings.

Before taking leave of pre-Christendom, a look at the summative Athanasian Creed is in order. The first and last lines of the creed form an *inclusio*, in which the believer is reminded of the requirement of orthodox belief in the Trinity and Christology for salvation:

> Whoever desires to be saved should above all
>   hold to the catholic faith.
> Anyone who does not keep it whole and unbroken
>   will doubtless perish eternally. . . .
> This is the catholic faith:
>   one cannot be saved without believing it firmly and faithfully.[11]

As such, the Athanasian Creed is a statement of the principle often articulated in the history of Christianity that outside of the parameters of orthodoxy, of which the church is guardian, there is no salvation (cf. Cyprian, Boniface VIII, the Council of Trent).[12] In the midst of Christendom, one can find this position generally assumed and articulated with some emphasis, as the following discussion will in due course demonstrate.

---

10. St. Augustine, *The City of God*, book 8.1.
11. "The Athanasian Creed," in *Ecumenical Creeds and Reformed Confessions* (Grand Rapids: CRC Publications, 1988), 9–10.
12. See Cyprian, "On the Unity of the Church," in *The Ante-Nicene Fathers: Translations of the Writings of the Fathers Down to a.d. 325*, trans. E. Wallis, ed. A. Roberts and J. Donaldson (Grand Rapids: Eerdmans, 1951), 5:421–29; Pope Boniface VIII, *Unam Sanctam*, in *The Papal Encyclicals in Their Historical Context*, ed. Anne Freemantle (New York: G. P. Putnam's Sons, 1956), 72–74; and "The Creed of the Council of Trent," in *The Church Teaches: Documents of the Church in English Translation*, ed. J. F. Clarkson et al. (St. Louis: Herder, 1955), 9.

CHRISTENDOM

The matter of Christianity's relationship to the religious traditions of the world was not by any means the central concern of the medieval period. For one thing, medieval Europe was hardly aware of the immensity of the globe and the complexity of humanity's religious history. For another, the Crusades aside, medieval thinkers were centrally concerned with other matters. Nonetheless, some theological developments that touch upon religious plurality are noteworthy.

If medieval theologians were primarily concerned with precision, rigor, system-building, and the logical presentation of the Christian faith, no theologian typified this approach better than Thomas Aquinas (c. 1225–74). In the host of topics treated in the *Summa Theologiae*,[13] the reader can sense Aquinas's desire to contribute to one of the tasks of his time, namely, the work of confronting non-Christians (especially Muslims) with the truth of the Catholic faith. He therefore emphasizes (1a.1.1) that although human beings are capable of knowing some things through the power of human reason—including the existence of God (1a.2.3)—they are in need of supplementary teaching drawn from divine revelation. This is so, Aquinas, argues, principally because God has set for human beings an end beyond what reason can know and, thus, teaching provided by God is required. If human beings were left with the power of human reason alone to discover such truths, few would be able to learn them, and then only after a long period of study, and then with only a limited degree of purity and certainty. Graciously, then, God revealed such teachings so that all might have access to them and thereby to God himself. A science is, therefore, needed—a science beyond philosophy, namely, theology, the highest of all sciences.

In order to move human beings toward the end that God has established, Aquinas says, God helps us to know truth and disposes us to do good—all by means of grace, of which we, in our fallen condition, stand in need. God bestows grace—and so eternal life—on whom he chooses (1a2ae.109.1–9; 1a2ae.114.8–9). Divine grace, Aquinas argues, instills dispositions in Christians, including the disposition to believe things that are true and revealed by God—in other words, faith. Unbelievers lack the disposition to believe for they do not see what Christians see. The essential content of faith, which directs us to eternal life, is expressed in the creeds. Believing what God the teacher

---

13. See Thomas Aquinas, *Summa Theologica*, 5 vols., trans. Fathers of the English Dominican Province (Westminster, Md.: Christian Classics, 1948).

has revealed pleases God; and it is even necessary to believe what can be demonstrated by human reason, such as the existence of God. Believing is necessary for several reasons: learning the things of God demands much study in many fields; not all people are capable of such study; and even the able are prone to error in such matters. In order that people would come to knowledge of God in a manner that is expedient, broad-based, and certain, then, one must believe what reason can demonstrate—in addition to what lies beyond the grasp of reason. At the core of what Christians must believe, Aquinas argues, is the mystery of the incarnation and atonement, for the name of Christ is the only name by which Christians can be saved. But believing in the incarnation requires antecedent belief in the Trinity (2a2ae.1.1–9, 2a2ae.2.3–4, 2a2ae.2.7–8).

What, then, of non-Christians (2a2ae.10.1, 2a2ae.10.8)? Failure to believe is sinful, although not believing for reasons of ignorance is different than willful unbelief. In distinguishing different kinds of unbelief (pagan, Jewish, heretical), Aquinas points out the necessity of conversion. But he is quick to add that unbelievers cannot be forced to believe, since believing is an act of the will. Aquinas understood the special challenges posed in confronting non-Christians with Christian teaching, for non-Christians do not accept the authority of Christian Scripture. But because some non-Christians (at least Muslims—the principal group that Aquinas had in mind) accept the authority of classical philosophy, truths known to reason are accessible to them, even though the other class of truths—revealed truths—remains beyond their grasp. With at least some non-Christians, then, there exists some common ground on which discussion can take place.

Aquinas's belief in the exclusive truth of the Christian faith was held on theological grounds. Some medieval thinkers, however, also held to a similarly exclusivistic position for reasons beyond theology. In 1302, Pope Boniface VIII issued a famous official edict or decree, known as a bull in the Roman Catholic Church, the first Latin words and title of which are *Unam Sanctam* (One Holy).[14] Embroiled in a political struggle with King Philip IV of France, the pope in this bull declares the supreme ultimate authority of his office in both earthly and spiritual matters. Submitting to the authority of the pope is furthermore declared a requirement for salvation, for there is no salvation outside the "one holy Catholic and apostolic Church," of which the pope is the one head. To this day, *Unam Sanctam* remains a famous declaration of the

---

14. See Boniface VIII, *Unam Sanctam*, 72–74.

principle that no salvation is possible outside the church—understood in this context as the Roman Catholic Church.

The medieval thinkers, then, while not primarily concerned with the question of religious plurality, did have some things to say about the matter. The period of the Middle Ages was notable for not only its grand system-building but for its harmonious holding together of sometimes unfriendly pairs: church and state, Christianity and culture, faith and reason, and theology and philosophy.

POST-CHRISTENDOM

The Renaissance and Reformation period would see the great medieval syn-thesis begin to come apart. With the nascent decentralization of Christianity, the question of religious plurality would slowly become more and more im-portant as the shape of the modern world began to emerge. Some thinkers seemed to sense immediately the challenge of religious plurality; others re-mained focused on intra-Christian problems.

The German Renaissance scholar Nicholas of Cusa (1401–64) represents something of a transition in the history of Western theology and philosophy. In some ways, he looks back to the medieval period and in some important ways he looks forward to the modern period. He thought that opposites could be reconciled and brought to harmonious unity, and applied this leitmotif in his work *De Pace Fidei* (On the Peace of Faith), which he wrote very soon after the Islamic conquest of Constantinople in 1453, an event that evidently both-ered him deeply.[15] *De Pace Fidei* proceeds from the assumption that the three great Western religious traditions—Judaism, Christianity, and Islam—can find a common substratum of belief upon which to build peace and harmony, rather than war and discord. Central to Nicholas's work is the view that there is one religion that takes a variety of forms. His position is very subtle. In assuming that Judaism and Islam are reducible to Christianity in some sense, he seems simultaneously to defend the truth of Christianity, open the door to inclusivism, and suggest the possibility of pluralism. Nicholas was ahead of his time in thinking about the problem of religious pluralism, suggesting that wisdom consists in recognizing that human beings are at best capable of learned igno-rance. This view can be regarded as a postmodern one, representative of what philosophers today call the "hermeneutics of finitude."

---

15. See Nicholas of Cusa, *De Pace Fidei and Cribratio Alkorani,* trans. J. Hopkins (Minneapo-lis: Banning, 1990), 33–71.

As the fifteenth century drew to a close, few could have anticipated the tumultuous ecclesiastical and theological events that the dawning sixteenth century would bring, centered on the figure of Martin Luther (1483–1546). In the "Preface to the Complete Edition of Luther's Latin Writings,"[16] written very near the end of his life, the greatest figure in the sixteenth-century Reformation ruminates about his life, his struggles, his conversion experience, and his new understanding of St. Paul's teaching concerning divine righteousness: humanity cannot justify or save itself but is instead justified and saved by grace, by the gift of faith.

Luther was a first-generation Reformer. Second-generation Reformers were able to build upon his work and further the cause of reforming the church in a variety of ways. Most notable among the second generation of Reformers is John Calvin (1509–64), who was clearly preoccupied with the problem of intra-Christian plurality but nonetheless provides a blueprint for thinking theologically about inter-religious plurality. In Book One of the *Institutes of the Christian Religion*,[17] Calvin points to a problem: on the one hand, he says, all people have a vague general veneration for God; but on the other hand, very few actually reverence God. Why is this so? Calvin answers that there is in the human mind by natural instinct an awareness of divinity *(sensus divinitatis);* people sense through the very fact of their humanness, through human experience, that there is a God. In other words, a certain God-orientation is in the very constitution of our human being. Putting this point another way, Calvin says that God, in order to remove the pretense of ignorance (Romans 1), implanted in all human beings a seed of religion *(semen religionis).* Idolatry, Calvin says, is proof that all have such a seed.

What are the implications of Calvin's position? First, religion is no arbitrary invention or construction; even those who deny God feel an inkling of divine fear or terror. Second, atheism is not really possible, because the sense of divinity cannot be destroyed, for it lies deep within us, in the marrow of our bones. This doctrine of the *sensus divinitatis/semen religionis* we learn, Calvin says, not in school but in the womb. If all human beings have a sense of divinity or seed of religion, it must also be recognized that few foster the sense or seed; most degenerate from true knowledge of God. Why is this so? Some, Calvin says, suppress

16. See Martin Luther, "Preface to the Complete Edition of Luther's Latin Writings," in *Martin Luther: Selections from His Writings,* ed. John Dillenberger (Garden City: Doubleday, 1961), 3–12.
17. See John Calvin, *Institutes of the Christian Religion,* trans. F. L. Battles, ed. J. T. McNeill, Library of Christian Classics (Philadelphia: Westminster, 1960), 20:35–69.

the truth in unrighteousness (Romans 1); some concoct their own picture of God, thinking that God must be as they conceive him (instead of seeking God in divine self-revelation); some consider God only in emergencies or when compelled to do so. Calvin concludes that simple zeal for religion is insufficient; true religion must be conformed to God's will.

After dealing with what might be called "internal general revelation," Calvin turns to what might correspondingly be called "external general revelation." In addition to "knowing" God by virtue of what lies within us, "knowledge" of God is also manifested in what lies outside of us in creation, as well as in providence: we "know" God in God's works.[18] Calvin says that one cannot open one's eyes in the universe (nature, the heavens) without seeing God. Creation is for Calvin the theater of divine glory. If further proof were required, Calvin argues, look at the pinnacle of creation—human beings, who bear the image of God and who provide ample evidence of divine activity. Despite all of this evidence, Calvin laments, human beings still tend to get God wrong and turn against God. It seems that human beings fail to see God in God's works. This leads to the inexorable conclusion that the signs (sparks) in the universe are not enough; we need the full revelation (light) of God. But we do see enough to render us without excuse. God attracts us to divine knowledge, but we refuse; the fault of dullness is ours.

And so in Book One, Calvin the Protestant Reformer comes to the point in his argument, which he has painstakingly set up: actual (i.e., saving) knowledge of God is bestowed only in Scripture. We do not really "know" God in creation. Accordingly, Scripture is necessary for a true knowledge of God (as both Creator and Redeemer). Using a most instructive analogy, Calvin says that Scripture functions as a set of spectacles and focuses our confused "knowledge" of God derived from the seed of religion and from creation. Without Scripture, we fall into error, for Scripture tells us what the revelation in creation cannot. Scripture truly reveals God. God calls us in the revelation in creation, and Scripture then answers this call by providing a true and adequate revelation of God, a sufficient knowledge of God.[19]

---

18. The words "know," "knowing," and "knowledge" are placed in quotation marks in order to draw attention to different kinds of knowing: knowing that (fact), knowing why (understanding), knowing who (personal), and the like. Unfortunately, the English language has but one verb for the complex phenomenon of knowing, whereas most modern Western languages have two: compare German *wissen* and *kennen*, French *savoir* and *connâitre*, and Spanish *saber* and *conocer*.

19. In Book 2 of the *Institutes of the Christian Religion* (20:270–89), Calvin enters into a discussion of the pervasiveness of sin in human life and the consequent limited role that reason can play in the life of the Christian. Calvin sees sin as pervasive in human life (cf.

While the sixteenth-century Protestant Reformers were busy rethinking such things as the nature of authority, the church, the sacraments, and so forth, the Roman Catholic Church did not sit idly by. In response to the Protestant up-starts, the Roman Church launched some initiatives of its own, among them the Council of Trent, which met on and off over eighteen years (1545–63). Trent rectified some problems in the Catholic Church of the day and, in the face of the Protestant challenge to its dominance, officially defined certain of its positions—including statements on authority (Scripture and tradition), justification, and the sacraments. In refusing to recognize or concede that Christendom was in decline and in the process of breaking down, the Roman Catholic Church in "The Creed of the Council of Trent" reiterates the neces-sity of the Catholic faith for salvation and so underscores a long-held Catholic teaching: "I, N.[ame], promise, vow, and swear that, with God's help, I shall most constantly hold and profess this true Catholic faith, outside of which no one can be saved and which I now freely profess and truly hold."[20]

---

the famous Calvinistic concept of "total depravity"). Since our original natural gifts were corrupted by sin, reason is also weakened and corrupted. Nonetheless, "We see among all mankind that reason is proper to our nature" (20:276). In its creationally proper but fallen, hampered condition, what can reason discern about things divine? Less inclined to be kind to philosophers and sanguine about the prospects of reason than, say, Aquinas, Calvin says that philosophers sometimes say fitting things, but overall they miss the point. Calvin writes:

> the greatest geniuses are blinder than moles! . . . the philosophers . . . always show a certain giddy imagination. . . . they saw things in such a way that their seeing did not direct them to the truth, much less enable them to attain it! They are like a traveler passing through a field at night who in a momentary lightning flash sees far and wide, but the sight vanishes so swiftly that he is plunged again into the darkness of the night before he can take even a step—let alone be directed on his way by its help. Besides, although they may chance to sprinkle their books with droplets of truth, how many monstrous lies de-file them! . . . Human reason, therefore, neither approaches, nor strives to-ward, nor even takes straight aim at, this truth: to understand who the true God is or what sort of God he wishes to be toward us. (20:277–78)

Philosophy and unaided human reason, according to Calvin, are not capable of under-standing things divine. In order to conceive who God is and what God wants by way of relationship and obedience—in short, in order to become wise—human beings must be illumined by the Spirit of God. Reason's role, according to the Augustinian Calvin, is not primary (establishing that God is and what God is like) in the life of the Christian but secondary (making sense of the faith once one has come to believe).

20.   "The Creed of the Council of Trent," 9.

There is yet one more voice of which to take note in the sixteenth century. The French scholar Jean Bodin (1530–96) was deeply troubled by the religious conflict in Europe, especially in his home country, as well as the discovery of a religiously diverse world beyond Europe. In other words, the problem in the sixteenth century was not just which kind of Christianity was true but which religion was true. Bodin gives voice to these concerns in his *Colloquium Heptaplomeres de Rerum Sublimium Arcanis Abditis* (Colloquium of the Seven About Secrets of the Sublime).[21] What is in part remarkable about this text, given the time in which it was written, is its form: the matter of truth in religion will not be settled by appeals to revelation, which are often mutually contradictory ("Who will be the arbiter of such a controversy?"[22] Bodin asks), but will be put up for conversation and rational debate. While clearly not an atheist himself, Bodin was hardly an orthodox Christian; his religious stance can best be characterized as in flux—a series of positions enthusiastically adopted and subsequently rejected. The seven participants in Bodin's colloquy—a Catholic (Coronaeus), a Lutheran (Fredericus), a Calvinist (Curtius), a Jew (Salomon), a Muslim (Octavius), and two nonconfessional and sometimes skeptical religionists (Toralba and Senemus)—seem to point to the conclusion that God is the ultimate source of all religions and that, therefore, all religions are in some sense legitimate. What is required is that one recognize harmony, and having recognized this fundamental reality, act accordingly—that is, with tolerance—a veritable proto-modern position.

The divisions that formed in and during the Reformation of the sixteenth century—to say nothing of scientific disputes about the geocentric or heliocentric nature of the cosmos—unleashed reactionary forces that today are recognized as the beginnings of modernity. By the late sixteenth century and extending into the seventeenth century, Europe was engulfed in a series of religious wars, which seemed to be fueled in part by mutually appropriated revealed claims. In an attempt to overcome the resultant impasse and arrive at

---

21. Jean Bodin, *Colloquium of the Seven About Secrets of the Sublime: Colloquium Heptaplomeres de Rerum Sublimium Arcanis Abditis,* trans. Marion Leathers Daniels Kurtz (Princeton, N.J.: Princeton University Press, 1975). Owing to its rather advanced thinking, the *Colloquium* was not published during Bodin's lifetime. In fact, it was not published until 1857. See Marion Leathers Daniels Kurtz, introduction to *Colloquium of the Seven About Secrets of the Sublime,* lxx.

22. Ibid., 170. Elsewhere in the text, as commentary on the cacophonous state of religious affairs in the sixteenth century, Bodin writes, "Who can doubt that the Christian religion is the true religion or rather the only one? Almost all the world" (ibid., 163). Elsewhere, "all are refuted by all" (ibid., 256).

some *certainty* (given great *uncertainty*), some early modern thinkers conceived
a new way of thinking about and solving humanity's problems. In humanity's
turn to itself to solve its own problems, human reason would come to be seen
in the emerging Enlightenment as virtually omnicompetent.[23] Christianity
would ultimately be judged to be rationally deficient given the new standard;
and its posture would become increasingly defensive and its status privatized.

Descartes (1596–1650) exemplifies perhaps better than any other the stance
of an early modern thinker who was heir to the complex of changes just described. Motivated in a reactive way by the strife of his time, he sought to forge
a new way of thinking and solving human problems. Inspired by the exemplary
rigor and unambiguousness of mathematics, Descartes sought certainty (centered on the notions of clarity and distinctness) in domains of life where uncertainty prevailed. He proposed to find such certainty through a particular
application of human reason, the faculty in which he had great confidence. More
particularly, he sought to find an indubitable, rock-solid foundation on which
to build the edifice of human knowledge by subjecting everything to rational
doubt. In his *Meditations on First Philosophy*,[24] Descartes applied methodological doubt, and ultimately concluded that a disembodied ego was doubting or
thinking, and that he could therefore be indubitably certain of his own existence
(and thus the famous *cogito ergo sum:* "I am thinking; therefore, I am"). He found
the Archimedean point for which he was searching in the famous *cogito*—or
better, *dubito ergo sum* ("I am doubting; therefore I am"). Descartes theorized,
however, that such a point was to be found in his own subjectivity and not in
God. Neither is the rock-solid, certain foundation derived from divine revelation or accumulated human wisdom—for the traditional authorities had been
discredited by the doubting ego. This reorientation of human thought toward
itself represents a major turning point in the intellectual history of the West.
Often characterized as the father of modernity, Descartes constructed a new
paradigm for human knowledge and certainty, and introduced a posture of doubt
and kind of skepticism into the business of human thinking and knowing. Such
a seminal thinker could but have extensive influence on the spirit if not the thinking of the period in which questions of religious certainty and plurality would
become increasingly intense.

23. See Alister E. McGrath, *Christian Theology: An Introduction,* 3d ed. (Oxford: Blackwell,
     2001), 91–92.
24. See René Descartes, *Meditations on First Philosophy with Selections from the Objections
     and Replies,* trans. John Cottingham (Cambridge: Cambridge University Press, 1986), 3–
     23, 37–43.

At approximately the same time as Descartes was fundamentally rethinking the nature of knowledge and first philosophy, a movement in European thought was recasting the nature of the divine, as well as relations among the religions. Recoiling at the post-Reformation wars of religion in Europe, some thinkers— instead of choosing to identify with a particular sect or to embrace secular nonbelief—sought a middle way that took into account both some form of religious belief and the emerging and increasingly credible scientific advances of the early modern period. The thinking went as follows: modern science seems to provide evidence that nature is regular, like a machine; a machine-maker seems a good explanation for such regularity. This machine-maker is none other than God, who established order and law in nature, which reason can decipher. In such natural religion, religion is purged of superstition and shown to be rational. There is still therefore a God, but this God is the engineer of the universe, a watchmaker, a machine maker—and not necessarily the God revealed in the Bible, or the God of Abraham, Isaac, and Jacob, as Paschal famously put it. This view came to be called deism, from the Latin term for God *(deus)*. It came to be associated with heterodoxy and was therefore distinguished from theism, from the Greek term for God *(theos)*, which came to be associated with orthodoxy. Deism became a key ingredient in many influential eighteenth-century Enlightenment views of religions and their relations.

The chief architect of this way of thinking was Edward Herbert (1583–1648), also known as Lord Herbert of Cherbury and the founder of English deism. Herbert articulated this view a century or so before it became influential. In the face of religious conflict and scientific skepticism, Herbert sought in his work *De Veritate*[25] (On Truth) to establish a new theory of knowledge and new criteria for determining truth. He concluded that natural instinct indicates that there are truths that reason can discover, the content of which he called the "Common Notions." The Common Notions are *a priori,* independent of other principles, universal, certain, and immediately apprehensible—as well as the final court of appeal for our beliefs and the essence of the deistic viewpoint. Concerning religion, Herbert argued, God has inscribed five Common Notions in the human mind; they deal with the existence of God, worship, piety, virtue, morality, eternal life, and the like. Religions are, therefore, according to Herbert, all *essentially* similar, differing only in regard to what they add to the original endowment. In the end, Herbert judged Christianity

---

25. Herbert of Cherbury, "Common Notions Concerning Religion," in *Christianity and Plurality,* 171–81.

to be superior for its faithfulness to—or least corruption of—the Common Notions.

Deism's establishment of religion and Christianity upon a rational and universal foundation implied, as the foregoing has shown, essential similarity. Recognition of such similarity calls for tolerance, the prime Enlightenment virtue regarding religion. A clever case for such tolerance was made in the eighteenth century by G. E. Lessing (1729–81), who believed that religion was not primarily a matter of creeds and doctrines but rather a matter of humanitarianism and tolerance. In his play *Nathan the Wise*,[26] the heterodox Lessing relates the famous parable of the ring. Whoever wore a certain priceless and magical ring and trusted in its strength was said to be loved of God and humanity. The ring was bequeathed by its owner to his son and passed down through the generations until it came into the possession of a man with three sons, whom he loved equally. Nearing death and having promised the ring to each of them, the father had two identical rings made. As all three rings were indistinguishable, the father called in each son, blessed him, and gave him the/ a ring. After the father's death, the sons squabbled about who possessed the true ring. But they argued in vain, says Lessing in a highly instructive and suggestive line, for "the genuine ring was not Demonstrable . . . almost as little as Today the genuine faith."[27] The sons went to a judge to swear out a complaint and have him decide the case. His refusal or inability to deliver a decisive verdict, coupled with a consequent plea for tolerance, comes close, the reader suspects, to the heart of Lessing's own view of the relations among Judaism, Christianity, and Islam.

Every so often in the history of ideas, a thinker comes along who gathers up the thinking of his or her time, gives marvelous expression to it, and advances the conversation. It could be argued that in the eighteenth century, that thinker was Immanuel Kant (1724–1804). Kant's famous definition of "enlightenment"— centered on the notion of "release from . . . self-incurred tutelage"[28]— tells us a great deal about both the eighteenth century and the greatest philosopher of that century. Kant wished humanity to muster up its will to use its own reason to decide any and all matters—and not to be slavishly dependent upon the authority of others (cf. Hans-Georg Gadamer's discussion of the Enlightenment's

---

26. See G. E. Lessing, *Nathan the Wise*, trans. B. Q. Morgan (New York: Ungar, 1955), 75–82.
27. Ibid., 77.
28. See Immanuel Kant, "What Is Enlightenment?" in *On History*, ed. Lewis White Beck, trans. Lewis White Beck et al., The Library of Liberal Arts (Indianapolis, Ind.: Bobbs-Merrill, 1963), 3.

prejudice against prejudice).[29] He himself applied this principle in his magisterial *Critique of Pure Reason*, his investigation into the nature and limits of knowledge.[30] Kant expresses his objective in this most challenging philosophical text by wondering if metaphysics, the erstwhile "Queen of all the sciences," is indeed possible at all. He concludes that it is not, that knowledge properly speaking is reserved for things that appear in space and time, and that, therefore, things-in-themselves are unknowable. With that conclusion, Kant implies that theoretical knowledge of God is not possible. About God one may have beliefs, but not theoretical knowledge. In his *Critique of Practical Reason* and *Religion Within the Limits of Reason Alone*, Kant thus reinterprets Christianity along moral lines.[31] In doing so, Kant emphasizes a distinction in Western thought that would cause mischief for an emerging pluralistic world, that is, the distinction between knowledge and belief (and its close cousin, the distinction between fact and value), wherein pluralism attends not the former but the latter. One may have aesthetic or ethical or religious beliefs or values, but one must recognize that others have them as well, and that there is no way to determine who is right in such a domain. Given the long shadow that Kant would cast over philosophy and theology in the succeeding centuries, methodological skepticism leading to material agnosticism would figure in important, if not always visible ways, in the debates about religious pluralism (cf. John Hick).[32]

One of the first thinkers, in fact, to see clearly the challenge that modernity posed for Christianity was Friedrich Schleiermacher (1768–1834). Schleiermacher's Pietist roots and Romantic affiliations brought him to a critical posture vis-à-vis the Enlightenment. In his effort to convince his Romantic colleagues that they had erred in rejecting religion in their critique of the

29. See Hans-Georg Gadamer, *Truth and Method,* 2d rev. ed., trans. J. Weinsheimer and D. G. Marshall (New York: Crossroad, 1989), 271–77.
30. Immanuel Kant, *Critique of Pure Reason,* trans. Norman Kemp Smith (New York: St. Martin's Press, 1965).
31. See Immanuel Kant, *Critique of Practical Reason,* trans. Lewis White Beck, The Library of Liberal Arts (Indianapolis, Ind.: Bobbs-Merrill, 1956); and idem, *Religion Within the Limits of Reason Alone,* trans. T. M. Greene and H. H. Hudson (New York: Harper, 1960).
32. Deism's bold judgment that God so engineered the universe that it needs no tinkering or providential care, or Kant's implication that God is unknowable, created truly first-order problems for orthodoxy. Less and less was God required to explain the workings of the cosmos. Here and there recourse to a *deus ex machina* would be necessitated to fill in a yet unaccounted for gap in the system. But the process of divine displacement was well underway. Even an anti-Christian such as Voltaire would concede the necessity for some kind of regulative idea as represented by God. Friedrich Nietzsche would be the first thinker in the West to break decisively with the notion of God.

Enlightenment, Schleiermacher argued that they had misunderstood religion, which he took to be neither knowledge nor doctrine (as Protestant orthodoxy and deism held), neither action nor morality (as Kant held), but something else: a sense of and taste for the infinite, the universe, the whole, or God—or, in his later formulation, the feeling of absolute dependence upon, or consciousness of relation to, God.[33] Religion so understood means that it can only be completely manifest in a multiplicity of religions (given the understanding of religion as a genus with attendant species, as having an essence and a myriad of manifestations); each positive religion emphasizes one relation of humanity to the infinite (i.e., each is a different *Anschauung des Universums*). And because in Christianity there is universal resistance of the finite (i.e., sin) to the infinite, and this resistance is overcome by God (i.e., redemption: Jesus was the most God-conscious person who ever lived), the highest of all God-consciousnesses is to be found in Christianity—the highest religion. This inclusivistic construal of Christianity's relationship to the religions of the world would in the succeeding centuries be found, in one form or another, in many of liberal Protestantism's distinguished figures, including Rudolf Otto, Gerardus van der Leeuw, Nathan Söderblom, and Joachim Wach. The history of religion is, according to this view, regarded as testimony to general revelation and *preparatory* to Christianity. In addition to general revelation, particular revelations—of which the revelation of God in Jesus Christ stands out as *fulfilling* and definitive—make Christianity the highest religion.[34]

---

33.   See Friedrich Schleiermacher, *On Religion: Speeches to Its Cultured Despisers,* trans. John Oman (New York: Harper and Row, 1958); and idem, *The Christian Faith,* ed. H. R. Mackintosh and J. S. Stewart, vol. 1 (New York: Harper, 1963), par. 3 and 4.

34.   Theologically speaking, the nineteenth century belonged to Schleiermacher; his response to the challenge of the Enlightenment and its effects, to mediate between Christianity and culture, to connect the devotional and the scientific, characterized the approach of many nineteenth-century (and some twentieth-century) Protestant theologians. This approach, broadly speaking, is characteristic of theological liberalism. If, as Schleiermacher argued, religion is a kind of nonrational experience, such experience is also available in religions beyond Christianity, albeit not as purely. Consequently, many Protestant theologians and scholars became interested in investigating the religious experience of non-Christians; in so doing, they came to certain theological conclusions. Wach (1898–1955) exemplifies this classic liberal approach to other religions. In his essay "General Revelation and the Religions of the World" (*Understanding and Believing: Essays by Joachim Wach,* ed. Joseph Kitagawa [New York: Harper, 1968], 69–86), which he wrote near the end of his life, Wach emphasizes the relation between the study of religion and Christian theology, and the relation between general revelation and special revelation. The history of religion for Wach is, in fact, to be understood as general revelation, as the experience of the Holy in the history of religion. In addition to general revelation, there are particular revelations, and the particular revelation of God in Jesus Christ stands out as unique.

Pausing briefly at this juncture, it bears mention that modernity forced Christianity into a two-front war—the very kind of war that the history of the twentieth century indicates is difficult to fight let alone win. These two fronts are atheism and pluralism. On the one hand, atheism's challenge—the death of God—would find Christendom in the post-Enlightenment West expending much of its intellectual energy justifying its belief in the *existence of God* and the rationality of Christian belief. On the other hand, pluralism's challenges to Christendom's construal of the *nature of God* would emerge. As a result of these two fronts, Christianity's posture in the post-Enlightenment West would be a fundamentally defensive one.

One of the first thinkers who lived into the twentieth century to take in all of these currents was Ernst Troeltsch (1865–1923), the eminent representative of the *Religionsgeschichtliche Schule,* which drew on the heritage of liberalism à la Schleiermacher as well as upon the scholarship emerging in the late nineteenth century about the history of religion. Nineteenth-century Protestant liberalism believed that God was not so much revealed in a book or in the church; rather, God was thought to be progressively revealed in the processes of history. Could the method of the history of religion applied to Christianity deliver a verdict of Christian uniqueness? Troeltsch did not think so.[35] Christianity must be regarded as one phenomenon among many in the Greco-Roman world. His historicist convictions prompted him to conclude that—because history is the realm of the transitory, the contingent, and the relative—history threatens standards of value (what might be called "Troeltsch's ditch"). Troeltsch thus articulates one of the first quasi-pluralist positions in the modern West. Christian attempts to respond to these difficulties by seeking to establish the ultimate validity of Christian revelation and truth over against historical relativity have all, in his judgment, failed. It must simply be recognized that the tendency of history is not toward unity and universality (i.e., Christianity) but toward individualities, of which Christianity is but one. Is Christianity in any sense true or valid? While it is not absolutely or ultimately true or valid, says Troeltsch, it is true for those of us who have developed in the cradle of Western civilization, with which

---

Jesus Christ is the *fulfillment* of revelation; Christianity is the highest religion. There is not just *one* revelation, but there is a *final* revelation. General revelation (history of religion and religious experience) is a preparation for Christianity, a *praeparatio evangelica* (it is difficult to miss the similarities to Justin Martyr's position). Christianity is the fulfillment of religious striving. The religious order of things thus reads: outside the temple (profane), forecourt, holy of holies (sacred).

35. See Ernst Troeltsch, "The Place of Christianity Among the World Religions," in *Christianity and Plurality*, 211–22.

Christianity is inextricably coupled. Christianity is, in some sense, our mother who made us what we are, and whom we cannot accordingly but honor and validate. Therefore, the conclusion must be that other religions are valid for the citizens of other civilizations in which they are resident. Bolstering his pluralist *cum* relativist position with a dash of methodological skepticism, Troeltsch asks, "Who will presume to make a really final pronouncement here? Only God himself."[36] It follows for Troeltsch that the idea of conversion—and missions in any meaningful sense—is folly.

Troeltsch died in 1923—living almost to the end of the first quarter of the twentieth century, to the time when the West underwent a time of profound crisis focused on the Great War and its aftermath. That crisis extended into the political turmoil of the 1920s and 1930s and ultimately into the second act of the world's violent conflict. This period, in which the West's decline would be paralleled by Asia's renewal, introduced the thundering voice of Karl Barth.

In 1911, the classically liberal and German-trained Barth (1886–1968) had taken up a pastorate in Safenwil in Switzerland, from which position he would come to rethink his theological training and the very nature of Christianity. As is so often the case in the history of Christianity, Paul's letter to the Romans proved to be the catalyst. With his book on Paul's letter to the Romans, Pastor Barth became Professor Barth—and a prolific pen began to detail the crisis of Protestant Christianity. With a theological identity forged in opposition to Schleiermacher and his heirs, Barth delivered his verdict on the nature of theology in the *Church Dogmatics*.[37] Theology is not talk about pious human feelings (i.e., anthropology, focused on religion), asserted Barth, but attentiveness to the word of the wholly other God (i.e., theology, focused on revelation). The task of the theologian is proclamation of the divine word in the church and not the engagement of the cultured despiser of religion in contemporary culture. With this conception of theology as his point of departure, Barth—drawing upon the ambivalent German philosophical notion of *Aufhebung*—judges religion to be unbelief, that is, literal contradiction of and resistance to revelation.[38] He argues that there can be true religion, however, just as there can be justified sinners; no religion *is* true, but some religion or other can

---

36. Ibid., 219.

37. See Karl Barth, *Church Dogmatics: The Doctrine of the Word of God*, 1.1, trans. and ed. G. W. Bromiley and T. F. Torrance (Edinburgh: T. & T. Clark, 1975), 47–347.

38. See Karl Barth, *Church Dogmatics: The Doctrine of the Word of God*, 1.2, trans. G. T. Thomson and H. Knight, ed. G. W. Bromiley and T. F. Torrance (Edinburgh: T. & T. Clark, 1956), 280–361.

become true by grace, by an act of justification. God has, in fact, designated the Christian religion as the true religion; by grace, revelation has more powerfully contradicted religion than religion has contradicted revelation. In light of his conviction that revelation means *the* revelation of God in Jesus Christ, the early Barth judges that anything like general revelation is an outright impossibility, as made amply clear by his famous dispute with Emil Brunner on the status of natural theology.[39] Accordingly, other than proclamation of true revelation, there is no "other task" of theology.

Barth's enormous influence on twentieth-century theology has functioned for some Christian thinkers as a perhaps unconscious justification for focus on Christianity and Christian revelation, and disregard of the challenge of religious plurality. To this general principle, at least one exception is notable: the Dutch missiologist Hendrik Kraemer (1888–1965). Kraemer lived through the sweeping changes that took place in Protestant missions in the first half of the twentieth century. He observed the significance of Edinburgh 1910, the First International Missionary Conference and originating inspiration of the twentieth century's ecumenical movement; he served as a missionary in Indonesia; was active at Jerusalem 1928, the Second International Missionary Conference; was a central figure at Tambaram 1938, the Third—and final— International Missionary Conference. Kraemer was indeed influenced by Barth in his rejection of liberal Protestantism's construal of Christianity's relationship to the religions of the world, especially as that construal was expressed in the famous *Laymen's Inquiry,* authored by W. E. Hocking and others.[40]

In Kraemer's classic work, *The Christian Message in a Non-Christian World,* which was composed for Tambaram 1938, he articulates his sense of the crisis of relativism in the West, the resurgence of the East, and the problems that these spelled out for Christian missions.[41] He adopts a revelation-centered (i.e., Christic) standpoint from which to judge the religions of the world. This was, to say the least, an unpopular stance both at Tambaram and in post-conference

39. See Emil Brunner and Karl Barth, *Natural Theology: Comprising "Nature and Grace" by Professor Dr. Emil Brunner and the Reply "No!" by Dr. Karl Barth,* with an introduction by John Baillie, trans. Peter Fraenkel (London: Geoffrey Bles/Centenary Press, 1946). The later Barth, however, seems to qualify his stark judgment about revelation. See Karl Barth, *Church Dogmatics: The Doctrine of Reconciliation,* 4.3.1, trans. G. W. Bromiley (Edinburgh: T. & T. Clark, 1961), 38–165.
40. See W. E. Hocking et al., *Re-Thinking Missions: A Laymen's Inquiry After One Hundred Years* (New York: Harper, 1932).
41. See Hendrik Kraemer, *The Christian Message in a Non-Christian World,* 3d ed. (Grand Rapids: Kregel, 1956).

discussions, for it clearly entailed that Christianity's relationship to the religions of the world was not one of continuity but of discontinuity. What is less clearly entailed is what Kraemer makes of the matter of extra-Christian revelation. He writes, "The problem whether, and, if so where, and in how far, God, i.e., the God and Father of Jesus Christ, the only God we Christians know—has been and is working in the religious history of the world and in man in his quest for goodness, truth and beauty, is a baffling and awful problem."[42]

In the end, Kraemer is ambivalent about what to make of revelation outside Christianity: although Christ is *the* revelation of God, Christians cannot limit God's revelatory activity; it must be recognized that God shines through in reason, nature, and history, although the revelation might be received in a broken way. Moreover, the idea of *sensus divinitatis,* expressed in both the Bible and the Christian tradition, necessitates the attempt to speak in a qualified sense of "general revelation" and "natural theology" (Kraemer did not like the terms), making Brunner's stance, over against Barth's, the right one in that historic debate. But, Kraemer hastens to add, glimpses of revelation in other religions are *not* a preparation for Christianity or the Christian revelation, for religions do not point naturally to Christ. To come to Christ, there is a need for regeneration, conversion—a position for which he was roundly criticized by the theological mainstream, although some evangelically inclined theologians such as Lesslie Newbigin have found his position in many ways congenial.[43]

---

42. Hendrik Kraemer, "Continuity or Discontinuity," in *The Authority of the Faith,* Tambaram Madras Series 1, ed. Wm. Paton (London: Humphrey Milford/Oxford University Press, 1939), 14.

43. For critical reactions to Kraemer's position c. 1938, see *The Authority of the Faith,* Tambaram Madras Series 1, ed. Wm. Paton (London: Humphrey Milford/Oxford University Press, 1939). For critical reactions c. 1988, see the *International Review of Mission* 78 (July 1988). On the more appreciative side of the ledger, consider the relatively lonely voice of Lesslie Newbigin (*International Review of Mission* 78 [July 1988]: 328): "If we are speaking about religious ideas, or about religious experiences, then certainly to claim uniqueness and finality for one's own is intolerable arrogance. Kraemer's whole point is that we are not; we are talking about facts of history. If, in fact, it is true that almighty God, creator and sustainer of all that exists in heaven and on earth, has—at a known time and place in human history—so humbled himself as to become a part of our sinful humanity and to suffer and die a shameful death to take away our sin and rise from the dead as the first-fruit of a new creation; if this is a fact, then to affirm it is not arrogance. To remain quiet about it is treason to our fellow human beings." For a more recent assessment, see Tim S. Perry, *Radical Difference: A Defence of Hendrik Kraemer's Theology of Religions,* SR eds., 27 (Waterloo, Ont.: Wilfrid Laurier University Press, 2001); and Richard J. Plantinga, "Missionary Thinking About Religious Plurality at Tambaram 1938: Hendrik Kraemer and His Critics" in *The Changing Face of Christianity: Africa, the West, and the World,* ed. Lamin Sanneh and Joel A. Carpenter (New York: Oxford University Press, forthcoming).

Kraemer lived through and participated in the great transition in the mid-twentieth century, an era in which international Protestant missionary discussions became midwife for the birth of the ecumenical movement and the rise of world Christianity. After the foundation of the World Council of Churches in Amsterdam in 1948, Kraemer became the first director of its Ecumenical Institute. He continued to write about the challenge of religious plurality in the post–World War II period, which forms a crucial divide for debates about the nature of Christianity's relationship to the religions of the world. In this period, the West was forced to confront Christianity's complicity with fascism, the holocaust and seeming inadequacy of theodicy, the end of colonialism, popularization of the death of God theme, the increasing presence of Asian communities and religions in Western societies, and the many-sided phenomenon of globalization.

As the challenge of religious plurality seemed increasingly unavoidable, the Catholic Church also sought to offer a response. Around the same time that the Second Vatican Council was in the process of planning, Karl Rahner (1904–84)—promoting and working in the spirit of *aggiornamento* (modernization) in the mid-twentieth-century Catholic Church—gave some consideration to the question of Christianity's relationship to non-Christian religions.[44] He argues that Christianity understands itself as the absolute religion intended for all and as such without equal; but Christianity *comes* to people as the true religion. Does this occur at the same time for all? Rahner answers *no*, and asserts that, *as regards destination,* Christianity is the absolute religion. But it becomes absolute for different cultures at different times; after a significant historical encounter with Christianity, Christianity becomes absolute and is necessary for salvation. Those who have not yet undergone a significant historical encounter with Christianity participate in lawful religions as anonymous Christians (i.e., such persons have an implicit faith and access to elements of grace—and therefore to the possibility of salvation, which God wills universally).

Whereas Rahner spoke as one Catholic theologian, the Catholic Church officially addressed religious plurality in a statement that it crafted at Vatican II. After its rather staunch historic conservatism and traditionalism, the first Church council in almost a century sought to open the arms of the Catholic Church to fellow Christians and even to members of non-Christian religions, choosing to underemphasize its traditional commitment to its *extra ecclesiam nulla salus est*

---

44. See Karl Rahner, "Christianity and the Non-Christian Religions," in *Theological Investigations,* trans. K.-H. Krueger (New York: Crossroad, 1983), 5:115–34.

(there is no salvation outside of the Church) doctrine. In its "Declaration on the Relationship of the Church to Non-Christian Religions" (*Nostra Aetate*),[45] Vatican II seeks to emphasize what religions have in common: a common origin and a common end (i.e., God); the recognition that God's plan of salvation extends to all; the recognition that all religions seek to answer the problems of human existence. In turning to specifics, the Declaration arranges the history of religion in a series of concentric circles, beginning at the outermost edge with non-Western religions and moving inward to the monotheistic faiths—Islam, Judaism, and Christianity. The Church understands itself to be duty-bound to proclaim the truth of the Catholic faith centered upon Christ and his bride, but it clearly expresses openness to other faiths.

Vatican II's rather startlingly open attitude to non-Christian religions is also shared by Pope John Paul II, who is generally considered to be a conservative. In various encyclicals and in his book *Crossing the Threshold of Hope*,[46] the pope, who was a participant at Vatican II, more or less holds the view espoused by Vatican II, spiced with some allusions to early Christian inclusivism (i.e., Latinized Justin Martyr: *semina verbi*). How this seemingly open position comports with recent different sounding statements from Rome, notably the Declaration "Dominus Iesus," cannot be explored here.[47]

As relatively open and tolerant attitudes toward non-Christian religions began to be articulated by *more* progressive Christian theologians, some *most* progressive Christian thinkers sought to bring about nothing less than a Copernican revolution in thinking about Christianity's relationship to the history of religion. The two most notable advocates of such a paradigm shift are the Canadian historian of religion Wilfred Cantwell Smith (1916–2000) and the British-American philosopher of religion John Hick (b. 1922). Smith wrote a charter essay in the 1960s signaling the fact of a religiously plural world and the end of Christian exclusivism and missions. This Copernican revolution, according to Smith, entails that Christian theologians are no longer justified in their ignorance of other religious traditions. Moreover, Christian exclusivism has fostered

---

45. "Declaration on the Relationship of the Church to Non-Christian Religions," in *The Documents of Vatican II* (Chicago: Association Press/Follett, 1966), 660–68.

46. See John Paul II, *Redemptor Hominis* (www.cin.org/jp2ency/redeem.html); idem, *Redemptoris Missio* (www.cin.org/jp2ency/rmissio.html); idem, *Ut Unum Sint* (www.cin.org/jp2ency/jp2utunu.html); and idem, *Crossing the Threshold of Hope* (New York: Knopf, 1994), esp. 77–100.

47. See "'Dominus Iesus': On the Unicity and Salvific Universality of Jesus Christ and the Church," from the Offices of the Congregation for the Doctrine of the Faith, Joseph Ratzinger, Cardinal Prefect, August 2000 (www.cin.org/docs/dominus-iesus.html).

attitudes of arrogance toward non-Christians, whereas Christ instructed his followers to adopt an attitude of humility. Smith would return to the theology of religious pluralism in his 1981 book, *Toward a World Theology*.[48]

But the thinker who has argued the pluralist position with greatest force and philosophical sophistication is John Hick. Hick has articulated his pluralistic position in any number of essays and books.[49] In seeking to respond with integrity as a Christian to the challenge of religious pluralism, Hick takes issue with inclusivism almost more so than with exclusivism, which he takes to be largely discredited. Given a changing world, to which Christian theology must respond, Hick avers that inclusivism makes Christians feel a little less bad about the dire implications of exclusivism. But for Hick, inclusivism is simply sweetened exclusivism or exclusivism presented with a happy face. That is, the core belief of the latter is still present in the former. That core belief might be expressed as follows: God is the God of Christians alone. Accordingly, God's saving activity is confined to one narrow strand in the thick rope that is the history of religion. If non-Christians are to be saved, they must be Christians without knowing it (i.e., Rahner).

But why not just take the next revolutionary, Copernican step and recognize that human beings in all religious traditions are in relationship with the one noumenal, transcendent being who answers to many names and who has taken up residence in many phenomenal religious communities? Why not simply declare a plurality of saving paths to God, wherein salvation is understood as the transformation from self-centeredness to Reality-centeredness? Hick locates Christian resistance to his proposal in the traditional Christian doctrine of the incarnation and this doctrine's "protective envelope," the Trinity. Hick pleads for Christians to give up a Christocentric view of the history of religion (characteristic of exclusivism and inclusivism) and adopt a theocentric position (characteristic of pluralism). To get Christians to do so, Hick recognizes, involves a radical revision of Christological orthodoxy. He alleges that the traditional

---

48. See Wilfred Cantwell Smith, *Toward a World Theology* (Philadelphia: Westminster, 1981), part 3; and idem, "The Church in a Religiously Plural World," in *Christianity and Plurality,* 309–21.

49. See, for example, John Hick, "Whatever Path Men Choose Is Mine," in *Christianity and Other Religions: Selected Readings,* ed. John Hick and Brian Hebblethwaite (Philadelphia: Fortress, 1980), 171–90; idem, "The Non-Absoluteness of Christianity," in *The Myth of Christian Uniqueness: Toward a Pluralistic Theology of Religions,* ed. John Hick and Paul Knitter (Maryknoll, N.Y.: Orbis, 1987), 16–36; idem, "A Philosophy of Religious Pluralism," in *Christianity and Plurality,* 335–46; and idem, *God Has Many Names: Britain's New Religious Pluralism* (London: Macmillan, 1980).

understanding of the incarnation has never made any sense and probably never will. Rather than accepting that the *logos* and second person of the Holy Trinity (f)actually became incarnate in Jesus of Nazareth, Hick suggests that one view the incarnation as a mythological idea expressed in metaphor. This metaphorical myth expresses the Christian experience of living contact with the noumenal, transcendent being. Jesus Christ should not be regarded as a divine-human person who was one in substance with and equal to the Father.

Rejecting substance Christologies, Hick prefers degree Christologies, which see incarnation as an activity of divine spirit or grace that various persons in the history of religion have had in greater or lesser quantity. The obvious advantage of this understanding of the incarnation for Hick is that it need not rule out the possibility of other saving points of contact with God. Another point in its favor, he opines, is its recognition that missions and conversion are things of the past. The flip side of this assertion is the good news that a ground for dialogue exists among the religions of a shrinking, interdependent, and unstable planet.

Hick's position is fraught with difficulties, both methodological and theological, that will be briefly addressed in the last part of this essay. Suffice it to say at this point that while Hick's position may be convenient, any orthodox Christian would be obligated to judge it radically out of step with the dictates of Christian Scripture and tradition. But before turning to the theological implications of the history that has here been under review, one more matter needs to be addressed. That matter concerns the revolutionary shift of Christianity's global center. Long at home in the West, Christianity in the second half of the twentieth century began taking up impressive residence in Africa and Asia. While Christianity in the modern and postmodern West dealt with the challenges of its two-front war—atheism and pluralism—the Christian center shifted. While the West fiddled and Rome burned, new cities sprang up elsewhere. This is a lesson that the West and its academies have been reluctant to learn. We will not be able to indulge this *agnosis* for much longer. Christian missionaries are now being dispatched with increasing regularity to the West from Asia and Africa. It seems likely that Christianity in the West and Christianity in the Rest are headed for conflict, as the one, prone to defensiveness and concession, will be found wanting by the other, which is prone to offensiveness and unabashed orthodoxy.[50]

---

50. For a recent, popularly presented account of this revolution in the history of Christianity, see Philip Jenkins, "The Next Christianity," *The Atlantic Monthly,* October 2002, 53–68. See also Lamin Sanneh, *Translating the Message: The Missionary Impact on Culture* (Maryknoll, N.Y.: Orbis, 1989); and Andrew Walls, *The Missionary Movement in Christian History* (Maryknoll, N.Y.: Orbis, 1996).

THEOLOGICAL: OF ISMS

The foregoing historical sketch of Christian responses to religious plurality suggests a series of positions. One might construe the range of positions in any number of ways—in terms of how they estimate the divine, the human prospect, knowledge of God, or truth. If, however, one focuses on the question of salvation, as is the tendency in theology at present, one might logically construct a spectrum with six positions: nihilism, skepticism, exclusivism, inclusivism, pluralism, and universalism. The first position, nihilism, is not a theological position, as no orthodox Christian theologian to my knowledge (and, obviously, one cannot consider death-of-God theologians and atheologians to be orthodox in any meaningful sense) has ever alleged that life should be viewed with despair because no truth or hope—that is, salvation—can be found in life. The second position, skepticism, must also, it seems, be viewed as a nontheological position, for it represents a defeat of the very notion of revelation, alleging and indeed despairing that no final way can be determined by which to know or decide which religion might be true or said to offer salvation. The fifth position on the spectrum, pluralism, is indeed a theological position as it suggests that all revelations are on a more or less equal footing and that salvation is available in all religions in which it is sought. Pluralism, however, violates historic Christianity's litmus test for orthodoxy, that is, it denies the necessity of belief in the Trinity and it radically compromises its doctrine of Christ (see the Athanasian Creed), making it wholly unacceptable. The last position, universalism, is also a theological position that has been suggested—and not entirely implausibly—by some in the history of Christian theology (e.g., Origen and the doctrine of *apokatastasis*[51]). But significant biblical and theological evidence counts against it. Left to be analyzed, then, are the first two positions of the generally employed triad—that is, exclusivism and inclusivism.[52] But before doing so, a few theological cards must be laid on the table in order to provide a framework for thinking about religious plurality from a theological point of view.

---

51. See Origen, "De Principiis," in *The Ante-Nicene Fathers: Translations of the Writings of the Fathers down to a.d. 325,* trans. F. Crombie, ed. A. Roberts and J. Donaldson (Grand Rapids: Eerdmans, 1956), 4:260–62, 344–48.
52. For a brief discussion of these terms, see Plantinga, *Christianity and Plurality,* 5–6. For examples of theologians who employ the triad, see McGrath, *Christian Theology,* chap. 17; and Lesslie Newbigin, *The Gospel in a Pluralist Society* (Grand Rapids: Eerdmans, 1989), chap. 14.

A balanced Christian view of non-Christian religions, a view rooted in a full-orbed and robust trinitarian understanding of God, requires attention to the themes of universality and particularity in Christian Scripture, as well as recognition of continuity and discontinuity, similarity and dissimilarity, in the history of religion. Such a balanced view also requires a conception of divine disclosure that does justice to both general and special revelation. The Christian God who is agapic love—Father, Son, and Holy Spirit—has never left his triune self without a witness. Human beings outside Christianity therefore respond to something real (i.e., revelational) in creation, which makes sense of the various human quests for transcendence. In other words, instead of seeing the non-Christian religions of the world either as areas of complete darkness (either theologically à la Tertullian or Barth, or psychologically à la Marx or Freud) or as equally efficacious paths to the divine (philosophically à la Hick), one could see such as legitimate products of revelation with a proper— that is to say, divinely ordained—point of departure but in need of further divine light in order to come to their proper *telos*.

That said, the standard exclusivism, inclusivism, pluralism typology seems flawed for at least two reasons.[53] First, the focus tends to be too narrowly trained on salvation, generally construed in an ultimate, other-worldly sense. Does not Christian faith also concern the here and now? Should not the Christian doctrine of creation be a key source for thinking about the significance of Christian life in the world for which the Son of God died? And for that matter, does not salvation itself also concern the here and now? Second, more distinctions are needed in order to discuss the complex of theological matters involved in thinking about religions. In particular, the need exists to address issues related to revelation, knowledge of God, truth, salvation, and the study of religion. In which of these domains should one be exclusivist or inclusivist? What is exclusively Christian and what is not? Where can the theologian recognize inclusivism, that is, where can non-Christian traditions be said to have a part of what Christianity has in full?

On the matter of revelation (Greek *apokalypsis*), one should be inclusivist in recognition that some kind of divine disclosure—evidenced internally in the *sensus divinitatis* and externally in creation—is available universally (i.e., both inside and outside Christianity). That is, the idea of natural or general

---

53. On the ideological origins and history of the typology, see Perry, *Radical Difference*, 9–28.

revelation is surely warranted by Christian Scripture and tradition.[54] But over and above general revelation, humanity needs special revelation to know God personally and salvifically. In the Christian tradition, Calvin has analyzed this matter admirably.

On the closely related matter of knowledge (Greek *episteme*) of God, one should also be inclusivist, but in recognition of different levels of knowing. On the basis of general revelation, one might argue that non-Christians "know" or at least sense *that* God exists, perhaps as Creator, but do not know God tripersonally as creator, redeemer, and sanctifier—as Father, Son, and Holy Spirit. Such personal and saving knowledge comes only by way of the incarnate Word revealed in Scripture.

On the matter of truth (Greek *aletheia*), one should also be inclusivist, but in recognition of different levels of truth: non-Christians can surely reach many true conclusions about the world and its workings (e.g., on a correspondence or coherence theory of truth) but cannot finally recognize the truth of the mystery of human existence, vis-à-vis the divine, apart from special revelation, that is, as exemplarily disclosed in the incarnation, *the* Truth.

On the matter of salvation (Greek *soter, soteria*), an orthodox Christian would want to be rigorously exclusivist. And here one might properly emphasize and defend Christianity's offensive, evangelistic claim. First to be considered is exclusivism from a *formal* point of view, looking at the way human beings hold beliefs in an ordinary, everyday way. Unless I hold simultaneously *all* beliefs that exist, which would make me both exceedingly busy and not very coherent, I will of necessity *not* believe some things. Moreover, many beliefs that I take to be true I must of necessity hold in an exclusivistic fashion. If, for example, if I believe that Toyota Camrys are the best cars around, it follows that I do *not* believe that Honda Accords can claim such status. More to the point, if I believe that Jesus Christ is the only-begotten Son of God and the Savior of the world, it follows that I do *not* believe that God has been most centrally revealed in the Qur'an through the mediation of the prophet Muhammad. To be an exclusivist, therefore, is not something that is arrogant,

---

54. This is an argument that cannot be systematically made here in plenary fashion. See the following *loci classici* in Christian Scripture: Genesis 1–2; Psalm 19; Acts 14:8–20; 17:16–34; and Romans 1:18–25. See also the following theological positions articulated throughout the Christian tradition: Justin Martyr, "The First Apology," 242–89; Aquinas, *Summa Theologica,* part 1, ques. 2 (see esp. 1a.2.3); Calvin, *Institutes of the Christian Religion,* 20:35–69; Brunner, "Nature and Grace" in *Natural Theology,* 16–60; John Paul II, *Crossing the Threshold of Hope,* 77–83.

irrational, impolite, embarrassing, or something for which one must make apology; we human beings have very little choice in this matter.[55] Second to be considered is soteriological exclusivism from a *material* point of view. If the sovereign God and the dependent world are indeed ontologically distinct, as Scripture clearly teaches, there can be no power or thing in creation that can save creation. God alone, in Jesus Christ, is the Savior of the world. And although Christ is the sole *means* of salvation, this truth does not necessarily entail that the *scope* of salvation must be exceedingly narrow; Christians have grounds, in fact, for hoping that the scope of salvation may be lovingly and gracefully expansive.

Finally, on the matter of the study of other religions, one would want to proceed in an empathetic (Greek *en, pathos*) fashion, recognizing in the religions of the world both protological propriety and eschatological misdirectedness. In other words, a Christian might rightly take a phenomenological approach to the religions of the world. This approach was forged by Christian and theologically inclined historians of religion in the first half of the twentieth century. Much misunderstood and criticized, this approach is currently rather out of vogue with hard-line practitioners of religious studies, who prefer a quasi-scientific approach to explaining religious belief and behavior by drawing upon the thinking of a series of methodological atheists and agnostics. But despite its current lack of popularity, the hermeneutically sophisticated phenomenological approach can, with some tinkering, well be utilized by Christian theologians—in large part because it is more consistent with core Christian beliefs than other approaches on the market. In this connection, it bears mention that long neglected scholars such as Gerardus van der Leeuw (1890–1950), who forged and championed the phenomenological approach, have important things to teach theologians in our time.[56]

To sum up, rather than declaring oneself to be an exclusivist or an inclusivist in a straightforward manner, a Christian theologian committed to both or-

---

55. See Alvin Plantinga, "A Defense of Religious Exclusivism," in *Philosophy of Religion: An Anthology*, ed. Louis P. Pojman, 4th ed. (Belmont, Calif.: Wadsworth/Thomson, 2003), 507–21. See also Newbigin, *The Gospel in a Pluralist Society*, chaps. 13–14.
56. Unfortunately, few of van der Leeuw's writings are available in English translation. For an introduction to his work as a scholar of religion, see Richard J. Plantinga, "An Ambivalent Relationship to the Holy: Gerardus van der Leeuw on Religion," in *Religion in History: The Word, the Idea, the Reality*, ed. M. Despland and G. Vallée (Waterloo, Ont.: Wilfrid University Press, 1992), 93–100. An excerpted version of this essay is available in Carl Olson, ed., *Theory and Method in the Study of Religion: A Selection of Critical Readings* (Belmont, Calif.: Wadsworth/Thomson, 2003), 139–42.

thodoxy (i.e., fidelity to Scripture and tradition) and coherence (i.e., fidelity to reason and experience) ought to be a qualified apocalyptic inclusivist, a qualified epistemic inclusivist, a qualified alethetic inclusivist, a soteriological exclusivist, and an empathetic phenomenologist in the study of religion. With a strong emphasis on particularity, one must also give adequate attention to the dimension of universality in Christianity. The triune God was revealed particularly and decisively in Jesus Christ; but the triune God is the God— Creator, Redeemer, and Sanctifier—of the *whole world*. But so to say is hardly to utter a novelty, for this position is as old as the sixteenth and seventeenth verses of the third chapter of the Gospel of John—as wonderful a synecdoche as ever there has been.

5

Biblical Faith and
Traditional Folk Religion

TITE TIÉNOU

EVANGELICAL MISSIONARIES AND missiologists have for a very long time paid attention to world religions. Yet the evangelical missiological interest in world religions usually revolves around two questions: Are the heathen lost? What is the fate of those who have never heard the good news concerning Jesus Christ? As important as these questions are, they cannot address all the theological and missiological issues involved in Christian responses to world religions. John G. Stackhouse is correct when he states that such questions "cannot . . . be answered fully outside the context of a comprehensive theology of religions."[1] Such a theology of religions is much needed today.

A Christian theology of religions is the necessary framework for Christian living in general and for pastoral care, evangelism, and mission. Whether they acknowledge it or not, like it or not, Christians live their faith and express it in the general context of human religiosity. My interest in folk or traditional religions stems, in part, from my social/cultural and geographical origins. My roots are African and my personal primary identity is Christian. I confess, however, that I once thought that "ridicule based upon ignorance" was the best Christian approach to African religions. Since my parents were Christian by the time I was born, I do not have firsthand knowledge of any African

---

1. John G. Stackhouse Jr., ed., preface to *No Other Gods Before Me? Evangelicals and the Challenge of World Religions* (Grand Rapids: Baker, 2001), 11.

religion. My parents made sure that my siblings and I did not participate in any pagan practices and warned us of severe spiritual consequences should we let ourselves be enticed by unbelieving idol worshipers into their rituals. Isolationism from "African idolatry" best describes the attitude I learned in my Christian community. This was my attitude until 1971, when I began my journey in Christian ministry in the city of Bobo-Dioulasso in Burkina Faso. I soon realized that many issues parishioners brought to me were related to African religions. I was unable to help them most of the time because I lacked knowledge of their religious traditions. Ridicule based upon ignorance could not help me address the concerns of my parishioners. Much learning was ahead of me. Along the way I encountered Anselme Titianma Sanon (now archbishop of Bobo-Dioulasso), in person and in his writings. I learned much about Bobo religion from Sanon: he was fully initiated into its mysteries prior to his conversion to Catholicism. His use of Bobo religious vocabulary, symbolism, and ritual also encouraged me to inquire about engaging in a similar practice within evangelicalism. In my quest to understand and use the elements of folk religion, I have encountered good and bad things, and I am still on the journey. I know that there are and will be many dangers and pitfalls along the way, but I do not want to return to the bliss of isolationism and ridicule based on ignorance.

I introduced this essay in the way I did for two reasons: first, Christian faith and identity are foundational in my study of other religions generally, and of folk religions specifically; second, I am a learner and have no insider's secrets to share with you. These two reasons establish, too, the background for the approach that I take in what follows. I raise more questions than I provide answers. But do humans ever embark upon a journey knowing everything in advance?

LOCATING FOLK RELIGION ON THE RELIGIOUS MAP

In his book *The Christian Message in a Non-Christian World*, Hendrik Kraemer observed,

> The West is inventing magnified tribal religions to invigorate its crumbling systems of life and its anarchic social and political order. Nothing can demonstrate more clearly that *the Christian Church, religiously speaking, in the West as well as in the East is standing in a pagan, non-Christian*

world, and has again to consider the whole world its mission field, not in the rhetorical but in the literal sense of the word.[2]

Folk religion—in Kraemer's terminology "tribal religions" or "pagan, non-Christian world"—is, indeed, the religion of the majority of the world's population. Its vitality can be seen on all continents. Yet it is still easier to acknowledge the reality of folk religions than to locate them on the map of religious studies.

Take, for example, African religions (often perceived as folk religion *par excellence*). Do they belong to the category *world religions?* This volume is not the place for a detailed examination of this question, but it is sufficient to note Laurenti Magesa's opinion that "even though the study of African religion engages the interest of many scholars, its status as a world religion has not yet been comfortably accepted in some quarters of the academic and Christian religious world."[3] Why?

At the World Parliament of Religions held in Chicago, September 11–27, 1893, African religions were invisible. In the absence of a direct mention of the religions of Africa, one may point to a remark by Reverend J. R. Slaterry of St. Joseph's Seminary (Baltimore, Maryland). He made his comment in his address "The Catholic Church and the Negro Race" and he was speaking about his perception of black populations in the United States. Negroes, he said, "love the worship of God; in their childish way they desire to love God; they long for and relish the supernatural; they willingly listen to the word of God; their hearts burn for the better gifts."[4]

People like Reverend Slaterry could not imagine that about a century later the global perceptions of various religions would be significantly different. Today, African religious ways are no longer consistently described as "childish," and in countless publications and Web sites, Africans and non-Africans alike extol the virtues of African religions. Could it be, then, that African religions are sometimes reluctantly admitted into the "club" of world religions? If not, why is

2. Hendrik Kraemer, *The Christian Message in a Non-Christian World,* 3d ed. (1956; reprint, Grand Rapids: Kregel, 1977), 16–17. Italics in the original.
3. Laurenti Magesa, *African Religion: The Moral Traditions of the Abundant Life* (Maryknoll, N.Y.: Orbis, 1997), 18–19.
4. J. R. Slaterry, "The Catholic Church and the Negro Race," in *Neely's History of the Parliament of Religions and Religious Congresses at the World Columbian Exposition,* ed. Walter R. Houghton, 3d ed. (Chicago: F. T. Neely, 1893), 603. It should be noted that the black/African presence at the World Parliament was "provided" by Bishop Arnett of the African Methodist Episcopal Church in his greetings "In Behalf of Africa" (ibid., 70–71) and in his address "Christianity and the Negro" (ibid., 605–7), and by Prince Momolu Masaquoi of Africa in remarks on closing day (ibid., 854).

the adjective *traditional*—a word commonly associated with the long-accepted practices of "major" religions—used so often with African religions? On the other hand, why do we think that the religions of a whole diverse continent, such as Africa, can be studied as a single entity? It is obvious that African religions are still on the road to recognition. And this situation will continue as long as doubt persists as to the "greatness" of African religions. For granting African religions the status of world religions "should not be considered a concession . . . but rather a reversal of long-standing prejudice."[5]

African Religion(s): The Ambiguity of Presence

What Magesa calls "long-standing prejudice" may explain the unending debate about terminology and the tendency toward oversimplification in matters related to religion in Africa. In regard to the former, considerable time and energy has been devoted to the issue of appropriate terminology. For instance, are African religions a variety of primitive, primal, tribal, pagan, or heathen religions? Or should we simply attach to them labels such as *idolatry* and *fetishism*? Moreover, should the singular or plural be used, whether one speaks of African religion(s) or African *traditional* religion(s)? Again, this volume is not the place for an extended discussion of these issues. I mention them because of their relevance to our present concerns.

By the middle of the twentieth century an enormous number of publications on African religions were available in many European languages. These publications contributed to a greater understanding of the religions of Africa by the outside world. The multiple publications, academic as well as popular, did not, however, put an end to "using the contemptuous word *fetish* for [the Africans'] sacred objects, or *magic* for their sacraments, [. . . or calling] their beliefs *superstitions*, or their religious officials *witch-doctors*."[6] Some evangelicals (Africans and expatriates alike) seem, in fact, not to mind the use of "contemptuous words." Such is the case for Lenard Nyirongo who, writing in 1997, stated emphatically, "The heart of African traditional religions is nothing but idolatry."[7] Nyirongo's assessment of African religions is in substantial agreement with J. Herbert Kane's

---

5. Magesa, *African Religion*, 24.
6. Mary Douglas, *Other Beings: Post-Colonially Correct* (Chicago: CCGM Publications, 2002), 2–3.
7. Lenard Nyirongo, *The Gods of Africa or the God of the Bible? The Snares of African Traditional Religion in Biblical Perspective* (Potchesfstrom: Institute for Reformational Studies, 1997), 37.

evaluation, which is revealed in his opinion about the factors accounting for the growth of Christianity in Africa:

> The missionaries encountered no opposition from existing religious systems. No such opposition developed in Africa, for the simple reason that such systems did not exist. . . . Africa is the heartland of animism and the people there knew nothing else until the coming of Islam and Christianity. . . . Animism has no books and no temples; nor has it produced great leaders, thinkers, or scholars. Of course, it has its medicine men, its witch doctors, and its devil dancers. . . . People with a modern education find it difficult to continue to practice the superstitious rites connected with animism. Little wonder that modern Africans are deserting animism by the millions every year.[8]

If Kane and others are right, how should we make sense of the resurgence of African religions, even among the African elite, so much so that African religions are now propagating themselves in the Americas and elsewhere?[9] How do we explain African intellectuals' (intellectual according to Western standards) extolling the virtues of African religions in publications such as *African Religion: The Moral Traditions of Abundant Life?*[10] Why is it that Henri Maurier could conclude in 1988 that the gap between the rate of growth for African religions and for Christianity was growing wider?[11] Could it be that the visible and rapid expansion of Christianity has caused many to overlook African religions' incredible capacity for flexibility? Lamin Sanneh reminds us that "the quasi-quiescent traditional African communities and their laissez-faire practice of toleration and inclusiveness"[12] is one dimension of the context for

8. J. Herbert Kane, *Understanding Christian Missions,* 4th ed. (Grand Rapids: Baker, 1986), 220–21. The first edition was published in 1978. One can find similar statements in Eugene A. Nida and William A. Smalley, *Introducing Animism* (New York: Friendship, 1959), see chap. 5, pp. 50–58, particularly.

9. On the resurgence of African religions, Achille Mbembe's *Afriques indociles: Christianisme, pouvoir et Etat en société postcoloniale* (Paris: Karthala, 1988) is must reading!

10. This book (*African Religion* by Magesa) was written by a Tanzanian Catholic priest and theologian. One can also read a three-page document titled "Elements to Admire in African Traditional Religions" on the Web at www.afrikaworld.net/afrel/atr_admire.htm

11. Henri Maurier, "Chronique sur la Religion Africaine traditionnelle," *Bulletin Secretariatus pro non Christianis* 23, no. 3, 69 (1988): 237.

12. Lamin Sanneh, *The Crown and the Turban: Muslims and West African Pluralism* (Boulder: Westview Press, 1997), 1. I have expressed myself on this issue in "The Church in the Pluralistic African Experience," in *Practicing Truth: Confident Witness in Our Pluralistic World,* ed. D. W. Shenk and L. Stutzman (Scottdale, Pa.: Herald, 1999), 148–55.

missionizing by Islam and Christianity. Commenting on religion and change in Africa, Johannes Fabian noted,

> The European in Africa mistakenly assumed that the flexibility and plasticity of African traditional religion, its ability to incorporate new symbolic expressions without changing its basic premises, was indicative either of childlike simplicity or of cunning dishonesty. In evaluating the history of mission and the impact of Christianity in Africa, however, the impression is that the Christian message for the most part was smothered in the embrace of African religion.[13]

These characteristics of relativism and tolerance in African religions may better be understood by demonstrating their parallel in American neopaganism. Danny L. Jorgensen and Scott E. Russell list the following six elements of neopaganism in the United States: "religious individualism," "emphasis on experience and faith instead of belief and doctrine," pragmatism regarding "matters of authority and practice," syncretism and "toleration of religions and worldviews," "a holistic (or monistic) worldview," and an "open, flexible organizational framework."[14] For these present-day American neopagans, then, as for "archaic or aboriginal peoples (as imagined by scholars of religion) . . . the function [of religion is] to create and sustain the whole cosmos or collective."[15]

I encountered another reason for the enduring vitality of African religions in the summer of 1983. I was in Burkina Faso, doing research for my dissertation. I interviewed many people, but one comment made by a well-known and seasoned evangelical pastor was particularly eye-opening. I asked him, "Why do Bobo Christians revert back to their ancestral religious practices?" He replied, "As older Bobo Christians sense the end of their life approaching, they feel more and more distant from Christ and they feel closer to their ancestors. They return to the religions of their ancestors because they know the

---

13. Johannes Fabian, "Religion and Change," in *The African Experience,* vol. 1, *Essays,* ed. John N. Paden and Edward W. Soja (Evanston: Northwestern University Press, 1970), 384. See also Ali A. Mazrui, "A Trinity of Cultures in Nigerian Politics: The Religious Impact," *Africa Events* 2, no. 10 (October 1986): 12–17.
14. Danny L. Jorgensen and Scott E. Russell, "American Neopaganism: The Participants' Social Identities," *Journal for the Scientific Study of Religion* 38, no. 3 (September 1999): 335.
15. Kathleen M. Sands, "Tracking Religion: Religion Through the Lens of Critical and Cultural Studies," *Bulletin of the Council of Societies for the Study of Religion* 31, no. 3 (September 2002): 68.

ancestors through kinship bonds. They do not know Jesus that way." There is some truth to this pastor's observation. I know a few people who "left the Jesus Way" many years after their conversion, and yet they appeared to be unwavering in their Christian faith. *Do African religions—does folk religion—smother the Christian message?* This is, perhaps, the most important question for us as we formulate a Christian response to the religious expression of many of our contemporaries.

BETTER UNDERSTANDING: THE FOUNDATION OF A CHRISTIAN APPROACH TO FOLK RELIGION

There can be no credible Christian response to folk religions without better understanding of these religions on the part of Christians in general and Christian theologians and witnesses in particular. Consider this exchange between Brother Fowles and missionary Nathan Price in the novel *The Poisonwood Bible:*

BROTHER FOWLES: Do you know the hymn of the rain for the seed yams, Brother Price?

NATHAN PRICE: Hymns to their pagan gods and false idols? I'm afraid I haven't got the time for dabbling in that kind of thing.[16]

Since the setting of the fictitious exchange is Africa in general and the Congo in particular, it is legitimate to wonder how many real-life Christian Africans or expatriate "Nathan Prices" have set their minds never to examine African religions or other "childish folk expressions of religion"? I know some. One, after more than thirty years on the field, gave a missionary report to his home church constituency. He described the religion of the people he claimed to have evangelized as "their form of football"![17] Such a blatant misunderstanding of a people's religion shows that the missionary did not think that their religion was worth studying. Like Nathan Price, this missionary focused his efforts on preaching the truth. He did not worry whether this truth was understood or reinterpreted by the people to fit their own religious categories.

Some raise a legitimate concern about the possibility of compromise when

---

16. Barabara Kingsolver, *The Poisonwood Bible* (New York: Harper, 1998), 252.
17. I have the audiotape of this report given on January 4, 1987, in my possession. I do not think it is appropriate to mention the names of the missionary, the church, the people, or the country of service.

Christians devote time and energy to the study of non-Christian religions. As Christians we must, indeed, remain committed to the truth revealed by God in his Word. Let us always contend for the truth and let us proclaim it boldly, but let us also know the religious context in which we communicate the truth. A call for Christians to seek better understanding of African and other religions must not, in itself, be viewed as a disguised plan to advance the cause of idolatry or paganism.

Missionaries and other cross-cultural communicators know the value of bilingualism and cultural competency. In today's world, Christian theologians also need competencies in other religions, especially folk religion. Thus, they must not hastily brush aside indicators of the paganism that thrives even on home soil. (Consider the recent "Pagan Pride Day" celebration in Chicago.) They must therefore acquaint themselves and their students with books like Loretta Orion's *Never Again the Burning Times: Paganism Revived*[18] or Marc Augé's *Le génie du paganisme*.[19] Theologians cannot afford to ignore publications such as these, thinking that paganism must be addressed only by missiologists or specialists in practical theology. To think so is to miss a great opportunity for missionary evangelization.

Competency in other religions is a necessary requirement of bilingualism for Western theologians today. As Walter J. Hollenweger wrote, "Western theologians have to become bilingual if they want to be competent Western theologians and not merely the religious rationalizers of the Western tribes to which they belong."[20]

REAL BIBLICAL THEOCENTRISM: THE WAY FORWARD

It can be argued that anthropocentrism is at the heart of many aspects of folk religion. In *Understanding Folk Religion* Hiebert, Shaw, and I, in fact, argue that the notion of "corporate anthropocentrism" is an essential component of the worldview of folk religion.[21] We assert that because of corporate anthropocentrism folk religion focuses on these four areas: the meaning of

---

18. Loretta Orion, *Never Again the Burning Times: Paganism Revived* (Prospect Heights, Ill.: Waveland Press, 1995).
19. Marc Augé, *Le génie du paganisme* (Paris: Gallimard, 1982).
20. Walter J. Hollenweger, "The Theological Challenge of Indigenous Churches," in *Exploring New Religious Movements,* ed. A. F. Walls and Wilbert R. Shenk (Elkhart, Ind.: Mission Focus Publications, 1990), 167.
21. Paul G. Hiebert, R. Daniel Shaw, and Tite Tiénou, *Understanding Folk Religion* (Grand Rapids: Baker, 1999), 80.

life and the problem of death, well-being in this life and the problem of misfortune, knowledge about how to deal with the unknown, and the management of evil and injustice and the promotion of justice.

African religions, indeed, provide illustrations of anthropocentrism. For many Africans, life is essentially good; ideally people should have health, prosperity, fulfillment, honor, and progeny. These Africans know, of course, that the world is not an ideal place. They are quite familiar with the reality of evil. In their understanding, the presence of evil forces in the world frustrates people's destiny because evil forces cause misfortune. Preventing misfortune and maximizing good fortune is, therefore, a major focus of religious activities. In this context, what Hendrik Kraemer called *eudæmonism* makes sense. For Kraemer, eudæmonism is consistent with "relativism" and "naturalistic monism" and is defined as a system in which "religion and ethics . . . in principle are always the means to an end, namely, to the *summum bonum* which consists in absolute happiness through the *summum* realization of life."[22]

As has been illustrated, in the spectrum of Christian responses to African and other folk religions, at one end lies ridicule based upon ignorance. At the other, however, may be too much concession to the prevailing anthropocentric ethos of these religions. Two such attempts are power encounter and prayer.

For many, power encounter is an especially relevant way for a Christian to respond to African religions. And I understand its validity and usefulness. Humanly speaking, I owe much of my Christian faith to my father's courage. He literally and publicly ridiculed one of the most sacred symbols of Bobo religion: the mask. For the Bobo the mask incarnates a spirit and no one is to reveal the identity of a human who incarnates such a spirit. A person who unmasks the mask dies. Soon after his conversion to Christ, my father revealed the identity of a mask by removing its head covering. Here was the so-called spirit, a man known by all the villagers, standing before horrified women, men, and children. This incident took place before I was born, and I am here to testify that my father did not die that day. But did literal unmasking of the mask convince the whole village of the superiority of the Christian faith? No! In fact, there was no significant Christian population in the village until thirty or so years later.

That power encounter does not necessarily produce the results we expect is shown in the well-known encounter between Elijah and the prophets of Baal (1 Kings 18:16–19:18) and in certain aspects of the ministry of Jesus, our Lord

22. Kraemer, *The Christian Message in a Non-Christian World,* 156. Cf. the subtitle of Laurenti Magesa's *African Religion: The Moral Traditions of Abundant Life.*

(John 10:22–39). In Elijah's experience, neither Ahab nor Jezebel turns to the one true God. On the contrary, Jezebel threatens Elijah. Moreover, God's powerful prophet is afraid, discouraged, and runs for his life! And in the gospel of John, even the miracles performed by Jesus did not turn everyone into a believer in him. I am not saying that power encounter is unnecessary. But in pointing out the limits of power encounter as a tool for response to African religions, I do suggest that we expand our resources for dealing with these religions.

In regard to prayer, it tends to be the sole focus of religion and Christian faith for many people in Africa. Consider, for example, the African Initiated Church, the Church of the Lord Aladura. *Aladura* means prayer and the Aladura Church practice of prayer seems to be based on Yoruba religious views of "compulsive prayer," which guarantees that the petition will be granted.[23] Guaranteed efficacious prayer, in fact, is perceived as a major reason for the success of the church. The efficacy of prayer, however, seems to depend upon proper ritual and appropriate fervor. "Compulsive prayer," then, is not unlike pagan prayer as Jesus characterizes it in Matthew 6:7, and should warn us not to accept uncritically everything that passes for prayer. Should we really organize seminars on *The Prayer of Jabez* in Africa? Does this book not unwittingly, perhaps, reinforce "compulsive prayer"? Should we spend so much effort hosting groups of prayer walkers coming from distant lands? Instead of working for the success of *The Prayer of Jabez,* should we not focus on making known the God of Jabez.

To the question, *How should evangelicals deal with folk religions?* there are many possible responses. Yet the ultimate focus of all Christian responses to human religions must be the uprooting of anthropocentrism and the planting of real biblical theocentrism, contributing to spreading the knowledge of the true God, who revealed himself through his Son and in his Word.

---

23. D. O. Olayiwola, "The Aladura: Its Strategies for Mission and Conversion in Yorubaland, Nigeria," *Orita* 21 (June 1987): 41, 43.

6

Biblical Faith and Islam

J. DUDLEY WOODBERRY

IN THE FALL OF 2002 MY WIFE and I returned to Kabul, Afghanistan, for the first time since we had been expelled by the Taliban three years before. When we went to worship at the house used as a church, I was handed the Bible from which I preached when I pastored the congregation in the 1970s. A large-caliber bullet had ripped through its pages. Like Islam, which encountered biblical faith fourteen centuries ago, the bullet left the Torah with only minor damage but took the heart out of the New Testament.

Islam, as the only world religion to arise after the advent of Christianity, accepts parts of biblical faith, omits others, and rejects still others—although it is not always clear historically whether it rejected orthodox Christian doctrines or heretical ones. Therefore, Islam presents a special case in the development of an evangelical theology of religions. First, it requires discernment regarding what foundational texts it accepted or rejected, which is not altogether clear in the light of the variety of Jewish and Christian sects that existed in the vicinity of Arabia at the time of Muhammad. Second, it necessitates discerning what Muslims understand to be the similarities and differences today between Islam and Christianity, where again there is far from unanimity of views.

When moving from theology to missiology, a variety of contexts are noted in which various missionaries and various Muslim-background followers of Jesus differ on what they may retain, what they may adapt, and what they must reject of their previous beliefs and practices. Even scholars differ on the accuracy of the traditional Arab Muslim accounts of the origins of Islam.[1] Nevertheless, Islam was clearly a contextualization of Jewish, Christian, and pre-Islamic Arab monotheism mixed with indigenous elements for not only the Arabs of Muhammad's day (A.D. 570–632) but for the subsequent period in which occurred the compiling, editing, and canonization of materials on his life and recitations (three hundred years).[2]

1. For contemporary revisionists, see Michael Cook, *Muhammad* (New York: Oxford University Press, 1983); Patricia Crone and Michael Cook, *Hagarism* (Cambridge: Cambridge University Press, 1977); and Crone, *Meccan Trade and the Rise of Islam* (Princeton, N.J.: Princeton University Press, 1987). For interaction with these and traditional materials, see Neal Robinson, *Discovering the Qur'an: A Contemporary Approach to a Veiled Text* (London: SCM Press, 1996); and Andrew Rippin, *Muslims: Their Religious Beliefs and Practices*, 2d ed. (New York: Routledge, 2001).
2. See Tor Andrae, *Les Origenes de l'Islam et le Christianisme* (Paris: Adrien Maisonneuve, 1955); Richard Bell, *The Origin of Islam in Its Christian Environment* (London: Macmillan, 1926); H. A. R. Gibb, "Pre-Islamic Monotheism in Arabia," *Harvard Theological Review* (October 1962): 269–80; J. Henninger, "Pre-Islamic Bedouin Religions," *Studies in Islam*, ed. and trans. Merlin Swartz (New York: Oxford University Press, 1981), 3–22; W. Stewart McCullough, *A Short History of Syriac Christianity to the Rise of Islam* (Chico, Calif.: Scholars Press, 1982); Gordon Darnell Newby, *A History of the Jews of Arabia* (Columbia: University of South Carolina Press, 1988); Chaim Rabin, *Qur'an Studies* (Oxford: Oxford University Press, 1957), 112–130; Arne Rudvin, "The Gospel and Islam: What Sort of Dialogue Is Possible?" *al-Mushir* 21 (Theological Journal of the Christian Study Centre, Rawalpindi, Pakistan) (1979): 82–123; C. C. Torrey, *The Jewish Foundation of Islam* (New York: Jewish Institute of Religion Press, 1933); J. Spencer Trimingham, *Christianity Among the Arabs in the Pre-Islamic Times* (New York: Longman, 1979); Arthur Jeffery, *The Foreign Vocabulary of the Qur'an* (Baroda: Oriental Institute, 1938); Jacob Neusner, Tamara Sonn, and Jonathon E. Brockopp, *Judaism and Islam in Practice* (London: Routledge, 2000); and J. Neusner and T. Sonn, *Comparing Religions Through Law: Judaism and Islam* (London: Routledge, 1999).

This present essay was for the most part written in a section of Kabul without telephone or electric lines or libraries, so it will focus on my reflections on the living Islam that I observed around us.

Two 9/11's: Our Variety

September 11, 2001, tended to polarize Christian attitudes toward Islam. Some—among them Pat Robertson, Franklin Graham, and Jerry Falwell—stressed the militant, evil side. Others like George W. Bush stressed the peaceful, good side. The inadequacy of monolithic, polarized views was evident as my wife and I compared our experience of September 11, 2001, with that of September 11, 2002. On the former one we were in our son's home one block from the major Taliban recruiting center in Peshawar, Pakistan. When news came that a plane had crashed into a tower of the World Trade Center in New York, a one-by-two inch picture on our computer screen confirmed the report.

Exactly one year later we arrived at the same location. As the sun rose that day we were flying over Iran, which produced both the Khomeini revolution and some of the most beautiful Muslim poetry on Jesus and the love of God. After performing their ablutions in the tiny airplane lavatories, Muslims were praying in the aisles the same prayers of divine adoration that the plane hijackers had prayed a year before.

When we changed planes in Dubai on the Arabian Peninsula, which produced most of the hijackers, we visited the *majlis,* or sitting room, of Sheikh Saeed al-Maktoum where, over many tiny cups of rich coffee, guests experienced the hospitality rather than the hostility of Muslims. Then we visited the old Ahmadiya Madrasa, or Qur'an school, where students under the sticks of *muttawa* teachers learned Islamic values, largely biblical or talmudic, rather than just the teaching of hate and holy war, which saturated the madrasas around Peshawar that nurtured the Taliban.

Finally, on the last leg of the flight to Peshawar that day, the illiterate Pakistani laborer beside me chanted the same Qur'an for the protection of our lives that the hijackers had chanted to steel their nerves to take lives with a similar plane just one year earlier.

In that intervening year I have been able to observe Muslims on most continents. They are divided into groups that are common within faith communities. *Adaptionists* adapt their faith to modern ideas, and include liberals and even secularists who still consider themselves to be Muslims. *Conservatives* try to conserve the classical Islam developed in the first three hundred years of the faith community. During that period, the major schools of law and theology were established along with the canonical collections of the sayings and practices of Muhammad *(hadith)* and sufficient decisions had been based upon them for the formulation of the varieties of Islamic law *(shari 'a)*. *Fundamentalists* try to return to their idealized understanding of the pristine Islam of Muhammad, the Qur'an, and the early Muslim community. The fundamentalists, plus some conservatives, comprise the Islamists who may be peaceful like the rulers of Saudi Arabia, or militant, like many of the Saudis. Another group are the *Sufi mystics*, some of whom are integrated into the major orthoprax/orthodox branches of Islam, while others form separate communities called Tariqas. Finally, the *folk Muslims* blend aspects of formal Islam with indigenous religious expressions. Most groups are struggling for the soul of Islam—especially since 9/11.

Some, like the Jews of Jesus' day from whom they borrowed so heavily, are not far from the kingdom. Others are like their father the Devil. When observing Islamic beliefs and practices, then, it can be seen that many reflect biblical faith, just as the crescent moon—which has come to symbolize Islam—reflects the light of the sun. Yet at the center of that crescent is darkness and emptiness, which biblical faith strives to fill with "the light of the knowledge of the glory of God in the face of Jesus Christ" (2 Cor. 4:6 NIV).

"GOD IS GREATER": OUR GOD

The first words we hear each morning in Kabul from the minaret of the mosque across the street are *Allahu akbar* (God is greater), which is similar to the benedictions in the daily Jewish *Tefillah* prayers that Muhammad would have heard in Medina.[3] We then hear "There is no god but God"—a common witness of the Jews and Christians. There has been some recent debate among Christians as to whether *Allah* may be considered as the God of the Bible. One prominent evangelical, for example, was quoted by NBC Nightly News (November 16, 2001) as saying that Allah was not the God of the Judeo-Christian faith.[4]

When we look at the use, derivation, and meaning of *Allah,* we note that Arab Christians used it before the time of Muhammad,[5] and it is still used by

---

3. E. Mittwoch, *Zur Entstehungsgeschichte des islamischen Gebets und Kultus,* in *Abhandlungen der königlich preussischen Akademie der Wissenschaften* (Berlin, 1913). Philosophisch—historische Kl. no.2.
4. See http://www.msnbc.com/news/659057.
5. Enno Littmann, *Zeitschrift fur semitistic und verwante Gebiete* (1929), 7:127–204, cited in Philip K. Hitti, *History of the Arabs,* 6th ed. (London: Macmillan, 1956), 101.

them today. Like almost every religious technical term in the Qur'an, it was most likely borrowed from the Aramaic spoken by Jews or Christians who used *alah/alaha* for God. Jesus, who spoke Aramaic, probably used the word.[6] It seems to have been both a generic designation for God and a name for him. The Qur'an understands it to refer to the One Creator God of the Qur'an and the Bible: "Our God and your God are one" (29:46).

Pagan Arabs considered Allah to be the High God with a pantheon of lesser gods beneath, as did pagan Semites understand El and Elohim when the Spirit of God inspired the writers of the Hebrew Scriptures to use these terms for Yahweh in the school house of God's people. As the Hebrews were called to get rid of false gods, so Muhammad cleansed the Ka'ba (the Meccan god house) of all idols, but not, we are told, a picture of Jesus and Mary on its inner wall.[7]

After the rise of Islam, Jews, Christians, and Muslims used *Allah* for *elohim* and *theos* when they quoted or translated the Bible in Arabic as they did in their dialogues together. Arabic versions have tended to transliterate *Yahweh* or use the word *rabb* (Lord) as Jews used *adonai*. The Malay translations of 1912 and 1988, however, used *Allah* even for Yahweh. *Allah* has also been used in Bible translations in other languages where Islam is dominant—for example, Turkish, Hausa, Javanese, Madurese, and Sundanese.[8] The biblical writers, guided by God's Spirit, adopted words like *theos* (even though it had been used for false gods like Jupiter), but in their new biblical context they acquired new meanings. The same is true of *Allah*.

When I walk down the street by our house, I see an old man fingering through the beads of a rosary as he recites a list of ninety-nine names of God. These names and the additional ones in other lists of God's names are similar to biblical ones although in a more talmudic form. God is even called the *wudud* (the loving one), although in the Qur'an itself, he only loves those who love him, not the sinners (3:31–32), whereas in the Bible he loves us while we are still sinners (Rom. 5:8; 1 John 4:10). There is no rosary bead for "Father" since the Qur'anic understanding of divine unity rejects God begetting or being begotten (112:3). This absence or presence of the notion of God as Father, however, qualitatively affects other divine attributes that Muslims and Christians hold in common—

---

6. Imad Shehadeh, "Do Muslims and Christians Believe in the Same God?" *Biblioteca Sacra* 161 (Jan.–Mar. 2004) 14–26.

7. According to Ibn Ishaq, Muhammad's earliest biographer. See Alfred Guillaume, *The Life of Muhammad: A Translation of* [Ibn] *Ishaq's Sirat Rasul Allah* (London: Oxford University Press, 1955), 552 n. 3, 774.

8. Kenneth J. Thomas, "'Allah' dans la traduction de la Bible," *Le Sycomore,* no. 11 (Dallas: SIL, 2002), 22–24.

such as God's mercy—since, for the Muslim, mercy is that of a Lawgiver and Judge while for the Christian it is also that of a Father.

This notion of Father raises, too, the question of the Trinity. In the Qur'an's rejection of pagan Arab ideas of God having wives (72:3) and children (2:116; 6:100), it also rejects what was apparently a misconception, that Christians believe in three gods comprised of Allah, Mary, and Jesus (4:171–172; 5:116). Whether or not that rejection was of a heretical tritheism, Muslims consider it a rejection, too, of the Trinity. The concept of Trinity, then, is a major difference in Christian and Muslim understandings of God, as is Muslim rejection of him as the God and Father of our Lord Jesus Christ. Judaism also rejects these understandings of God, yet most Christians believe that they and Jews worship the same God. Although Islam, unlike the Judaism of the Old Testament, is not the divinely chosen instrument to lead to the coming of God in Christ, the Qur'an by *Allah* means the One Creator God whom Jews and Christians worship.

To the question, *Do Christians and Muslims worship the same God?* it must be answered both *yes* and *no*. Various scholars distinguish between God as subject, the One to whom we refer, and as predicate, what we say about him. Since there is only one Supreme Being and Muslims mean that One described in the Bible, this is the *yes*. Anything we say differently about him is the *no*.

Each Muslim day starts with the words *Allahu akbar*, but how is the greatness of God expressed? In the November 2002 riots in Kabul, the Afghan police chanted *"Allahu akbar"* as they marched quickly into action. In these days of terrorism the words are also shouted with clenched fists raised high as a sign of power. But does God demonstrate his greatness primarily by the clenched fist or the outstretched hand with the nail prints? This question leads to my next reflection.

TWO MINARETS: OUR MESSENGERS

As I wrote this essay, the muezzin from the minaret of the mosque across the street had been proclaiming that "Muhammad is the messenger of God." Abu Hamid al-Ghazali (d. 1111), the most celebrated Muslim theologian in history, on two occasions gave the confession in a form that both Muslims and Christians can accept by substituting the name of Jesus for Muhammad in the confession of faith.[9]

---

9. V. Chelhot, ed., *Al-Qustas al-Mustaqim,* 68, cited in V. Chelhot, "La Balance Juste," *Bulletin d'Etudes Orientales* 15 (1958): 62; Jamil Saliba and Kamal 'Ayyad, eds., *al-Munqidh min al-Dalal* [The Deliverer from Error], 3d ed. (Damascus: n.p., 1358/1939), 101; and W. Montgomery Watt, trans., *The Faith and Practice of al-Ghazali* (London: Allen and Unwin, 1953), 39.

Another minaret has stood in the middle of Afghanistan for over eight hundred years, the Minaret of Jam, built by the Ghorid Sultan Ghiyas ad-Din Muhammad (1157–1202). In an inscription upon this monument, the Sultan is called "King of kings." Yet by inscribing on it also the entire nineteenth chapter of the Qur'an, which is largely about Jesus, the Sultan unwittingly identified the real King of kings. Here are listed biblical characters we hold in common: Adam, Noah, Abraham, Isaac, Jacob, Ishmael, Moses, Aaron, Zechariah, John the Baptist, and Mary. Jesus is described in this chapter in ways and with words that are also used of him in the New Testament, even though the meaning is often different. He is virgin born (vv. 18–20; Luke 1:26–31), a sign (v. 21; Luke 2:34), the truth (v. 34; John 14:6), faultless (v. 19; Heb. 4:15), a servant (v. 30; Phil. 2:7), and a prophet (v. 30; Acts 7:37).

In this same chapter, however, the Book is given to him (v. 30) rather than it being the divine interpretation of him as the Word made flesh. And his sonship is denied (vv. 35, 88–92). Yet these passages are in a context wherein the Qur'an notes that "the sects among them [Christians] differ" (v. 37). It is evident that the Qur'an understands sonship as involving carnal relations between God and Mary (5:116), which, of course, Christians reject, too. The rendering of John 3:16 in KJV as "only begotten son" is, of course, better rendered by the Revised Standard Version as "only son," indicating uniqueness rather than physical birth. The Fourth Lateran Council in A.D. 1215 makes a parallel rejection: the divine nature "does not beget nor is begotten."[10]

The Qur'anic chapter 19 on the Minaret of Jam portrays Jesus as referring to his coming death and resurrection (v. 33) in words identical to those used by John the Baptist in referring to his coming death and resurrection (v. 15). There is no hint of the Muslim belief—based upon the apparent rejection of the crucifixion in the Qur'an 4:157—that Jesus was raised to heaven before he died and will come again and die and be raised. In fact, in the Qur'an 5:117, Jesus says to God, "I was a witness over them [the disciples] as long as I was among them, and when you caused me to 'die' you were their overseer." The word translated "you caused me to 'die,'" *tawaffaytani,* is elsewhere in the Qur'an always understood to mean death.

Consequently, major Muslim commentators of the Qur'an have allowed for a real death and resurrection of Jesus as a legitimate interpretation of the Qur'anic text—although few Muslims know this. These commentators include

---

10. Robert Caspar, *Trying to Answer Questions* (Rome: Pontificio Instituto di Studi Arabi e Islamici, 1989), 36n. See additional discussion in Timothy C. Tennent, *Christianity at the Religious Roundtable* (Grand Rapids: Baker, 2002), 184.

al-Tabari (d. 923), al-Razi (d. 1210), al-Qurtubi (d. 1272), al-Baydawi (d. 1286), and Sayyid Qutb (d. 1966).[11] For most Muslims historically, the crucifixion did not happen; theologically, it need not happen (God can forgive without it); morally, it should not happen (we all bear our own sins).[12]

These differences between Muslim and Christian theology are surely important, yet the major difference is that Islam, like the Minaret of Jam, has given the glory due to Christ to another. The Qur'an switches attention to Muhammad, and the Muslim community historically has elevated him still higher than his position in the Qur'an.

The Madrasa: Our Scriptures

Attached to the mosque across the street is a *madrasa,* or Qur'an school, where young boys go early in the morning to memorize the Qur'an in Arabic. Arabic is not their mother tongue. But, as Wilfred Cantwell Smith has noted, in Islamic thought the Word became book, so to take it into oneself by memorization is somewhat similar to the feeling High Church persons have when they take the Word became flesh into themselves in Holy Communion.[13] In Islamic thought, God dictated the Qur'an in Arabic through Gabriel to the Prophet Muhammad. The first recension is commonly believed to be a year or two after his death and the second about fifteen years later.

This high view of the Qur'an was certainly brought into question by scholars like Arthur Jeffery, whose book *Materials for the History of the Text of the Qur'an* in 1937 noted the variants in the ancient codices of the Qur'an from manuscripts and quotations in commentaries.[14] More recent revisionist theories have been offered by scholars such as John Wansborough, who considered the Qur'an to be "Salvation History" and the result of ideas from the ninth century read back into the seventh century.[15] But these studies were buried in academic books, which were not translated for the Muslim masses.

11. Joseph L. Cumming, "Did Jesus Die on the Cross? The History of Reflection on the End of His Earthly Life in Sunni Tafsir Literature," to be published in J. Dudley Woodberry, Osman Zümrüt and Mustafa Köylü, eds., *Muslim and Christian Reflections on Peace: Divine and Human Dimensions* (London: University Press of America, forthcoming).
12. Cf. Kenneth Cragg, *Jesus and the Muslim: An Exploration* (London: George Allen and Unwin, 1985) 178.
13. Wilfred Cantrell Smith, "Some Similarities and Differences Between Christianity and Islam," in *The World of Islam: Essays in Honour of Philip K. Hitti,* ed. James Kritzeck and R. Bayly Winder (London: Macmillan, 1959), 56–58.
14. Arthur Jeffery, *Materials for the History of the Text of the Qur'an* (Leiden: E. J. Brill, 1937).
15. John Wansborough, *Qur'anic Studies* (Oxford: Oxford University Press, 1977).

That changed in January 1999 when the *Atlantic Monthly* published an article on Qur'anic manuscripts that had been found in Yemen and were written in Medinan script, making them older than the Kufan texts, which was used for today's standard Egyptian edition of the Qur'an.[16] The Medinan text indicates a period of editing, as sections in a different handwriting are interspersed, apparently to correspond with the present order of the chapters and verses. Also, many small variants are seen between the Egyptian and Medinan texts, as well as places wherein the text says of God "He said" rather than the command "say" that is in today's text. The "He said" translation is harder to reconcile with a dictation view of revelation.[17] Since very little has been published about these Medinan texts, detailed results are yet awaited.

An author with the pseudonym Christoph Luxenberg has published a book *Die Syro-Aramaeische Lesart des Koran,* which suggests that parts of the Qur'an reflect parts of Syriac lectionaries, and the meaning changes if the vowel pointing of the latter is used.[18] Again, if this information were confined to scholarly books it might not raise Muslim concerns very much, but it was reported on the front page of the *New York Times.*[19] Currently these materials seen in mainstream publications are interpreted as a Western attack on Islam, but eventually Muslims will have to deal with them, although scholars are divided on the conclusions.

Most Muslims believe the text of the Bible has become corrupted. When my family and I first went to Kabul to pastor the church in 1971, two visitors from Pakistan were arrested for giving out four Gospels of Luke. In coming to the defense of these visitors, we, through a Muslim lawyer, argued that, although there are Qur'anic charges that the Jews changed some scripture orally (2:75, 146) and some even pretended that what they wrote was scripture (2:79), still the following holds true:

1.   The Qur'an bears witness to the Bible's accuracy (3:3; 10:94).
2.   Christians are told to make judgments based upon their Scriptures, implying their reliability (5:47).

---

16.   Toby Lester, "What Is the Koran?" *Atlantic Monthly,* January 1999, 43–56.
17.   E-mail from Jay Smith in London, June 27, 1999, concerning interview with Dr. Gerd Puin in Erlangen, Germany, and seeing photocopies of some of the Hijazi manuscripts. Additional information on http://www.domini/org/debate/home.htm.
18.   Christoph Luxenberg, *Die Syro-Aramaeische Lesart des Koran* (Berlin: Das Arabische Buch, 2000).
19.   Alexander Stille, "Scholars are Quietly Offering New Theories of the Koran," *New York Times,* March 2, 2002, Al, 19.

3. Muslims are required to believe the Bible (3:84).
4. The Scriptures are protected (5:48; 6:34).

All of the original religious charges were dropped.

It is obvious, though, that the Bible creates a problem for some Muslims. When my wife and I went to Afghanistan during Taliban rule, they searched for Persian Bibles and, although they found none, they sealed the guesthouse where we were staying. And as noted earlier, my old Bible was found in the church office in Kabul. A shell had been shot through it at close range.

"COME TO SALVATION": OUR SALVATION

The call to prayer from across the street includes the words, "Come or rise up, for salvation *(falāh)*." The word here translated as "salvation" gives more the sense of "happy result," so it is not as comprehensive as the Christian concept.

In the Qur'an, human nature is seen as good or neutral (30:30); in the Bible humans reflect both the image of God and its own fallenness (Gen. 1:27; Eph. 2:3). Therefore, Muslims see only the need for the law and forgiveness, and Qur'anic law is based on rabbinic law.[20] Thus, because human nature is not fallen, people can be changed by the habit of following the law, making the kingdom of God fully realizable here.

In the Bible, the law shows us how to please God without giving us the power to do it (Rom. 7:13–25). Thus there is the need for what Jesus calls the new birth (John 3:5) and Paul calls the spirit of life in Christ Jesus (Rom. 8:2–3). At times the Qur'an indicates that the problem is greater. In Sura 16:61, for example, it says, "If God were to punish people for their wrongdoing, he would not leave on earth a single creature." This is hard to reconcile with human nature being good. Also, even after resisting temptation, Joseph notes that "truly the soul inclines to evil" (12:53).

Shi'ites, like the Imam Khomeini, have developed the concept of evil as innate. At the inauguration of President Khamenei, the Imam said, "Man's calamity is his carnal desires, and this exists in everybody, and it is rooted in the nature of man."[21] But Shi'ism still expects the law to remedy the situation.

---

20. See, e.g., Robert Roberts, *The Social Laws of the Qoran* (London: Williams and Norgate, 1925).
21. Imam Khomeini, "Islamic Government Does Not Spend for Its Own Grandeur," *Kayhan International*, September 4, 1985, 3.

It is obvious, then, that there is still the need for the good news of newness of life offered by Christ Jesus.

THE MOSQUE: OUR WORSHIP

A mosque a few blocks from us was reportedly built with materials from the church building that was torn down by the government in Kabul in 1973. Thus, the mosque illustrates the historic course of Muslim worship; all of the worship forms used and all the technical religious terms in the Qur'an, except references to Muhammad and Mecca, were first used by Jews and/or Christians. I have elsewhere documented in detail this borrowing of forms and terms, so will omit the details here.[22]

Some of these forms may have accumulated unbiblical meanings, such as earning merit during their sojourn in Islam, something they probably were not without in their Jewish or Christian use. In the case of some Christians, they—having seen the common heritage of these words and forms—have felt more free to use them in translating the Bible and in the worship of God through Jesus Christ.

THE SHRINE: OUR FOLK EXPRESSIONS

Above Kabul University is the blue-domed Ziarat-i-Sakhi, which briefly housed what Afghans believe was the cloak of Muhammad. The Ziarati-Sakhi represents a mixture of formal Islam and pre-Islamic folk beliefs and practices, similar to those of the Christo-paganism in certain parts of Latin America. A comparison of formal and folk Islam might look as follows:

	FORMAL	FOLK
The focus:	truth, righteousness	power or blessing, existential crises
Names of God:	how they express his attributes	how they can be used for power

---

22. "Contextualization Among Muslims: Reusing Common Pillars," in *The Word Among Us,* ed. Dean S. Gilliland (Waco, Tex.: Word, 1989), 282–312, and with more complete documentation in the *International Journal of Frontier Missions* 13, no. 4 (October–December 1996): 171–86.

	FORMAL	FOLK
Place of prayer:	mosque	shrine
Written authority:	Qur'an, reports of the practice of Muhammad	Qur'an as a fetish, books of magic
Practitioners:	imam, ulama (scholars), males	pir, wali, people of power, can be females
Authority:	learning	power[23]

In the realm of folk Islam, with its fear of beings and forces, real or imagined, the relevance of a savior from fear is often felt more than a savior from sin. The challenge is how to show the relevance of the gospel to the felt needs of the folk Muslims without substituting a Christian magic for a Muslim magic.

THE TOMB OF AL-AFGHANI: OUR POLITICS

At Kabul University is the tomb of Jamal al-Din al-Afghani (1838–97), champion of Islamic reform and a Pan-Islamism that proposed uniting all Muslims around a Caliphate that combined religion with all of life, including politics. The model would be that of Muhammad and the early Muslim community.

In this regard a common comparison with Jesus is instructive. Both Muhammad and Jesus preached a message of "Repent for the kingdom is near." (Matt. 3:2 NIV) Both were rejected in their hometowns, but each made a different formative decision for their followers. Muhammad in 622 fled from Mecca to Medina to rule rather than suffer, while Jesus went to Jerusalem to suffer rather than rule in an earthly sense. The Arabian prophet chose an earthly kingdom that could be extended by force, but Jesus said, "My kingdom is not of this world. If it were, my servants would fight" (John 18:36a NIV).

---

23. For a description of folk Islam and its implications for Christian witness, see Bill Musk, *The Unseen Face of Islam* (London: Monarch, 2004).

The Prophet believed that law could bring in the kingdom of God, while for Jesus the law was not enough: a new birth, a transformation, was required. For Muhammad what we today call religion and politics overlapped, whereas Jesus defined a realm for Caesar and a realm for God, which indicated that his followers could live under godless rule or in Calvin's Geneva.

Very quickly a Muslim Empire grew, ruled by law, while for three hundred years Christians remained as a suffering minority. With the Holy Roman Empire and the Crusades, however, Christians soon forgot the lessons of their founder.

Muhammad's early message in Mecca was of repentance and peace while his later message involved military expansion. Conversely, the Old Testament message included elements of military expansions while the New Testament focused on repentance and peace. Both communities are wrestling with which elements of their history they should draw upon today.

"I BEAR WITNESS": OUR MISSION

In the call to prayer across the street from us, the confession of faith "There is no god but God" is always introduced with the words "I bear witness" *(ashhadu)*. In 2002 the U.S. State Department brought Muslim leaders from a number of countries to Fuller Theological Seminary. I was asked to speak to them on "Distinctives of Evangelism among Muslims."

After starting with major beliefs that we held in common, I referred to our common but competing claims. We are both missionary religions with a message for all people (Qur'an 25:1; 38:87; 3:20; John. 3:16). We both claim the final messenger (Qur'an 33:40; Heb. 1:1–2). Both groups of followers are to be witnesses (Qur'an 2:143; 22:78; 33:45; Matt. 28:19–20; Acts 1:8). Both have exclusive claims for their message (Qur'an 3:85; John 14:6; Acts 4:12), yet both enjoined all to bear witness in a kind manner (Qur'an 16:125; 29:46; 1 Peter 3:15).

I then went on to show that, as has been indicated earlier, our analysis of the human problem was different. The Qur'an considers human nature as good or neutral (30:30), while the Bible sees human nature as in the image of God but fallen. Therefore, the Muslim sees forgiveness and the law as sufficient, for the kingdom can come by the habit of following the law. Conversely, the Christian sees the law as insufficient (Rom. 3:20; 7:14–15, 18, 21–24). A transforming new life is necessary (John 3:3, 5; Acts 2:38; Rom. 8:2–3, 9–11). Finally, for the Muslim the crucifixion is unnecessary because God forgives whom he pleases (2:284), but for the Christian it is the means by which we are saved (Rom. 3:23–26; 1 John 2:1–2). As noted, although most Muslims do not know it, some of their major commentators on the Qurʾan have allowed for a real crucifixion and resurrection of Christ.

Since September 11, 2001, we have seen among Muslims both more opposition and more receptivity to the gospel. The opposition has been heightened by events in Afghanistan, Palestine/Israel, and Iraq. On the other hand, terrorism and the imposition of Islamic law in certain countries have led to disillusionment and consequent receptivity when there are friendly Christians present. Thus, increased openness to the gospel has occurred among Iranians after the Khomeini revolution, among Pakistanis after Zia al-Haq in a previous military coup tried to impose Islamic law, and among Afghans after the rise of the Taliban.

CONCLUSION

The present topic of "Biblical Faith and Islam" began by looking at the Bible from which I used to preach in Kabul. A large-caliber bullet had ripped through its pages. Like the Islam that encountered biblical faith fourteen centuries ago, that bullet left the Torah with only minor damage but took the heart out of the New Testament. As Christians, we are called "People of the Book," but a book having the heart taken out of it is what we have in common with Muslims. Our task, then, is to use what Christians and Muslims hold in common and painstakingly repair what is missing.[24]

---

24. Parts of this presentation in a different framework were also given at the annual meetings of the Evangelical Missiological Society in Orlando, Florida, October 5, 2002.

Scripture Index

GENESIS

1 . . . . . . 67–68, 85, 87, 88n. 29
1:1–2:4 70
1–2 . . . . 89, 135n
1:1 . . . . 82, 84
1:14–19 68
1:20–23 67
1:26 . . . . 89n. 30
1:26–27 83
1:27 157
1:27–28 . . . . 84n. 17, 86n. 20
1:28 . . . . 83, 86, 87–88
1:29 . . . . 85, 86n. 20
2 . . . . 85, 87
2:7 . . . . 84n. 17, 85, 86n. 20
9:1 . . . . 86, 87
9:1–7 . . . . 85–86n. 20
9:3 . . . . 85–86n. 20
9:6–7 87
9:7 86
10:5 86
10:20 86
10:31–32 86
31:19 . . . . 61n. 47
31:30–35 70
31:34–35 . . . . 61n. 47

EXODUS

1:16 . . . . 72n
3:14 95–96
9:16, 21 . . . . 51n. 18
13:12 . . . . 51n. 18, 57
15:11 . . . . 58n. 36

19 68
20 85
20:2 68
20:3 . . . . 55n. 30
20:3–6 62–63
20:11 . . . . 82, 84, 90
20:23 . . . . 63n. 61
24 68
29:39 51
32 43
32:1–6 . . . . 71n. 79
32:4, 8 . . . . 61n. 50
32:20 68
32:21–24 . . . . 71n. 68
32:28 68
34:6 . . . . 58n. 35
34:7 . . . . 60n. 44
34:11–17 . . . . 63n. 61
34:14 62
34:17 . . . . 61n. 50

LEVITICUS

1–5 46
19:4 . . . . 61n. 50, 62n. 52,
    63n. 61
26 . . . . 46, 55
26:1 . . . . 62n. 52, 63n. 61
26:30 . . . . 62n. 58

NUMBERS

21:8–9 69
21:29 65
33:4 57

33:15 . . . . 61n. 50
33:52 . . . . 61n. 49

DEUTERONOMY

. . . . 56n. 33
3:24 . . . . 58n. 35, 60n. 42
4 . . . . 66n. 72
4:5–8 75
4:7 78
4:8 78
4:14 56
4:15–18 . . . . 66, 68
4:15–24 . . . . 63n. 61
4:16 61
4:17–18 67–68
4:19 66
4:20 68
4:23 61
4:24 62
4:24–27 63
4:25 . . . . 61, 63
4:25–31 . . . . 63n. 61
4:28 . . . . 61, 62, 71, 78
4:31–40 71
4:32–34 60
4:32–40 . . . . 56, 68
4:35, 39 . . . . 57, 62, 66–67
5:6 68
5:7–10 62–63
5:9 62
6:4–5 62
6:5 . . . . 60n. 63
6:14–15 . . . . 63n. 61

6:15 .... 60n. 62
7:3–5 .... 63n. 61
7:9 57–58
7:9, 12 .... 60n. 43
7:9–10 58–59
7:13–14 50
7:21 59–60
7:25–26 64
8:8 51
8:19–20 64
9:12, 16 .... 61n. 50
10 .... 66n. 72
10:14–18 59
10:17 .... 56, 60n. 45
11:16–18 63
13 .... 63n. 61, 64, 69
13:5 63
13:15 .... 62n. 60, 64n. 66
14:26 51
16:21–22 .... 63n. 61
17:4 .... 62n. 60
18:9–14 48–49
18:17–18 .... 61n. 50
27:15 .... 61n. 50
28 .... 46, 55, 63–64
29:16 .... 62n. 59, 64n. 67
29:19 .... 62n. 58
32 89
32:8 86
32:8–9 .... 66n. 73
32:12, 21 .... 58n. 35
32:16 .... 62n. 60
32:23–25 53–54
32:39 96
33:26–29 52

JOSHUA
14:1 .... 67n. 73
18:2 .... 67n. 73
22:8 .... 67n. 73

JUDGES
2:11 .... 63n. 64
2:17 .... 64n. 65
3:7, 12 .... 63n. 64
4:1 .... 63n. 64
5:20–22 .... 54n. 28
6:1 .... 63n. 64
6:25–27 69
6:25–32 70
8:27, 33 .... 64n. 65
9:23 .... 56n. 32
10:6 .... 63n. 64
11:24 65
13:1 .... 63n. 64
16:23 51

17–18 .... 71n. 79
17:3–4 .... 61n. 50
17:5 .... 61n. 47
18:14, 17–18, 20 .... 61n. 47
19–21 49

1 SAMUEL
5:1–5 .... 71n. 78
8:1–12 51
8:5, 19–20 49
15:23 .... 61n. 47, 62n. 53
16:14 .... 56n. 32
19 .... 49n. 12
19:13, 16 .... 61n. 47
26:19 65
28:3–25 49
28:4, 18, 51 .... 51n. 18
28:6 49
28:13–18 49
31:1–13 .... 49n. 12
31:9 .... 61n. 51

2 SAMUEL
5:21 .... 61n. 51

1 KINGS
7:29–36 48
12:25–13:6 .... 71n
14:9 .... 61n. 50
15:12 .... 62n. 58
16:13, 26 .... 62n. 55
18 70
18:16–19:18 146
18:27 .... 70, 71n
18:40 69
21:26 .... 62n. 58

2 KINGS
5:15–19 .... 71n. 79
10:18–28 69
17:5 .... 62n. 55
17:12 .... 62n. 58
17:16 .... 61n. 50
18:1–5 69
19:18 .... 61n. 48
21:11, 21 .... 62n. 58
23:1–25 69
23:4 69
23:6 69
23:12 69
23:14 69
23:24 .... 61n. 47, 62n. 59

1 CHRONICLES
10:9 .... 61n. 51
16:26 .... 62n. 52, 66n. 72

28:11–19 46

2 CHRONICLES
15:8 .... 62n. 59
28:2 .... 61n. 50
31:1 69
32:19 .... 61n. 48
33:7 61
34:3–4 .... 61n. 50
34:25 .... 61n. 48
34:33 69

EZRA
7:12 .... 57n

NEHEMIAH
9:18 .... 61n. 50
9:32 .... 60n. 43

JOB
.... 53n. 26
5:7 .... 54n. 27
18:13–14 .... 55n. 29
28:22 .... 55n. 29
31:24–28 .... 66, 74
38:17 .... 55n. 29
41:17 .... 58n. 37
42:11 .... 56n. 32

PSALMS
2:7 93
4:2 62
4:3 .... 62n. 56
6:5 .... 55n. 29
8 .... 60n. 46
9:13 .... 55n. 31
9:14 .... 55n. 29
19 .... 135n
24:4 .... 62n. 54
29 52–53
29:1 .... 58n. 37
31:7 .... 62n. 55
33:4–18 89–90
40:5 .... 62n. 56
44:20 .... 58n. 35
49:15 .... 55n. 29
72:1 96
74:12–17 89–90
76:4 .... 54n. 27
77:13 .... 58n. 35
78:48 .... 54n. 27
81:9 .... 58n. 35
82:1 .... 58n. .37
89:7 .... 58n. 37
91:5–6 54
96:5 .... 62n. 52, 66n. 72

97:7 . . . . 62n. 52
104 52–53
104:1–4 53
104:10–17 53
104:18–30 53
106:19 . . . . 61n. 50
106:36, 38 . . . . 61n. 51
107:18 . . . . 55n. 29, 31
115:1–8 74
115:4 . . . . 61n. 48
135:15 . . . . 61n. 48
135:15–17 78
135:15–18 74
136:1–2 56–57
136:3 . . . . 57n
139:24 62
141:7 . . . . 55n. 29
148:3–10 89–90

PROVERBS
1:12 . . . . 55n. 29
7:27 . . . . 55n. 29
27:20 . . . . 55n. 29
30:15–16 . . . . 55n. 29

SONG OF SONGS
5:2 104
8:6 . . . . 54n. 27, 55n. 29

ISAIAH
1:13 . . . . 62n. 53
2:8 . . . . 61n. 48, 61n. 51
    62n. 52
2:18, 20 . . . . 62n. 52
5:14 . . . . 55n. 29
9:6 . . . . 60n. 42
10:10–11 . . . . 62n. 52
10:11 . . . . 61n. 51
11:4 93
19:1, 3 . . . . 62n. 52
19:18 50
28:15, 18 . . . . 55n. 29
30:7 62
30:22 . . . . 61n. 50
31:3 . . . . 58n. 35
31:7 . . . . 62n. 52
37:19 . . . . 61n. 48
38:10 . . . . 55n. 31
40:18–20 . . . . 64n. 68
40:19–20 71
41–48 98
41:4 . . . . 95, 96n, 98n
41:5–14 71
41:6–7 . . . . 64n. 68
41:29 . . . . 61n. 50, 62n. 53
42 . . . . 84, 85, 89

42:5 . . . . 82, 84–86
42:6–7 85
42:6–8 74
42:16 85
42:17 . . . . 61n. 50
43:10 . . . . 58n. 35, 95, 98n
44:6 . . . . 95, 96n, 98
44:6–20 . . . . . 66n. 72, 71, 73–74
44:9–20 . . . . 64n. 68
44:10, 15, 17 . . . . 58n. 35
45:20 . . . . 58n. 35
46:1 . . . . 65n
46:1–2 . . . . 64n. 68
46:6 . . . . 58n. 35
46:21 . . . . 61n. 51
48:2 . . . . 58n. 35
48:5 . . . . 61n. 50, 62
48:12 . . . . 95, 98n. 55
49 85
49:2 93
49:4 62
49:6 85
49:6–7 75
66:3 . . . . 62n. 53

JEREMIAH
1:16 . . . . 61n. 48
2:5 . . . . 62n. 55
2:9–13 . . . . 66n. 72, 78
2:11 65–66
4:1 . . . . 62n. 59
5:7 . . . . 66n. 72
7:30 . . . . 62n. 59
8:19 . . . . 62n. 55
10:1–6 71
10:1–10 . . . . 64n
10:3, 9 . . . . 61n. 48
10:8, 15 . . . . 62n. 55
10:14 . . . . 61n. 50, 62n. 57
12:14–17 66
13:27 . . . . 62n. 59
14:22 . . . . 62n. 55
16:18 . . . . 62n. 59
16:19 . . . . 62n. 57
16:20 . . . . 66n. 72
18:15 . . . . 62n. 54
25:6–7 . . . . 61n. 48
32:34 . . . . 62n. 59
44:8 . . . . 61n. 48
48:7 . . . . 65n
48:46 65
49:1 65
49:3 . . . . 65n
50:2 . . . . 61n. 51, 65n
50:35–40 66
50:38 62

51:17 . . . . 61n. 50, 62n. 57
51:18 . . . . 62n. 55

EZEKIEL
1:1–3:15 49–50
2:9–10 104
5:11 . . . . 62n. 59
5:16–17 . . . . 54, 55
7:20 . . . . 61n. 49, 62n. 59
8:3 61
8:5 61
8:10 . . . . 61, 64n
8:12 61
11:18, 21 . . . . 62n. 59
20:7–8, 30 . . . . 62n. 59
21:21 . . . . 48, 61n. 47
26:7 . . . . 57n
37:23 . . . . 62n. 59

DANIEL
1:12, 14 104
2:28–29 102–3
2:29, 45 . . . . 103n. 68
2:37 . . . . 57n
2:45 . . . . 100n
2:45–47 102
2:47 . . . . 56, 57
3 . . . . 93n. 44, 94n. 44
3:26, 49, 93 . . . . 93n. 44
4:37 104
7:9–13 95
7:13 . . . . 89, 93
10 . . . . 93n. 44, 95
10:6 . . . . 92, 93, 94–95
10:16 . . . . 93, 94–95
11:8 . . . . 61n. 50
11:30–38 95
11:36 . . . . 56, 57, 58n. 36
11:45 95

HOSEA
3:4 . . . . 61n. 47
4:15 . . . . 62n. 53
8:4 . . . . 61n. 51
8:4–6 71
8:6 . . . . 66n. 72
10:8 . . . . 62n. 53
12:12 . . . . 62n. 53
13:2 . . . . 61n. 50
13:2–3 71
13:14 55
14:4 . . . . 61n. 48
14:9 . . . . 61n. 51

JOEL
3:1 . . . . 103n. 68

AMOS
.... 87n. 23
2:4 .... 62n. 56
5:26 .... 61n. 49
9:11–12 86

JONAH
2:9 .... 62n. 55

MICAH
1:7 .... 61n. 51
5:12 .... 61n. 48
5:12–13 71

NAHUM
1:14 .... 61n. 50

HABAKKUK
2:5 .... 55n. 29
2:14 89
2:18 .... 61n. 50, 62n. 52
2:18–19 71
3:5 54

ZEPHANIAH
2:10–11 71

ZECHARIAH
10:2 .... 61n. 47, 62n. 53
12:10ff 93
13:2 .... 61n. 51

MALACHI
1:9 .... 47n. 6
2:11 .... 58n. 35

MATTHEW
6:7 147
28:19–20 160

LUKE
1:26–31 154
2:32 85
2:34 154

JOHN
2:1–25 .... 100n
3:3 160
3:5 .... 157, 160
3:16 160
10:22–39 147
14:6 .... 154, 160
18:36 159

ACTS
1:8 160

2:17 .... 103n. 68
2:38 160
4:12 160
7:37 154
7:48 82
13:47 85
14:6–23 90
14:8–20 .... 135n
14:11–18 79
14:15–17 .... 89n. 33
15:16 .... 87n. 23
15:16–17 86–87
17 .... 88n. 19
17:16–34 ...... 79, 80–90, 135n
17:18 82–83
17:24 .... 82n. 13, 84, 90
17:24–25 .... 81–82, 84–86
17:24–30 85
17:25 .... 85–86n. 20, 87
17:26–27 .... 83, 86, 87
17:26–31 83
17:27 88
17:28 .... 82, 87n. 25
17:29 82
17:31 89
26:18 85

ROMANS
1:18–25 .... 135n
1:18–2:10 .... 89n. 33
1:21ff 67n. 74
3:20 160
3:23–26 161
5:8 152
7:13–25 157
7:14–15, 18, 21–24 160
8:2–3 .... 157, 160
8:9–11 160
11:36 .... 96n. 49

1 CORINTHIANS
12:2 .... 59n. 41
15:33 79

2 CORINTHIANS
4:6 151

EPHESIANS
2:3 157
4:11 .... 59n. 41

PHILIPPIANS
2:7 154

1 TIMOTHY
6:15 .... 57n

TITUS
1:12 79

HEBREWS
1:1–2 160
4:14 .... 59n. 41
4:15 154

1 PETER
3:15 160

1 JOHN
2:1–2 161
4:10 152

REVELATION
.... 91–92, 99
1:1 .... 93, 102
1:4 .... 95–97, 100
1:5 94
1:6 95
1:7 93
1:8 .... 97–99, 100
1:9 95
1:12–19 .... 100n
1:13–15 .... 93, 94–95
1:15 92
1:16 93
1:17 97–99
1:18 .... 55n. 31
1:19 ... 93, 99–104, 103n. 68
1:20 93
2–3 93
2:1 93
2:10 104
2:18 92–94
3:20 104
4–5 104
4:1 .... 103n. 68
4:8 100
11:17–18 .... 96, 100
16:5–7 96
17:14 .... 57n, 104
19:16 .... 57n, 104
21:6 97–99
22:13 97–99

Subject Index

Aaron 154
Abraham 87, 154
Abraham, William 39
absolute dependence, feeling of 124
Adam 83–84, 154
Adamic commission 85–86, 87, 88, 89, 90
adaptionists, Islamic 150
Advaita Vedanta 23, 40
Afghani, Jamal al-Din al- 159
Afghanistan 148–50, 153, 154, 157, 161
African Initiated Church 147
African religion 12, 132, 138–39, 140, 141–44
African Religion: The Moral Traditions of Abundant Life (Magesa) 142
aggiornamento (modernization) 129
agnosticism 21, 36, 136
Ahab 147
Ahmadiya Madrasa 150. See also *madrasa*.
Ain Dara temple 48
Aion 97
Akiba 96
Akkadian 76n. 83
aleph and *tau*. See Alpha and Omega.
"all paths lead to God" 131–32, 134
Allah 152, 153
all-inclusiveness formulas 95–104
Alpha and Omega 97–99
Alston, William P. 25, 31–32, 34, 35
ambiguity 27, 29–30, 35, 37–38
Ammonites 48, 65
Amos 55n, 87
ancestors, veneration of 143–44
Ancient of Days 94

Ani 97n. 53
animism 142
anthropocentrism, corporate 145–46, 147
Apocryphon 100
apokatastasis 133
Apollo Tyrimnaeus 92–93, 94
apologetics 23, 30, 105
    early church 108
    inclusive 115
Apostolic Constitutions 89n. 33
Arab Christians 151
Arabian Peninsula 150
Aratus 82, 88, 89, 90
Areopogus address 79, 80–92
Arguments for the Existence of God (Hick) 30
Arnold, Clinton E. 79
arrows, divination with 48
Asherah 58, 69
Ashurbanipal 75–78
Asia Minor, religions of 93n. 41
Asian Christianity 132
Assyria 12
Athanasian Creed 112, 133
atheism 21, 22, 23, 30, 116, 119, 125, 132, 136
Athena 96–97
Athens Acropolis 81–82
atheologians 133
Atlantic Monthly 156
attributes of God 60n. 45, 88–89, 98, 100, 152–53, 158
Aufhebung 126
Augé, Marc 145
Augustine 110–12

Aune, David 97–98, 104
authority
    basis for 22, 23, 122
    in Islam 159
    nature of 118
    neopagan 143
    Scripture's 118, 132

Baal 50, 51, 58, 69, 70, 146–47
Babel, Tower of 86, 87, 90
Babylon 12, 57, 69
Baha'ism 12
Balch, D. L. 83–84n. 16
Barnabas 90
Barr, James 44n. 4
Barrett, David 21n
Barth, Karl 126–27, 128, 134
"basic belief" 33–34
Bauckham, R. 87n. 23
Baydawi, al- 154–55
Beale 104
being
    contingent 41
    necessary 41
Bel 65n
Belet-ili 72n
belief
    components of 113–14
    formation 32
    neopagan 143
    problem of 22
    shared 45
    warrant for 34n. 27
Benjamites 49
Berger, Peter 22
Bible
    Muslim view of 156–57
    purpose of 44n. 4
    truth claim of 22
biblical faith 13
bilingualism 145
Bobo religion 139, 143, 146
Bodin, Jean 119
Boniface VIII 112, 114
Bristol, University of 40
Bronner, Leah 71n. 79
bronze serpent 69
Brunner, Emil 127, 128
Buddhism 11, 12, 30, 34, 40, 22, 34
    truth in 22–23
    incoherence of 40
"Bull El" 58
"burnished bronze" 92, 93, 94
Bush, George W. 150

Calvin, John 116, 117–18n. 19, 135

Canaan 12, 67n. 73
    mythology 50–53, 58, 60, 71
    people of 63–64
"Catholic Church and the Negro Race, The"
    (Slaterry) 140
causation 41
cereal offering 47
certainty, foundation for 119–20
chariot 49–50
Chemosh 65
cherubim 49–50
Christendom 107, 108, 113–15, 118
Christian Message in a Non-Christian World, The
    (Kraemer) 127, 139–40
Christianity 115, 134, 142–43, 152
    Arabic 149
    culture and 110, 115, 124n. 34
    epistemology of 30
    faith of 21, 134
    monotheism of 130
    uniqueness of 125
    validity of 125
Christology 112, 132
Church
    as revelation 125
    salvation in 114–15
    state and 115
    in world 91, 110
Church Dogmatics (Barth) 126
Church of the Lord Aladura. See African
    Initiated Church.
Cleanthes 88
Clement of Alexandria 108
"Cloudrider" 52
cogito ergo sum 120
cognitive function 34
coins 93
Colloquium Heptaplomeres de Rerum Sublimium
    Arcanis Abditis (Bodin) 119
colonialism 129
commission
    Adamic 88
    human 85–88
    Israel's 85
Common Notions 121
commonality of religions 109, 114, 130
"compulsive prayer" 147
Confucianism 11, 12
conservatives, Muslim 151
Constantinople 115
contingent existence 40–41
continuity 108, 109, 127–28, 134
conversion 116, 128, 132
cosmological argument 26
cosmos 59, 60n
    God in 123n. 32

nature of 119
covenantal relationship 46, 60, 62, 63–64, 66–67n. 73, 68
craft-deities 73
Craigie, Peter C. 53
creation 60n. 46, 67–68, 70, 82, 83–84, 85–86, 88, 89–90, 112, 117, 134
of human beings 117
mythologies 83–84n. 16
preservation of 89–90
shared belief in 46
Creator 117, 135, 137, 153
"Creator of Creatures" 58
Creed of the Council of Trent, The 118
creeds 110, 122
crisis of liberalism 126
Critique of Pure Reason (Kant) 122–23
Crossing the Threshold of Hope (John Paul II) 130
Crusades 160,113
Cyprian 112

Dagon 51
Daniel 57, 92–95, 102–3
dating issues 56n. 33, 66n. 72
David 47
De Pace Fidei (Nicholas of Cusa) 115
De Veritate (Herbert) 121
death 45, 46, 54, 59n. 41, 145–46
death of God theology 125, 129, 133
deductive reasoning 26
Deir ʿAllā texts 51
deism 121, 123n. 32, 124
depravity 117–18n. 19
Descartes, René 120–21
design plan 34n. 27
dharmata 41
dialectic faith 110
dialogue, interfaith 39, 105, 115
Dibelius, Martin 81
Dick, Michael 71–72
discontinuity, Christian-pagan, 108, 109–10,127–28, 134
diversity, religious 23, 27, 28–36
divination 48–49, 72
divinity of Christ 132
Domitian 93, 94, 104
doubt, methodological 120
doxastic practices 31–32
Driver, S. R. 67n. 74
Dubai 150

earth 45, 46, 59
Eastern religions 127, 129, 130. *See also* Buddhism; Hinduism.
Eck, Diana 23
Ecumenical Institute 129

ecumenism 129
Edinburgh Missionary Conference of 1910 127
Egypt 12, 53, 60, 64, 68, 71
Eighteen Benedictions 89n. 33
El 57–60, 152
El Gibbor 60n. 42
Eleusis 97
Elijah 69, 70, 71n. 79, 146–47
Elisha 69, 71n. 79
ʾĕlōhîm 61, 70, 152
Elyon 66n. 73
Emar texts 51
Emerson, Ralph Waldo 106
empathy toward religions 136
emperor worship 93n. 41
emptiness 34, 39
Enlightenment 119–24
enlightenment, mystical 22–23, 34
Epimenides 82, 87, 88
Epistemology
challenges of 23
framework of 27, 28
Reformed 26–27, 32, 33
of religious experience 39
of truth 22–23, 119–32
Epistula Apostolorum 89n. 33
eudæmonism 146
Europe 119, 121
evangelical 12–13
evangelism 9, 23, 91, 128n. 43
evidence, apologetic 32–33. *See also* evidentialism.
evidentialism 26–27
evil
problem of 129, 145–46
spirits 56n
exclusivism 79, 107, 110, 114–15, 130, 133, 134–35
Exodus 57, 60, 64, 68
experience 36
as epistemology 30
of God 32
neopagan 143
rational 36
"experiencing-as" 29
exploited pagan religion 48–60
external general revelation 117
extra ecclesiam nulla salus est 129–30
Ezekiel, 48, 49–50, 53, 64n. 69

Fabian, Johannes 142–43
fact and value 123
faith 44, 116
implicit 129
neopagan 143
rational 110, 111,115

Faith and Knowledge (Hick) 29, 31, 36
Fall 89, 157
fallenness 160
Falwell, Jerry 150
fascism, Christianity and 129
Father, God as 58, 135, 152
"Father of Humanity" 58
"Father of Years" 58
fear as faith 44, 116
fellowship offering 47
fertility divinity 50–51, 53
fetishism 141
final revelation 124–25n. 34
"first and last." See Alpha and Omega.
First Clement 89n. 33
First International Missionary Conference. *See*
    Edinburgh Missionary Conference of
    1910.
"flame of fire" 94n. 44
folk religion 13, 138–47, 151, 158–59
Freud, Sigmund 134
Fudge, Edward 81, 85
Fuller Theological Seminary 160
fundamentalism, Muslim 151

Gabriel 155
general revelation 86, 88, 113, 116, 124, 127, 128,
    134–35
    external 117
    internal 117
"General Revelation and the Religions of the
    World" (Wach) 124n. 34
génie du paganisme, Le (Auge) 145
Gentiles, Israel and 85
German theology 123–30
Ghazali, Abu Hamid al- 153
Gibeah 49
Gideon 69, 70
global center, Christian 132
globalization 23, 129
Gnosticism, 100, 110
God
    attributes of 58–60, 78, 82–83, 88–89, 95–96,
        98, 100, 152–53, 158
    belief in 33–34
    -consciousness 124
    death of 125, 129
    "divine being" of 57–58
    of gods 56–57
    immanence of 87
    knowledge of 116–17, 117–18n. 19, 121, 135
    names of 151–52, 158
    nature of 134
    offspring of 87–89
    perceptions of 31
    shared views of 45–47

sovereignty of 59n. 41
transcendence of 112, 132
"watchmaker" 121
wholly other 126
will of 117
gods of Egypt 57
golden calf 68, 69
Goodenough, E. R. 81
gospel, necessity of 138
Gowan, Donald E. 55n. 30
grace 116, 127
Graham, Franklin 150
Greco-Romans 108
Greece 12
Griffiths, Paul 38

Habakkuk 71
Hadad 50
Hadith 151
Haq, Zia al- 161
Hasel, Gerhard 70
heaven 45, 46, 59
heaven of heavens 56, 59n. 41
heavenly bodies 59n. 41, 67–68, 74
heavens 117
    seven 59n. 41
    three 59n. 41
Hellenism 79–82, 91, 92, 97–99, 104
Hemer, Colin 82n. 13, 92, 94, 104
henotheism 44, 67
hepatoscopy. See sheep liver, divination with.
Herbert, Edward 121
Herbert of Cherbury. *See* Herbert, Edward.
hermeneutics of finitude 115
Hermes 90
Hesiod 98n. 56
Hezekiah 69
Hick, John, 24–25, 29–31, 32, 32, 34, 36, 123,
    130–32, 134
Hiebert, Paul G. 145
Hinduism 11, 12, 23, 40
History
    God's control of 98–104
    meaning of 100–4
    of religion 124–25n. 34
Hittites 61
Hocking, W. E. 127
Hollenweger, Walter J. 145
holocaust 129
holy 124n. 34
    of holies 48, 73, 124–25n. 34
    One 58
    Place 48
Holy Roman Empire 160
Holy Spirit 118n. 19, 135
Homer 99

Hosea 71
hostility against idols 61, 68–69
household idols 70
human
 hands 82
 nature 157, 160
 rights 39
humanitarianism 122
Hume, David 26

iconography, religious 49–50
idols/images 61
 African 141
 manufacture of 61, 71–73, 82
 polemic against 61–62, 82–83, 85, 90, 92, 93, 98
 terms for 64n. 69
 worship of 44, 60–74, 139, 141
illumination of Holy Spirit 118n. 19
immanent God 59, 60, 87, 89
implicit faith 129
Incarnation 114, 128n. 43, 131–32, 135, 154
inclusivism 107, 110, 115, 130, 131, 133, 134–35
individualism, neopagan 143
Institutes of the Christian Religion (Calvin) 116, 117–18n. 19
integrity of the human person 40
internal revelation 117
Iran 150
Iraq 161
Irenaeus 110
Isaac 154
Isaiah 65n, 71, 73–75, 85, 90, 95
Ishmael 154
Ishtar/Astarte 51
Isis 96–97
Islam 22, 115, 130, 142–43, 148–61
 ascendancy of 11
 Christianity and 11, 113, 114
 empire 160
 epistemology of 30
 isolationism 139
Israel 71
 commission of 85, 87
 Gentiles in 85
 land given to 66–67n. 73
 pluralism and 107
 Yahwism in 43

Jacob 70, 154
Jam, Minaret of 154, 155
James 87n. 23
Jeffery, Arthur 155
Jehovah's Witnesses 11
Jehu 69
Jenkins, Philip 23n

Jephthah 65
Jeremiah 55n. 30, 65n, 66, 71
Jerusalem 48, 57, 69
Jerusalem Missionary Conference of 1928 127
Jesus Christ 100–4, 147, 153, 159
 atonement of 128n. 43, 154–55
 doctrine of 133
 Islamic conception of 154
 as metaphorical myth 132
 nature of 124
 as revelation 124–25n. 34, 127, 128
 in Revelation 92–104
 salvation in 87, 135–37, 138
 servanthood of 85
 titles of 92, 95–96, 97–99
 as Truth 135
 uniqueness of 41, 79, 83, 91
Jews 152
Jezebel 147
Joash 70
Job 56n. 74
John, apostle 92–104
John Paul II 130
John the Baptist 154
Johnson, Luke Timothy 84n. 17, 89
Jorgensen, Danny L. 143
Joseph 157
Joseph and Asenath 89n. 33
Josiah 69
Judaism 12, 115, 130, 153
 Arabic 149
 Christianity and 108
Judge, God as 152–53
justice, achieving 145–46
justification 116, 118, 157–58, 160–61
 Barthian 126–27
 for belief 31–32
Justin Martyr 108–9, 110,112, 125n. 34, 130

Ka'ba 152
Kabul University 158, 159
Kane, J. Herbert 141–42
Kant, Immanuel 26, 122, 123n. 30, 124
Khamenei, Sayyed Ali 157
Khomeini, Ruhollah 157, 161
King of kings 57n, 104, 154
knowledge
 belief and 123
 epistemology of 117n. 18, 122–23
 of folk religion 146
 of God 89–90, 116–17, 121, 133, 134, 135
 levels of 135
 nature of 120–21
 sin and 117–18n. 19
 of truth 116–17
Köstenberger, Andreas 90–92

172 SUBJECT INDEX

Kraemer, Hendrik 127–29, 139–40, 146

Laban 70
Larkin, W. J. 86
Lateran Council, Fourth 154
law, God and 152–53, 157, 160
Laymen's Inquiry (Hocking, et al.) 127
learned ignorance 115
Leeuw, Gerardus van der 124, 136
legitimacy of religions 24–25, 119
Lessing, G. E. 41, 122
Leviathan 53
liberalism, theological 123–25. *See also* modernism.
Life
    and breath 85–86
    in the world 134
    meaning of 145–46
logical positivism 26
logos 109, 132
logos spermatikos 109
"lord of kings" 57n
Lord of lords 104, 56, 57
Luther, Martin 116
Luxenberg, Christoph 156
Lycaonia 90

McKim, Robert 34–36
McNamara, M. 96
madrasa 155–57
Magesa, Laurenti 140, 141
magic 97–98, 141, 159
Maktoum, Saeed al- 150
Malasia 152
manufacture of idols 61, 71–73, 82
Marduk 57, 59n. 41, 65n
Mari texts 51
Marx 134
Mary 153, 154
mask, Bobo 146
Masoretic Text 103n. 68
Materials for the History of the Text of the Qur'an (Jeffery) 155
mathematics 120
Maurier, Henri 142
Mavrodes, George 39
mediators, early church 108
medical incarnations 59n. 41
medieval period 107, 113, 115
Medina Qur'an texts 156
Meditations on First Philosophy (Descartes) 120
medium of Endor 49
mercy of God 152–53
merism 98–99, 100
Merodach. *See* Marduk.
Mesopotamia 71–72

messianic
    hope 46
    kingdom 94
metaphor 101n. 63
metaphorical myth 132
methodological skepticism 126
mighty acts of God 60n. 42
Milcom 65
minaret 153–55
misfortune 145–46
mission of church 91
missions 127–28, 132, 138, 149
    decline of 130–31
    mandate, 160–61
    to West 22
Moab 65
Moberly, R. W. L. 63
modern era 107
modernism, 119–32
monism 143, 146
monotheism 43
    Arab 149
    Israelite 66n. 72
    practical 55n. 30
    theoretical 55n. 30
Monson, John 48
moral obligation 39
Mormonism 11
Moses 50–52, 56, 57–60, 61, 63–64, 66–67, 71, 75, 78, 95, 154
mosque 158, 159
Mot 54, 56, 58
mother goddess 72n
Mount Carmel, Elijah on 69, 70, 146–47
Muhammad 149, 151, 152, 155, 158, 159, 160
Muhammad, Ghiyas ad-Din 154
multiculturalism 42
Muslims. *See* Islam; *Qur'an*.
mythological references in Scripture 50–56
mythological truth 132

Nabu 65n
names of God 151–52, 158
Nathan the Wise (Lessing) 122
natural revelation. *See* general revelation.
natural theology 25–26, 27, 32, 41–42, 67n. 74, 89, 116, 121, 127, 128
    diversity and 36–42
    Pauline 81
    soft 37
naturalism 21–22, 30
naturalistic monism 146
Nauck, Wolfgang 89
NBC Nightly News 151
Near East religion 45–47
Nebuchadnezzar 48, 56, 57, 94n. 44

necessary being 41
neighbors, mission to 9
neopaganism 143, 145
Never Again the Burning Times: Paganism Revived (Orion) 145
New Testament studies 79–80
New York Times 156
Newbigin, Lesslie 22, 128
Nicholas of Cusa 115
Nicholson, E. W. 70
Nietzsche, Friedrich 123n. 32
nihilism 133
nirguna Brahman 39
Noah 85–86n. 20, 87, 154
noetic effects of sin 117–18n. 19
non-Christian religions, Christianity and 134
Nostra Aetate 130
Nudimmud (Ea) 73
Nyirongo, Lenard 141

"offspring of God" 82–83, 87–89
"old man" 100n
Old Testament context 93, 94, 97–99, 104
omnipresence 88–89
ontological argument 26
Origen 133
Orion, Loretta 145
Otto, Rudolf 124
"overriders" 31

paganism
    challenging 50
    New Testament and 79, 80–105
    West 22
    worldview 70
Palestinian Targum 86
Pan-Islamism 159
Pao, David 85, 87
parallel development in religions 46
particularity in Scripture 134
Paschal, Blaise 121
patristic era 107
patron deities 46, 57, 64–65, 92
Paul 75, 79, 80–92, 116, 126. *See also* Areopogus address.
Pausanius 96
peace offering 47
"perfect Man" 100n
Persia 12
Philip IV of France 114
philosophical theism 113
philosophy 106–32
    authority of 114
    gospel and 109, 110, 111–12
    limits of 117–18n. 19
    of religion 23, 25–36

Phoenicia 47–48, 52n. 21
pietism 123
placating the deity 46, 47
Plantinga, Alvin 25, 26–27, 32–34, 35
Plato 97
platonists 110, 112
pluralism. *See also* plurality.
    ethos of 24–25
    incoherence of 25
    issues of 25–36
    meaning of 23–25
    New Testament on 91
    religious 21–42
    response type of, 107, 115, 119, 123, 125–26, 132, 133, 134
plurality. *See also* pluralism.
    in history 115
    responses to 106–32
    theological view of 133–37
Plutarch 96
poetry, Islamic 150
Poisonwood Bible, The (Kingsolver) 144
polemic against idols 61, 70–74, 82–83, 90, 92, 93, 98, 105
polished bronze 94n. 44
political
    correctness 42
    power 159–60
polytheism 67n. 74
Posidonius 87n. 25
post-Christendom church 107, 108, 115–32
post-Enlightenment West 125
postmodernism 107, 115, 132
power
    encounter 146–47
    in folk Islam 158–59
practical monotheism 55n. 30
practice in forming belief 32
praeparatio evangelica. See preparation for faith.
prayer 47, 146, 147
Prayer of Jabez (Wilkinson) 147
Prayer of Manasses 89n. 33
"Prayer to Every God, A" 75–78
pre-Christendom church 107, 108–12
preaching 110
preparation for faith 125n. 34, 128
prohibition of idolatry 61, 62–68
proper function 34
properly basic belief 33–34
prophets 49, 64, 71
providence 89–90, 117, 123n. 32
Punic texts 51
puns 101n. 63
Pythagorean cosmology 59n. 41

Quinn, Philip 33–34

Qur'an 22, 151, 152, 153, 154, 155–57, 158, 159
Qurtubi, Tafsir al- 154–55
Qutb, Sayyid 154–55

Rachel 70
Rahner, Karl 129, 131
Rand, E. K. 108–9
Ras Shamra/Ugarit texts 71
Rastafarianism 12
rationalism 119
rationality
    of faith 27, 32–33, 36, 37–38, 109,120,
        121–22, 125
    in religious experience 39
    truth and 25–36
Razi, Fakhr al-Din al- 154–55
Real, the. See ultimate reality.
reason, limits of 117–18n. 19
redemptive history 85–90, 117, 124, 135, 137
Reformation 107, 115, 116, 118, 119, 121
Reformed epistemology 26–27, 32, 33
regula fidei 110
relativism 25, 38, 126, 146
    African 142–43
    moral 42
    Western 127
religion 44
    adherents of 21n
    Christianity and 106–37, 127–28, 138
    commonality of 121
    folk 158–59
    New Testament view of 90–91
    as preparation 128
    study of 124n. 34
    validity of 67n. 74
    vs. revelation 126–27
Religion Within the Limits of Reason Alone (Kant)
    123
Religionsgeschichtliche Schule 125
religious ambiguity. See ambiguity, religious.
Religious Ambiguity and Religious Diversity
    (McKim) 34–36
religious concepts
    exploitation of 48–60
    repudiation of 60–74
    sharing of 47–48
religious diversity. See pluralism, religious.
religious experience 27, 124–25n. 34, 128n. 43
religious pluralism. See pluralism, religious.
Renaissance 107, 115
repentance 159
repudiated pagan religion 60–74
Resheph 54, 55
revelation
    -focused theology 126–27
    general 86, 88, 116, 124, 127, 128, 134–35
    outside Christianity 128

pagan allusions in 92–104
rejection of 133
religionvs. 126–27
special 86, 89, 90, 113, 116–17, 124–25n. 34,
    134, 135
universality of 134–35
rhabdomancy. See arrows, divination with.
Robertson, Pat 150
Roman Catholic Church 118, 129
Romanticism 123
rule of faith. See regula fidei.
Russell, Scott E. 143

sacraments 118, 141
sacrifice in Near East religion 47, 73
salvation 89–90, 117, 118, 128, 128n. 43, 135
    basis for 131
    in Christ 87, 88
    in church 114–15
    history 98–99, 103–4
    in Islam 157
    nature of 133, 134
samadhi. See enlightenment, mystical.
Samuel 49
Sanctifier, God as 135, 137
Sanneh, Lamin 142
Sanon, Anselme Titianma 139
satori. See enlightenment, mystical.
Saudi Arabia 151
Saul 49
saving points of contact 132
Schleiermacher, Friedrich 123–24, 125
Schnelle, Udo 80
science 113, 121
Scripture
    as "spectacles" 117
    authority of 118, 132
    revelation and 117, 135
Second International Missionary Conference.
    See Jerusalem Missionary Conference of
    1928.
secularism 21–22
    faith of 36
    Muslim 150–51
seeking God 86–88
semen religionis 116
semina verbi 130
sensus divinitatis 116, 128, 134
September 11, 2001 11, 150–51, 161
Septuagint 83n. 16
seven seals 104
seven stars 93
Shaggar/Sheger 51
shared pagan religion 47–48
shari'a Islamic law 151
Shaw, R. Daniel, 145
sheep liver, divination with 48

Shema' 63
sheol 45, 46, 55–56, 59
Shi'ites 157
Sibylline Oracles 89n. 33
"Sick Man of Europe" 36
sin 60n, 152, 157
   modernist view of 124
   in Near East religion 46, 47, 76–78
   noetic effects of 117–18n. 19
   of unbelief 114
Sinai, revelation at 68
skepticism 120, 121, 133
   methodological 126
   religious 27
Slaterry, J. R. 140
Smart, Ninian 26, 36, 38
Smith, Wilfred Cantwell 130, 155
Söderblom, Nathan 124
"soft natural theology" 37, 41–42
Solomon 47–48
Son of God 92, 93, 94, 100n, 135
Son of Man 89, 92, 93, 94
sovereignty 59n. 41, 98, 100
space-time world 41
special revelation 26, 89, 90,113, 116–17, 124n.
   34, 134, 135
spectacles, Scripture as 117
spiritism 12, 56n. 32
Stackhouse, John G. 138
Stephen 82
Stephens, F. J. 76n
Stoics 83–84n. 16, 110
storm god 53
Strecker, Georg 80
subjectivity 120
substance Christologies 132
Sufis 151
Sumer 75–78
Sunyata. See emptiness.
sutras 41
symbolic pictures 101n. 63
symbols, divine 46
syncretism 44, 65
   Israelite 56
   neopagan 143
Syrian temple 48
Syro-Aramaeische Lesart des Koran, Die
   (Luxenberg) 156

Tabari, Abu Ja'far Muhammad al- 154–55
tabernacle 48
Taliban 148, 157, 161
Tambaram Missionary Conference of 1938 127
Taoism 12
teleological argument 26
temple 57
   ancient 48

idol 85
Jerusalem 47–48
structures 82
true 87
"ten days" 104
teraphim 48, 61, 70
Tertullian 109–10, 112, 134
theatre of divine glory 117
theism
   argument for 27, 29, 30
   philosophical 113
theodicy 129, 145–46
Theodotion 93, 103n. 68
theogony 72n
theoretical monotheism 55n. 30
Thesaurus Linguae Graecae (Wettstein) 79–80
Third International Missionary Conference. *See*
   Tambaram Missionary Confernce of 1938.
Thomas Aquinas 26, 40, 113, 117–18n. 19
Three-fold name 95–97
throne of God 49–50
Thyatira 92–95
Tiénou, Tite 145
Tigay, J. 67n. 74
Tirshu/Tirash 51
toleration 119, 122
   African 142–43
   neopagan 143
Toward a World Theology (Cantwell Smith) 131
tradition 132
   authority of 110, 118
   revelation and 135
traditional religion 141
transcendence
   of God 59–60, 112, 132
   quest for 134
transformation in Christ 160
Trent, Council of 112, 118
Trinity 112, 114, 131–32, 133, 134, 135, 137, 153
Troeltsch, Ernst 125–26
"Troeltsch's ditch" 125
truth
   in Christian theism 25–42
   claims 22, 80
   epistemology of 33–34, 119–32, 133
   knowledge of 116–17
   levels of 135
   meaning of 21–42
   nature of 109, 134
   non-Christian 109, 158
   religious 126–27
   suppression of 116
   ultimate 125–26
   unique 30–31, 36
Ugarit texts 51, 52, 54, 71
"Ugly Ditch" 41
U.K. Association of Buddhist Studies 40

ultimate reality 24–25, 125–26
Unam Sanctam (Boniface VIII) 114–15
Understanding Folk Religion (Hiebert, Shaw,
    Tiénou) 144, 145
Unexpected Way, The (Williams) 40
uniqueness of Christianity 79, 91, 125, 128n. 43
United States
    demographic shifts of 23
    State Department 160
universalism 133
universality in Scripture 134
universe, three-tiered 45
unknown, facing 145–46
Upanishads, truth claims of 23

Validity
    of Christian revelation 125
    of idol worship 61
    of religions 67n. 74
Van Unnik, W. C. 81, 99–104
Vatican Council II 129–30
Voltaire, Francois-Marie 123n. 32

Wach, Joachim 124
Wainwright, William 38
Walker, Christopher 71–72
Wansborough, John 155
warrant for belief 34n. 27
wars of religion 119, 121
watchmaker God 121
West
    Christendom in 108
    intellectual progress of 117n. 18, 120
    paganism of 22
    post-Enlightenment 21, 125
    relativism in 42, 127
    religious illiteracy in 106
    theology 115, 132
whole burnt offering 47
wholly other God 126
will of God 117
Williams, Paul 40
Wisdom 89n. 33
Witherington, Ben 86
World Council of Churches 129
World Parliament of Religions of 1893 140
World War I 126
World War II 129
worldview
    assessment 38
    folk religion 145–46
    neopagan 143
    nonreligious 21

worship
    of God 111–12
    interfaith, 11–12
    pagan 62–68, 72

Yahweh 43, 60n. 45
    Allah and 152
    paganism and 45–75
    supremacy of 57n
    uniqueness of 52, 55n. 30
Yamm 58
Yandell, Keith 38, 40
Yemen 156
Yoruba religion 147

Zechariah 154
Zen. *See* Buddhism.
Zephaniah 71
Zeus 82, 83–84n. 16, 88n. 29, 87–89, 90, 94, 97
    omnipresence of 88–89
    three-fold description of 96
Ziarat-i-Sakhi 158